New Historicism and Renaissance Drama

LONGMAN CRITICAL READERS

General Editors:

RAMAN SELDEN, late Emeritus Professor of English, Lancaster University and late Professor of English, Sunderland Polytechnic;

STAN SMITH, Professor of English, University of Dundee

Published titles:

K.M. NEWTON, *George Eliot*

MARY EAGLETON, *Feminist Literary Criticism*

GARY WALLER, *Shakespeare's Comedies*

JOHN DRAKAKIS, *Shakespearean Tragedy*

RICHARD WILSON AND RICHARD DUTTON, *New Historicism and Renaissance Drama*

PETER BROOKER, *Modernism/Postmodernism*

PETER WIDDOWSON, *D.H. Lawrence*

RACHEL BOWLBY, *Virginia Woolf*

FRANCIS MULHERN, *Contemporary Marxist Literary Criticism*

ANNABEL PATTERSON, *John Milton*

CYNTHIA CHASE, *Romanticism*

MICHAEL O'NEILL, *Shelley*

STEPHANIE TRIGG, *Medieval English Poetry*

ANTONY EASTHOPE, *Contemporary Film Theory*

New Historicism and Renaissance Drama

Edited and Introduced by

Richard Wilson And Richard Dutton

Longman
London and New York

Longman Group Limited,
Longman House, Burnt Mill, Harlow,
Essex CM20 2JE, England
and Associated Companies throughout the world.

Published in the United States of America
by Longman Publishing, New York

First published 1992
Second impression 1994

British Library Cataloguing-in-Publication Data
New historicism and renaissance drama.
– (Longman critical readers)
   I. Wilson, Richard II. Dutton, Richard
   III. Series
   809.2

ISBN 0–582–04562–2
ISBN 0–582–04554–1 pbk

Library of Congress Cataloging-in-Publication Data
New historicism and renaissance drama / edited by Richard Wilson and Richard
Dutton.
       p. cm. — (Longman critical readers)
    Includes bibliographical references and index.
    ISBN 0–582–04562–2. — ISBN 0–582–04554–1 (pbk)
    1. English drama–Early modern and Elizabethan, 1500–1600–History and
    criticism. 2. English drama–17th century–History and criticism. 3. Renaissance–
    England. 4. Historicism.
I. Wilson. Richard, 1950–. II. Dutton, Richard, 1948–. III. Series.
PR654. N49 1992
822′.309–dc20

Set by 2K in 9/11$\frac{1}{2}$ pt Palatino
Produced by Longman Singapore Publishers (Pte) Ltd.
Printed in Singapore

Contents

General Editors' Preface   vii
Acknowledgements   ix
Preface   xi

RICHARD WILSON   Introduction: Historicising New Historicism
New Historicism and New Philosophy   1
Cultural Poetics   4
History and the Market   8
Cultural Materialism   11

1   JEAN E. HOWARD   The New Historicism in Renaissance Studies   19

2   CATHERINE BELSEY   Literature, History, Politics   33

3   JONATHAN DOLLIMORE   Shakespeare, Cultural Materialism
and the New Historicism   45

4   STEPHEN GREENBLATT   Marlowe and the Will to Absolute
Play   57

5   STEPHEN GREENBLATT   Invisible Bullets: Renaissance Authority
and its Subversion, *Henry IV* and *Henry V*   83

6   LOUIS MONTROSE   *A Midsummer Night's Dream* and the
Shaping Fantasies of Elizabethan Culture: Gender, Power, Form   109

7   CATHERINE BELSEY   Alice Arden's Crime   131

8   RICHARD WILSON   Shakespeare's Roman Carnival   145

9   FRANCIS BARKER   Hamlet's Unfulfilled Interiority   157

10 ALAN SINFIELD   *Macbeth*: History, Ideology
and Intellectuals   167

11 JONATHAN DOLLIMORE   *The White Devil*: Transgression
Without Virtue   181

12 LEONARD TENNENHOUSE   Family Rites: City Comedy and
the Strategies of Patriarchalism   195

13 PETER STALLYBRASS AND ALLON WHITE   Smithfield and
Authorship: Ben Jonson   207

RICHARD DUTTON   Postscript   219

New Historicism And Renaissance Drama

Key Concepts   227
Notes on Authors   233
Further Reading   235
Bibliography   240
Index   245

General Editors' Preface

The outlines of contemporary critical theory are now often taught as a standard feature of a degree in literary studies. The development of particular theories has seen a thorough transformation of literary criticism. For example, Marxist and Foucauldian theories have revolutionised Shakespeare studies and 'deconstruction' has led to a complete reassessment of Romantic poetry. Feminist criticism has left scarcely any period of literature unaffected by its searching critiques. Teachers of literary studies can no longer fall back on a standardised, received methodology.

Lecturers and teachers are now urgently looking for guidance in a rapidly changing critical environment. They need help in understanding the latest revisions in literary theory, and especially in grasping the practical effects of the new theories in the form of theoretically sensitised new readings. A number of volumes in the series anthologise important essays on particular theories. However, in order to grasp the full implications and possible uses of particular theories it is essential to see them put to work. This series provides substantial volumes of new readings, presented in an accessible form and with a significant amount of editorial guidance.

Each volume includes a substantial introduction which explores the theoretical issues and conflicts embodied in the essays selected and locates areas of disagreement between positions. The pluralism of theories has to be put on the agenda of literary studies. We can no longer pretend that we all tacitly accept the same practices in literary studies. Neither is a *laissez-faire* attitude any longer tenable. Literature departments need to go beyond the mere toleration of theoretical differences: it is not enough merely to agree to differ; they need actually to 'stage' the differences openly. The volumes in this series all attempt to dramatise the differences, not necessarily with a view to resolving them but in order to foreground the choices presented by different theories or to argue for a particular route through the impasses the differences present.

The theory 'revolution' has had real effects. It has loosened the grip of traditional empiricist and Romantic assumptions about language and literature. It is not always clear what is being proposed as the new agenda for literary studies, and indeed the very notion of 'literature' is questioned by the post-structuralist strain in theory. However, the uncertainties and obscurities of contemporary theories appear much less worrying when we see what the best critics have been able to do with them in practice. This series aims to disseminate the best of recent criticism, and to show that it is possible to re-read the canonical texts of literature in new and challenging ways.

RAMAN SELDEN AND STAN SMITH

The Publishers and fellow Series Editor regret to record that Raman Selden died after a short illness in May 1991 at the age of fifty-three. Ray Selden was a fine scholar and a lovely man. All those he has worked with will remember him with much affection and respect.

Acknowledgements

We are grateful to the following for permission to reproduce copyright material : the author Catherine Belsey for her article 'Literature, History, Politics' in *Literature and History*, 9 (1983), pp. 17–27 (Thames Polytechnic), © Catherine Belsey; The Johns Hopkins University Press and the author Richard Wilson for his essay '*Julius Caesar*: Shakespeare's Roman Carnival' in *English Literary History*, 54, 1 (Spring 1987), pp. 31–44; Harvester Wheatsheaf for Jonathan Dollimore's '*The White Devil* (1612): Transgression Without Virtue', Chapter 15, pp. 231–46 in *Radical Tragedy: Religion, Ideology and Power in the Drama of Shakespeare and His Contemporaries* (2nd edition, London: Harvester Wheatsheaf, 1989) © 1984, 1989 Jonathan Dollimore; Manchester University Press for an extract from Jonathan Dollimore's, 'Shakespeare, Cultural Materialism and the New Historicism' in *Political Shakespeare: New Essays in Cultural Materialism* (1985), pp. 2–17, and Stephen Greenblatt's 'Invisible Bullets: Renaissance Authority and its Subversion: *Henry IV* and *Henry V*' in *Political Shakespeare*, ed. J. Dollimore and A. Sinfield (1985), pp. 18–47; Routledge for '*Hamlet*' in *The Tremulous Private Body: Essays in Subjection* by Francis Baker (Methuen, 1984), 'Alice Arden's Crime' in *The Subject of Tragedy: Identity and Difference in Renaissance Drama* by Catherine Belsey (Methuen, 1985), 'Smithfield and Authorship: Ben Jonson' in *The Politics and Poetics of Transgression* by P. Stallybrass and A. White (Methuen, 1987) and 'Family Rites: City Comedy and the Strategies of Patriarchalism' (edited) in *Power on Display: the Politics of Shakespeare's Genres* by Leonard Tennenhouse (Methuen, 1986); the author Alan Sinfield for his essay '*Macbeth*: History, Ideology and Intellectuals' in *Critical Quarterly* 28, 1/2 (Spring/Summer 1986); University of California Press and the author Louis A. Montrose for his essay '*A Midsummer Night's Dream* and the Shaping Fantasies of Elizabethan Culture: Gender, Power, Form' in *Representations*, 2 (Spring 1983), © 1983 by the Regents of the University of California; The University of Chicago Press and the author Stephen Greenblatt for his essay 'Marlowe and the Will to Absolute Play' in *Renaissance Self-Fashioning: from More to Shakespeare* (1980), pp. 193–221; The

University of Massachusetts Press for the article by Jean E. Howard, 'The New Historicism in Renaissance Studies' in *Renaissance Historicism: Selections from English Literary Renaissance*, ed. Arthur F. Kinney and Dan S. Collins (Amherst: University of Massachusetts Press, 1987), copyright © 1980, 1983, 1984, 1986, 1987 by *English Literary Renaissance*.

Preface

This collection of essays offers a survey of one of the most dynamic and controversial movements in contemporary criticism, focused on the literature with which it claims to have a special affinity. New Historicism and Renaissance Drama have been firmly associated since the 'turn to history' in criticism was signalled at the beginning of the 1980s, and one of the aims of this collection is to examine the reasons for this connection. Another is to review the range of New Historicist work as it has developed on both sides of the Atlantic, since it is over the interpretation of Renaissance Drama that the American and British wings of the movement have diverged most sharply. By the end of the Eighties New Historicism was coming to be considered, like every school of criticism, a product of its era, and the intention of this anthology is to set its debates and contributions within the specific context of a decade of consumer capitalism, of a political New Right and of a demoralised Left. A retrospective, therefore, on the most striking critical phenomenon of the Eighties, this volume sets out to initiate a critique that has only now become possible : to historicise New Historicism.

By no means all the authors included in this collection would recognise themselves as New Historicists, and the term has been applied in a somewhat cavalier fashion to both its practitioners and opponents as a general sign of the recent turn towards and discussion of a historicist reading of Renaissance drama. Necessarily excluded is 'old historicist' work by critics who apply to Elizabethan and Jacobean plays an unproblematic concept of history, since the defining quality of these essays is that each addresses the notion that has come to characterise New Historicism: a theoretical awareness of both 'the historicity of texts and the textuality of history'. The different emphasis given to one or other side of this formulation is what effectively divides these contributions.

The essays collected are preceded by headnotes that are intended as a commentary on the debates within New Historicism as they unfolded during the Eighties. The key concepts of the movement, printed in the Headnotes in bold type, are alphabetically listed and defined at the end of the book, while the Introduction and Postscript offer a theoretical guide to the issues and an account of their continuing significance. For reasons of space and ease of reference, footnotes from the essays have been concentrated in a single Bibliography. Since the brief of this Series has been to provide a conspectus of current theory, the Bibliography omits references to primary Renaissance sources, and readers are referred to the original published versions of the essays for this information.

In memoriam Raman Selden
1937–1991

Introduction: Historicising New Historicism

RICHARD WILSON

New Historicism and New Philosophy

New Historicism is the name given to the return of history in literary criticism over the last ten years. According to one account, it was a movement that began punctually at the beginning of the 1980s, when the American critic Stephen Greenblatt edited a selection of Renaissance essays and announced that they constituted a 'new historicism'. Greenblatt later remarked that for reasons he could not have predicted, the name stuck and proliferated, until by the end of the decade its momentum had become such a roller-coaster it made him 'giddy with amazement' (Greenblatt 1989, p. 1). In fact, the circulation of the name which Greenblatt imagined he invented is itself a prime instance of New Historicism's own premise that, contrary to 'the humanist trivialization' of history (p. 8), no author is the origin or owner of her / his meaning, but that all statements are written through by pre-existing texts, which having intersected then disperse. If the New Historicism burst suddenly into existence around 1980, it did so, by its own definition, as the conjunction of a number of prior *discourses*, or ways of speaking, about literature and language, and not by inspiration of any single individual. And if it was associated momentarily with a time and place and person, its dissemination during the next decade was a perfect illustration of its thesis that meaning can never be fixed, since language is in perpetual contest. This Introduction will trace the strands of theory that fused to create New Historicism, in an attempt to locate it as a historical phenomenon, while the Postscript will examine some of the ways in which the movement has since fragmented as it has collided with and generated other kinds of criticism.

Stephen Greenblatt himself proposes a big bang theory of the origin of New Historicism, with speculation that the lectures of the French social thinker Michel Foucault at Berkeley in October 1980 ignited a theoretical explosion (Greenblatt 1989, p. 1). But there is irony in this tribute, since the message Foucault brought to America was that there is no founding moment, because every utterance or event has to be understood as part of something else. Thus, Foucault's thesis that truth is an effect of words, and knowledge the exercise of power, has to be understood itself in the context of the rejection of the totalising drive of Marxism in the aftermath of May 1968. The Events of that month in France – when students and strikers almost toppled the government but were outflanked as the Communist Party sided with de Gaulle – were described by Foucault as 'profoundly anti-Marxist', and they had crucial repercussions for intellectuals who had credited Marx's claim to have located the dynamo of history in economic change. Instead, the generation of '68 learned what Saussure propounded: that men and women are not primarily economic beings, but talking animals, created by and in words. This lesson was turned against the revolution itself, when at the height of the crisis de Gaulle disappeared, and for twenty-four hours there was no head of state in France. Like a crafty Shakespearean duke, he had secretly flown to Germany to monitor the carnival; but what his absence and return dramatised was that power, as Roland Barthes saw, was not concentrated in some centre but dispersed throughout society. 'In our innocence', Barthes recalled, 'we believed power was a political object; we learned that power is an ideological object, that it creeps in where we do not recognise it, into institutions, teaching... even the forces of liberation themselves. Power is plural, we discovered.... Make a revolution to destroy it, power will spring up again. And the reason why power is invincible is that the object in which it is carried for all human eternity is language: the language that we speak and write' (Barthes 1982, p. 459) .

The Events of 1968 amounted to ' the greatest strike in the history of the world', concluded the Marxist theoretician Louis Althusser (Althusser 1977, p. 49), but they failed because they did not win the ideological war. Though he was reviled for his attempt to restore Marxism's credibility, Althusser's importance lay in his recognition that now Marx would have to be entirely rethought. In his essay of 1969, 'Ideology and Ideological State Apparatuses', he broke the ground for all Post- or Anti-Marxist theory, when he conceded that it was in institutions such as the school, the family and the media, that the domination of a ruling class was first installed 'in words' (Althusser 1984). Cued by the Chinese Cultural Revolution, which waged class struggle in the 'superstructural' fields of education, literature and art, Althusser thus overhauled the Marxist base/superstructure theorem of economic determinism, by detailing how labour power is reproduced through prior forms of ideological subjection. The Italian Marxist Antonio Gramsci had deduced in his prison notebook of 1929 that 'the supremacy of a social group manifests itself in two ways, as "domination" and as "intellectual and moral leadership"... A Social group must already exercise "leadership" before winning governmental power' (Gramsci 1971, p. 57); and it was Gramsci's notion of cultural leadership or *hegemony* which enabled Althusser to grasp that an 'Ideological State Apparatus' is as crucial as a repressive one, such as the police, in maintaining the status quo. It does this, he explained, by securing our consent through a subtle kind of indoctrination, an *interpellation* or 'calling' of individuals into line. Jacques Lacan had theorised how the individual subject was constituted by entry into language; Althusser adopted this psycholinguistic axiom that it is language with its pre-existing order that 'speaks us', to suggest how we enter capitalism through the cradle and the crèche. So, if for Marx, ideology had been an illusion and a lie, for Althusser it was the very material of daily life.

May 1968 seemed to prove that the modern Prince has no need to turn his army on the people, whose subjection is cemented in the unconscious conditioning of their lives. Moreover, in an era of mass communication, power was contested through the electronic media, and not, as Marxists imagined, through occupations and strikes. It was when he reasserted mastery of television that de Gaulle was re-elected, and when he fumbled with it again in 1969 he resigned. So the myths of the bourgeoisie that Barthes had ridiculed in his book *Mythologies* – the myths of the good life of steak and chips, the Persil Family, quiz shows and the Citroën Car (Barthes 1972) – which meshed together into the ideology of French capitalism, proved stronger than either barricades or flower power. It had been the anthropologist Claude Levi-Strauss who taught intellectuals that a culture is regulated like a language, and now the students of Levi-Strauss discovered that in an advanced industrial society the structures of consumerism bound them with a thread as irresistible as the label on their jeans. As the *Internationale* faded and demos melted in exams, it did seem, as Barthes lamented in his Inaugural Lecture at the Collège de France, that it is language which is 'fascist', because it *compels* speech and obliges those who use it to subject themselves to the order it prescribes. 'Language is legislation', Barthes intoned, 'speech its code. We do not see the power that is in speech because we forget that all speech is classification, and that all classifications are oppressive.... But if we call freedom not only the capacity to escape power but also the capacity to subjugate no one, then freedom can exist only outside language. Unfortunately language has no outside: there is no exit from words' (Barthes 1982, p. 460). As Gilles Deleuze and Felix Guattari likewise warned, 1968 had been a rebellion of 'desire' against power, but it had been thwarted by the patriarchal oppression inscribed in the symbolic order, including that of theory such as Marxism itself (Deleuze and Guattari 1972).

The dark wisdom that *power* is *productive rather than repressive*, since there can be no escape from the prison-house of words, underlies the problematic that developed during the 1970s from which New Historicism would emerge. It was a cultural paranoia exemplified by Foucault's pronouncement that 'Power is everywhere; not because it embraces everything, but because it comes from everywhere' (Foucault, 1981b, p. 93). Alongside the Freudian pessimism of Lacan, Foucault's Nietzschean collapse of 'knowledge' into 'power' and refusal of the 'truth' of science inspired the Parisian movement that called itself the New Philosophy, with which New Historicism would share much ground. Like New Historicism, New Philosophy was politically diffuse, with leftist and conservative tendencies, but it was characterised by an unexamined hypostatisation of power that made it liable to be coopted to the libertarianism of the New Right. Believing, with Foucault, that 'Power is reinforced by the complicity of those who are dominated.... it is transmitted by and through them' (Foucault 1981a, p.16), New Philosophers, such as the ex-Maoist Andre Glucksmann, opposed all institutions as coercive, but identified socialism as the true enemy of freedom. Championship of Soviet dissidents went hand-in-hand with a rejection of Western rationality, of which the Gulag was assumed to be the logical end, and a refusal to totalise or intellectualise in systematic terms. The result was a strategic eclecticism, which Foucault likened to guerrilla warfare, with philosophy seen as a 'tool kit' for dismantling the state. Against totalitarian reason, New Philosophy valorised the irrational and marginal: 'the poets and vagabonds, peasants and shopkeepers, dissidents and dreamers' whom the 'Masters' of the Enlightenment had excluded or confined (Benton 1984, p. 176). Its 'hermeneutics of suspicion' may have been Nietzschean, therefore, but the ideology of the New Philosophy was every bit the Orwellian fashion of a decade that voted to 'deregulate' the Welfare State. Both the ideology and the agenda would surface in American New Historicism.

Cultural Poetics

For all its subversiveness, the trouble with Foucault's claustrophobic model of power, Umberto Eco commented, is that if power is immanent in language, 'it can never be a place of revolution'. It was this theoretical 'knot to do with a centreless universe where there is no longer any "heart" of anything' (Eco 1986, p. 255), that Foucault took to America, where critics had long been alert to the avidity with which capitalism thrives by incorporating the forces that oppose it. As he conceded, at Berkeley Foucault learned that his analytics of power had been anticipated by the Frankfurt School of sociology, and in particular by

Herbert Marcuse's description of the 'repressive tolerance' with which opposition is neutralised by the West's permissive society (Marcuse 1964). Foucault's dismal prognosis likewise coincided with the foreboding of New York liberals such as Lionel Trilling, whose writings mourned the 'socialization of the anti-social, the acculturation of the anti-cultural and the legitimation of the subversive' by the colleges and broadcasting networks of Middle America (Trilling 1968, p. 26). And if the generation of '68 was alive to the ploys with which its counter-culture was orchestrated by the 'culture industry' (Adorno and Horkheimer 1972), it was primed by pundits such as Marshall McLuhan that in the electronic age, when the world is a 'global village' and' the medium is the message', power circulates in instantaneous images (1964). Thus, *Amusing Ourselves to Death* was the title of one best-seller of the Eighties, in which Mark Postman tabulated the mesmerising impact of television on the society which elected a movie actor President. It was a theme that condensed the panic-stricken poetics of New Historicism. For as Greenblatt himself noticed, Ronald Reagan and New Historicism were both manifestations of a culture of triumphant capitalism which, by short-circuiting simulation and reality, appeared to offer no escape from the interminable circularity of representations (1989, p. 8).

What distinguished New from old historicism was the knowledge that the historic moments of the Reagan Presidency were not only projected onto film, but turned out to be stolen from Hollywood. Where criticism had been concerned with the historicity of texts, New Historicism grasped the textuality of history with an acuity born of a decade when the leader of the West lived, as Greenblatt observed, 'within the movies' that shaped his identity and rhetoric, and which he was unable or unwilling to separate from reality (1989, p. 6). New Historicism, shared, that is to say, the post-modern vertigo about what Jean Baudrillard melodramatised as 'the disappearance of reality'; the sensation that 'today the image is not only a mirror or counterpart of the real, but begins to contaminate reality and to model it, conforms to reality the better to distort it: it appropriates reality for its own ends, anticipates it to the point that the real no longer has time to be produced' (Baudrillard, 1988, p.16). The awareness that 'a government is sustained not by the gun, but by the effects of texts' (Debray 1980, p. 61) was common to all varieties of post-structuralism, but New Historicism was marked by the alacrity with which it adopted Jacques Derrida's maxim that 'There is nothing outside of texts'. Where Glucksmann courted controversy in arguing that 'German fascism was born not in a territory but a text instituted long before Hitler', (Glucksmann 1977, p. 48) Greenblatt and others were equally 'strong textualists' in tracing the West's domination to 'the wonderful self-validating circularity' of its textual 'construction of reality' (Chapter 5). Thus, perhaps the most influential of Foucauldians, Edward

Said, adumbrated in his book, *Orientalism* (1978), how Europe's superiority complex was grounded in a fictional East that is ' less a place than a mirage, and that seems to have its origin in a quotation, or fragment of text, or some previous bit of imagining'. But for all its fantasy, Said charged, this occidental dream of oriental delight was crucial to colonialism, which has depended as much on poets as marines.

New Historicism dates from the last days of the Cold War, when critics of the nuclear age were eager to follow up on Derrida's deconstruction of 'The White Mythology', by which the texts of Western reason oppose their light to the opaque materiality of the heart of darkness (1974). Another of the seminal works of the movement, published in 1982, was therefore *The Conquest of America* by the linguist Tzvetan Todorov. 'The Question of the Other' was the subtitle of this book, which also related how European power has been inscribed in a binary antagonism between light and dark, and invested in a crusade to exterminate the 'evil empire' of the alien. As Greenblatt remarks, of all the encounters between the West and its Other, the meeting between colonist and Amerindian was the most 'privileged anthropological moment', when the Old World was able to 'test upon the bodies and minds of non-Europeans' the superiority of its map of reality (Chapter 5). Todorov interprets the confrontation, then, as a battle not so much of weapons, as of signs. The Indians fell victim to the Spaniards, he submits, because of their cumbrous system of signification, overwhelmed, despite their numbers, by Cortez's capacity to decipher their cultural codes, while baffling them with his own. Europeans, he concludes, conquered the New World by *writing*. 'The pen is mightier than the sword' might be the motto of such criticism, which is founded on the premise that, while sticks and stones may break our bones, words will surely kill us. Certainly, this was to be the axiom of New Historicism, which is best seen as an annexation of history by linguistics. As Greenblatt wrote, in America during the Seventies Marxist historicism made way for 'courses with names like "Cultural Poetics" ' (1989, p. 2), with the implication that any new historicism would be a science, like structuralist anthropology, of culture viewed as a self-regulating and synchronic system. The new history would slice across time, keeping the past pure in its difference from the present with methods as ahistorical as those of Saussurean linguistics.

When the Inca asked to see the Christian God, the *Conquistador* gave him a Bible, which the king attempted to eat but spat out in disgust: it was then that the outraged Spaniards began their genocidal slaughter. The episode is a complex parable, not only of the clash of signifiers, but of the materiality of language. The fatal power of texts is the theme of one of the most quoted of New Historicist essays, by Greenblatt himself, which takes its title from the fact that, decimated by smallpox, to which they had no immunity, Indians thought the Europeans were killing them with 'invisible bullets' (Chapter 5). Greenblatt deploys this tale of grim misreading as a metaphor for the Machiavellian manipulation of texts by western rulers. Shocked by the Indians' beliefs, he surmises, the settlers grasped the arbitrariness of religion, yet exploited this insight to threaten the natives with a God about whom they were themselves now sceptical. But when the Indians began to die, their faith was restored, since savagery, they rejoiced, was punished. 'Power defines itself', Greenblatt infers, 'in relation to that which threatens it'; and in a deft analogy, he explains how in Shakespeare's *Henry IV* plays, Hal is an *agent provocateur* who incites the crimes which he will afterwards condemn, in order to reinforce his own authority. The judge, as Foucault teaches, needs the criminal; the prince requires subversion. So 'the modern state is based on deceit, calculation and hypocrisy', Greenblatt inveighs, and 'theatricality is power's essential mode'. This is the subject of his important 1980 book, *Renaissance Self- Fashioning*, which explored the way the self was constructed in Tudor England through the displacement of contradiction onto the demonized Other. Catholic and Protestant were twinned in a deadly double-bluff, in this view, while those who trumped the game courted disaster. Though Marlowe's 'Will to Absolute Play' broke every rule, therefore, even his ludic self-improvisation was crushed by 'the immense power' of the orthodoxy against which he wagered (Chapter 4).

Under the shadow of Foucault, each chapter of *Renaissance Self-fashioning* ended in murder or execution, with the subject overpowered by social institutions. Struggling to be free, like Othello, the Elizabethans only tied themselves the more in ideological chains. So, 'There is subversion, no end of subversion', Greenblatt quoted Kafka, 'only not for us ' (Chapter 5). Marxist critics, such as Walter Benjamin or Mikhail Bakhtin, divined a glimmer of utopia in art and carnival; but for New Historicism, literature, play or transgression were merely pretexts for redoubled oppression. And this meant that our pleasure as consumers of the text submitted us also to the cunning provocation of what Greenblatt termed 'the massive power structures that determine social and psychic reality' (1980, p. 254). The illusion of freedom art promises he compared to Desdemona's kiss of death, since, though he had set out to analyze 'the role of human autonomy' in the choices that we make in representing ourselves, 'as my work progressed', he reported bleakly, 'I perceived there were, so far as I could tell, no moments of pure unfettered subjectivity; indeed the human subject came to seem remarkably unfree, a cultural artefact' (p. 256). So, it was as if the disillusion of 1968 had for ever curdled aesthetic experience for New Historicism, and the course of the May Events was doomed to be repeated in every work of art, where the Duke would inevitably return to punish us for the desires he incited. Nor was a preference for Renaissance literature accidental to this daunting scenario. Every school of criticism has an elective affinity with a particular period, and New Historicism gravitated, like Foucault, to the threshold of the modern era to explore the dialectic of repression and desire at a time when even a sentimentalist such as Bakhtin could recognise a narrowing of carnival culture as popular laughter was outlawed (1968, Chapter 3). If New Historicism had a favorite line, then, it would have been Kent's from the end of *King Lear*: 'All's cheerless, dark, and deadly' (V, iii, 289).

History and the market

Earlier theorists, such as the New Critics, had valorised Renaissance culture as the ideal of organic unity and order; but New Historicism followed Foucault in reading it as the site of the 'dividing practices' that have made us modern subjects. And where criticism had mystified Shakespeare as an incarnation of spoken English, it found the plays embedded in other *written texts*, such as penal, medical and colonial documents. Read within this archival continuum, what they represented was not harmony but the violence of the Puritan attack on carnival, the imposition of slavery, the rise of patriarchy, the hounding of deviance, and the crashing of prison gates during what Foucault called 'the Age of Confinement' at the dawn of carceral society. ' My subject', Foucault told the Californian professors, 'is our subjection: how we turned ourselves into the objects of our own social science, our prisons, asylums and hospitals, and of our own conscience' (Ignatieff 1984, p. 1). So compelling was this account of the genesis of our subjectivity, that even a Marxist critic, such as Louis Montrose, found it hard to resist. His 1983 essay on *A Midsummer Night's Dream* (Chapter 6), printed in *Representations*, the New Historicist flagship, typified the manoeuvres of the American Left when faced with the premise that the 'will to power' circumscribes the human subject not in economic relations but in signs. Shakespeare's comedy is powerful, Montrose proposes, to the extent it 'creates the culture by which it is created, shapes the fantasies by which it is shaped', and thereby engenders 'the cycle of sexual and familial violence, fear, and betrayal' which constitutes the relations of the sexes. The 'intertextual irony' that pervades *A Midsummer Night's Dream* 'contaminates' the play with 'recurrent bestiality and incest... rapes and disastrous marriage', which, together with the 'habitual victimization of women', the Elizabethan text then recycles. But there is, it seems, no historical ground from which to end the vicious circle.

If it was Barthes who spelt out the homology between this cycle of oppression and the system linguists call *langue* – the given language – with its regime of syntax and grammar, it was Foucault who made language identical with power. The Catholic confessional and Freud's consulting room have this in common, he reasoned, that they both require us to produce ourselves as docile subjects by coaxing us to talk. The 'talking cure' was paradigmatic, in his account, of the 'formidable materiality' of all discourse, as, imagining we are liberated or absolved, we manacle ourselves in words. This was the 'discourse theory' that allowed New Historicism to equate the transactions of language with those of capitalism, by conflating verbal with market forces, as Greenblatt did in his book *Shakespearean Negotiations*. For though 'the circulation of social energy' in the production and consumption of Renaissance drama was not, he insisted, part of any 'totalizing system', the exchanges of 'cultural capital' he described turned out to be those of the marketplace, as, 'by moving certain things – principally ordinary language, but also metaphors, ceremonies, dances, emblems, items of clothing, well–worn stories, and so forth – from one cultural zone to another', poetics obeyed the hidden hand of 'trade and trade-offs' (Greenblatt 1988, p. 7). Written at the climax of the speculative boom fuelled by junk bonds, this subsumption of language into the techniques of the dealing room chimed with Reaganomics and its campaign to universalise market competition as human nature. Likewise, Greenblatt's claim that capitalism generates an 'inexhaustible oscillation' of 'boundary making and breaking' (1989, p. 8) echoed the neo-liberal proposition that since 'the economic approach provides a framework for all human behavior', the oppressed only make it worse for themselves by struggle (Becker 1976, p. 14). As the Marxist critic, Fredric Jameson, remarked at the close of the decade, with these theories the market had ironically come to occupy the place formerly held by 'socialism', as a totalitarian Utopia (Jameson 1990, p. 110).

The history restored by New Historicism was a history, then, oddly recalling that of modernism, with its gyre and wheel of fire. Modernism replaced history with eternally recurrent myth: in the Eighties New Historicism repressed historical reality in favour of what Greenblatt called 'the circulatory rhythms of American... production and consumption' (1989, p. 8). With such worship of the market, criticism was in tune with the historian Francis Fukuyama, who in 1989 proclaimed 'the end of history' with the universality of consumer capitalism. The textuality of history was a function, it transpired, of the ubiquity of the shopping mall, where image and commodity were one, the media produced desire, and there seemed to be no reality exterior to 'virtual space'. According to Jameson, all postmodernism fuses form with content (1990, p. 107); and the dogma that a historical referent no longer exists, because history is a story, suited English departments drilled in formalist New Criticism. To be fair, New Historicists never stated that fact and fiction were one, but encouraged by historians such as Natalie Davis and Robert Darnton, their quest for fiction in the archives was liable to efface the historicity of texts. In 1968 Barthes predicted that the historian would become a literary critic, since ' History is henceforth not so much *the real* as *the intelligible* ' (1986, p. 140); but the consequence of reading history for rules governing discourses about the body, pleasure, sexuality or crime, was that all these discrete *histories*, as Foucault termed them, converged in a monologue of mastery. By the mid-Eighties New Historicism was being applied to later periods, but, as Mark Seltzer showed with *Henry James and the Art of Power*, even the nineteenth–century novel was complicit in the same mechanism of discipline and surveillance. Thus, by fetishising power as coterminous with language, New Historicism had mistaken what linguists call *parole* – specific individual utterance – for the entire potential system, so 'confusing life under capitalism with the nature of reality as it must always be' (Graff 1989, p. 180).

It was the fallacy of modernism, Lukács wrote, that 'Man is now what he always was and always will be' (1963, p. 21). New Historicism, which demystified the human condition, threatened by siting itself within 'the lines of credit', of 'money and prestige' (Greenblatt 1989, p. 12), to essentialise capitalism instead. But those who objected that Greenblatt devoted no more space than Foucault to the possibility that the hapless victims of history might resist, misunderstood his equation of representation with power. If 'reality for each society is... constructed out of the qualities of its language and symbols', as he declared in *Learning to Curse* (1991, p. 32), there could be no emancipation, since power and its subject were locked in a hermeneutical circle of mutual exchange. 'You taught me language', Caliban rails at Prospero in *The Tempest*, 'and my profit on't / Is, I know how to curse'; and for the *Representations* school the fact that Prospero endowed his slave's purposes with English words meant that the freedom to curse was empire's most victorious ruse (I, ii, 359–66). Caliban fears his master's art is indeed 'of such pow'r' (374); but one of the first and sharpest New Historicist works, *The Illusion of Power*, by Stephen Orgel, had explicitly disowned the myth that reality is constructed out of signs. Though the drive 'to purify and reform a whole culture was realized in the apparitions and machinery' of the court masques, Orgel commented, as 'Year after year designer and poet created an ideal commonwealth under rational control... Power was asserted only through analogies', which history would expose as a 'charade' (1975, p. 87–9). Likewise, D.J. Gordon, in a study which laid a cornerstone for New Historicism, ended his survey of *The Renaissance Imagination* with a caution not to take theatre for the world: if Renaissance drama was an exorcism, it was 'singularly ineffectual', he observed, as 'Imagery works only to sustain a group's image of itself. Outside (the theatre) a far different vocabulary was directing thought and act' (1975, p. 50). It was a warning his American students did not always heed.

New Historicism broke the base/superstructure, text/context dichotomy, by insisting that works of art are themselves events, which intervene materially in history, rather than mirrors of reality. But the danger in this iconolatry was that history would be aestheticised into a spectacle or game. Nietzsche was often cited as a precursor of such an ironic disinterest, but Greenblatt's identification of Elizabethan theatre with market capitalism, on the ground that 'everything produced by society' was circulated 'through the stage' (1988, p.19),was closer to the idea of 'the state as a work of art' in Jakob Burckhardt's *The Civilization of the Renaissance* (1865), itself rooted in the pessimism of Schopenhauer. Burckhardt had been a subject of New Historicism, when Hayden White demonstrated in a pioneering study that his exaltation of the Renaissance as 'a period when the "cultural" cut itself free of subordination to politics and religion, to float above, dominate, and determine the forms they would take', had more to do with Swiss conservatism after the aborted revolution of 1848, than pre–1600 Italy. Burckhardt's irony before the brute force of the *condottieri*, 'realistic' refusal to moralise, and sense of 'the Renaissance as nothing but the free play' of individuals, was the cynicism, according to this reading, of a middle class that had betrayed its former liberal ideals (1973, pp.244–7). But though Greenblatt traced to Burckhardt his concept of 'the self and state as works of art' (1980, p.162), he did not connect his own ironic stance as a man of '68 with that of the ex-Liberal of 1848. Yet it was precisely *irony* which Alan Liu, in a monumental extension of New Historicism to Wordsworth in 1989, feared in its 'demystifying strategies'. 'How can historical criticism prevent itself from hardening into (in)difference,' Liu asked, if it robs history of a 'material determinant'? If history was a mere play of 'difference', he considered, with no relation to the present, it could provoke only 'Foucauldian laughter, wonder, shock, and irony', but 'irony', he added,'is not by itself criticism' (1989, p.457).

Cultural Materialism

The heyday of New Historicism was the mid-Eighties. After the Crash of 1987, and notwithstanding Fukuyama, it became more difficult to declare 'the end of history', or simply to admire winners and losers for the entrepreneurialism of their will to play against the invisible croupier of the market. What was required of criticism, Liu advised, was 'to identify

with the past', rather than to spectate, by discerning within it its own
'sense of history: its emergent awareness that it is at once an ideological
formation' and a process. Instead of irony, 'the greatest of the holdovers
of New Criticism', a *new* New Historicism would admit 'a certain
"foreknowledge" of the past within the present'. Thus, criticism would
need to defy postmodern fashion, and reinstate something of the 'grand
narrative' of Marx, if it was to make sense of the historicity of texts as well
as the textuality of historicity. To read the past for 'the history of the
present', Foucault always said, had been his Marxian project; and he had
given warrant for the turn back towards what Liu called 'the past's own
worry over the fact that it is not simply the past' (p. 458), when he
observed in an essay called 'The Order of Discourse', that every text is
scored by the conditions of its existence, since 'as history teaches,
discourse is not simply that which translates struggles or systems of
domination, but is the thing for and by which struggle takes place'
(Liu 1989: 52–3). Access to discourse and controls upon it, such as
censorship or means of distribution, are its material determinants; so
discourse, which shapes struggle, is shaped by struggle as it evolves, and
if language constructs reality, it is also constructed *within* it. This theory
of dialectical meaning was very close to that proposed by Althusser, who
also wrote of the 'internal distantiation' within each work, caused by the
friction of surrounding ideologies; and for critics such as Liu it was vital
to grasp the dialectic if 'the sense of history' was ever to be restored to
literary texts.

Himself a founder of a prisoners' aid association, Foucault unlocked a
door, with his concept of contested discourse, not only for the critique of
dominant culture, but also for the possibility of resistance. And while in
Reagan's America Cultural Poetics threatened to swallow history, in
Thatcher's Britain a criticism developed which countered that, if language
does mediate reality, the meanings it assigns may still be challenged,
seized and altered. As Catherine Belsey vigorously declared (Chapter 2),
what was at stake in 'the elision of the signified' – history – by signifying
practice, was access to power itself, since from the European side of the
Atlantic it was evident that 'meaning is not a matter of infinite play'. In
Britain, in the aftermath of the 1982 Falklands war, it was plainer than
ever, she protested, that criticism 'collaborates with the operations of
power' by reducing meaning to free play, for

> It was explicitly in a contest for meaning that British and Argentine
> soldiers killed and mutilated each other in the South Atlantic, both
> sides using might to establish that might is not right. In this as in all
> other wars it was evident that the letter kills. The control of meanings
> is political power, but it is a mistake to suppose that the abolition of the
> signified is the abolition of power.

For Belsey then, the importance of Foucault was not in his depressing scenario of panoptic power, but in his insight that history is 'fictioned from a political reality that renders it true'; and it was the duty of the historicist critic to apply this axiom to the category of Literature, so as to bring out the contradictory definitions assigned to men and women as subjects whose meanings 'slide in history'. From the Renaissance onwards, she saw, canonical works like *Macbeth* had served to install the nation-state, nuclear family and individual subject, but these institutions had been constructed over other practices, such as witchcraft or regicide, which a historical reading would recover within the text as a means of encountering the contingency of every discourse.

If the 'ism' of New Historicism bracketed history within irony, British historicist critics stressed the reality of combat in which people were 'killed and mutilated' for control of meaning. As Belsey noted, even 'the word "I" meant something new in the late sixteenth century', making it the site of contest; and in *The Subject of Tragedy* she analyzed this conflict as it was acted out in Renaissance drama, whose tragic subject was subjectivity itself. Absent from medieval plays, the autonomy of the freeborn Englishman was defined, she showed, in opposition to his mute, submissive wife. But for feminists, the value of Renaissance texts was that they exposed the instability of this system of difference. In the story of Alice Arden, condemned for murdering her husband in 1551, Belsey traced a battle over marriage itself, in which an 'unruly woman' defied subordination (Chapter 7). If the meaning of man or woman is culturally determined, such criticism averred, cultural struggle is no game. Unlike those Whiggish Marxists who read Shakespearean drama as a cutting-edge of the English Revolution, Belsey took the Foucauldian point that authority produces resistance as its 'difference, its visibility'; but 'Subjects exceed the space allotted to them', she asserted, 'work to challenge as well as confirm the existing order', since 'The subject, however defined... does not stay in place. Meaning, the condition of subjectivity, is a location of change' (1985, p. 224). To British historicist critics in the Eighties, therefore, Renaissance texts were sites of conflict, not containment. As Richard Wilson demonstrated in his essay on *Julius Caesar*, they read Shakespearean carnival for its vulnerability to, rather than mastery of the popular violence from which it arose. Where Bakhtin had idealized the crowd, materialist criticism would admit that 'power uses circuses'; but it would also affirm that no sign system, however dominant, is truly global. As the London apprentices proved when they commandeered the Globe, if a culture aspires to universality, it is also likely to be gatecrashed (Chapter 8).

'The history of the subject in the seventeenth century', Belsey decided, 'indicates that our subjectivity is not natural, inevitable or eternal; on the contrary, it is produced and reproduced in and by specific power relations' (1985; p. 223). Where British historicists differed from their American counterparts, then, was in the latters' structuralist assumption that cultures maintain themselves somehow by self-regulation, without effective social agency or transformations. Thus, in *The Tremulous Private Body* of 1984, by Francis Barker (Chapter 9), the story told is again the grim Foucauldian one, of how the body came during the seventeenth century to be dissected on the anatomy table, while the rational, interiorised subject was distilled in the self-censored and gendered discourse of a diarist such as Pepys. But what compels Barker is not the ineluctability of this process, but the inconsistencies in the construction of the bourgeois subject; so that *Hamlet* may be read as an exemplary text precisely because it does *not* conform to modern critical standards of individual psychology or motivation. Barker starts, therefore, from the prince's statement that he has 'that within which passes show', taking this to mean that he refuses the 'forc'd breath... . Together with all forms, moods, shapes' of the ancient regime, as he gropes towards an 'inner reality'(*Hamlet*, I, ii, 75–86). '*Hamlet* is nothing but the prince's evasion of a series of positions offered him', Barker deduces; yet 'the point is not to supply this absence, but to aggravate its historical significance... . From its vantage on the threshold of the modern the text reveals the emptiness of the myth of the autonomous individual. Rather than a gap to be filled, Hamlet's mystery is a void to be celebrated, therefore, against the individualist illusion of man as free and full of meaning: a fable which it is still ours to undo today' (1984, p. 116). Nothing could contrast more with Greenblatt's existential panic, at the end of *Renaissance Self-Fashioning*, that 'to abandon the craving for freedom... in our culture, is to die' (1980, p. 257).

As it hardened into Cultural Poetics, American New Historicism imitated linguistics in its retreat from history, privileging synchrony over diachrony, paradigm over syntagm, and *langue* over *parole*. Paradoxically, it was the very continuity of the English monarchy between the reigns of the two Elizabeths that convinced British critics, by contrast, that 'our culture' was not a closed, self-generating or inescapable system. As Alan Sinfield pointed out in his essay on *Macbeth*, the 'uncanny resemblance between the Gunpowder Plot and the 1984 Brighton Bombing' of the Conservative Cabinet by the IRA, was enough to remind those in the vicinity that in writing of Renaissance drama they were 'dealing with live issues' still in violent contention (Chapter 10). The incomplete nature of England's seventeenth–century revolution had long preoccupied Marxist historiography, but the new literary historicism coincided with a Revisionist history that repudiated economic determinism and emphasised the stability of English society, particularly at local level (Cust and Hughes 1989: 3–17). Without sharing a Tory tendency in this Revisionism, critics such as Sinfield accepted its main thrust, that the British monarchy has been as innovative as those who resisted its aggression. In *Macbeth*, therefore, it was possible to uncover the strategies by which the British state has been perpetuated despite 'persistent structural difficulties'. And since the Eighties were the most confrontational decade in recent British political history, when Margaret Thatcher's spurning of consensus unmasked a ruthless will to power in battles with trade unionists, pacifists, poll tax protestors and civil rights campaigners, Sinfield read Shakespeare's tragedy as a blueprint for the legitimation of state violence. Macbeth's bloody deeds are applauded when they serve Duncan, we are reminded, and questioned only when he himself becomes a usurper; but it is by identifying this contradiction at the root of the Absolutist state, Sinfield argued, that oppositional criticism can unravel the ideology sustaining its successor, the so-called United Kingdom.

As Cultural Poetics hermeticised culture, then, into a self-sustaining sign system, British critics were engaged in a reading of Renaissance drama that located the material struggles inscribed in literature. Cultural Materialism was the name they adopted in contradistinction to Cultural Poetics and as a statement of a conviction that 'writing, teaching, and other modes of communicating all contribute to the long-term establishment of legitimacy' (Chapter 10). Though the name had been coined by Raymond Williams, Cultural Materialism was above all inflected by Althusser's theory that though ideology is produced 'in words', it has a material existence since it is *reproduced* in institutions such as the theatre or university. So, like the Althusserian 'Regulation Theory' economists, Cultural Materialists recognised that capitalism has no developmental logic, but without abandoning a belief in struggle as the means of transition from one regime to another. Their recurring refrain, quoted by Jonathan Dollimore in a 1985 collection entitled *Political Shakespeare*, was that 'ruling culture does not define the whole of culture... and it is the task of the oppositional critic to re-read culture so as to amplify the voices of the ruled, exploited, oppressed, and excluded' (Chapter 3). For Dollimore, therefore, a tragedy such as *The White Devil* indicates both the Jacobean domination of women, and the way their fate was tied to an entire system of exploitation (Chapter 11). We inherit a narrative of oppression, he acknowledged, but our duty as re-readers is to show that 'It did not, and still does not, need to be so'. In this stress on the ongoing potential for resistance, Cultural Materialism was thus encouraged by Gramsci's proposition that hegemony is decided in a ceaseless 'war of position' that occurs between the world's great battles. 'Pessimism of the intellect: optimism of the will': Gramsci's famous dictum could apply to these critics, who insisted that texts can be rewritten, as Brecht rewrote Shakespeare, since there is indeed 'subversion, no end of subversion' to be carried onward.

Representations do shape history, Cultural Materialists agreed, but are shaped by history in turn, since they are terrains of struggle as well as of submission. This was also the finding of the American critic Leonard Tennenhouse in *Power on Display*, which endorsed the Foucauldian line that Renaissance 'stagecraft collaborated with statecraft in producing spectacles of state', but then described the Shakepearean theatre as a place where real events punctured the stage-managed frame. So, though Jacobean city comedy strove to bind London to patriarchy, it could not permanently cow its freemen or Levellers (Chapter 12). Feast table and festival became irrelevant to the marketplace when the servile began to call the tune. Bakhtin, who had dreamed of a mystic carnival in Stalin's Russia, had theorised such contestation with his more convincing notion of *heteroglossia*, whereby the fair became the intersection of colliding dialects and languages (1968, p. 470). Out of such a contest, the dominant accent would not always emerge victorious, as Peter Stallybrass and Allon White observed in *The Politics and Poetics of Transgression*. In *Bartholemew Fair* Ben Jonson bid adieu to the dirt and laughter of the crowd, but the role he then assumed was the dictatorship of the library, where 'His plays were to become fitting companions' to unread tomes. So if Kafka provided the slogan that an empire of words brooks no subversion, Cultural Materialists responded that, by imagining itself all-powerful, Literature struck the pose of Kafka's 'Fasting Showman', whose fate is to die of starvation in a side-show, whilst 'the crowds hurry on past' (Chapter 13). For no sooner did the pundit preach the end of history than history erupted in the greatest popular movement since 1789. When the Berliners razed the wall, when the Romanians stormed the TV studio, when the Czechs elected a playwright President, people learned that history is not necessarily a Kafkaesque prison. Though it destroyed the Marxist state, 1989 proved Marx right; if not in circumstances of their choosing, men and women *do* make their own lives.

References

THEODOR ADORNO and MAX HORKHEIMER, *Dialectic of Enlightenment*, New York: Herder and Herder, 1972.

LOUIS ALTHUSSER, *22ème Congrès*, Paris: Maspero, 1977.

— 'Ideology and Ideological State Apparatuses', in *Essays in Ideology*, London: Verso, 1984.

MIKHAIL BAKHTIN, *Rabelais and His World*, trans. Helene Iswolsky, Bloomington: Indiana University Press, 1968.

FRANCIS BARKER, *The Tremulous Private Body : Essays on Subjection*, London: Methuen, 1984.

ROLAND BARTHES, *Mythologies*, ed. and trans, Annette Lavers, London: Jonathan Cape, 1972.

— 'Inaugural Lecture, Collège de France', in *A Barthes Reader*, ed. Susan Sontag, London: Jonathan Cape, 1982, 459–69.

— 'The Discourse of History', in *The Rustle of Language*, trans. Richard Howard, Oxford: Basil Blackwell, 1986.

JEAN BAUDRILLARD, *The Evil Demon of Images*, Sydney: Power Institute, University of Sydney, 1988.

GARY BECKER, *An Economic Approach to Human Behavior*, Chicago: University of Chicago Press, 1976.

CATHERINE BELSEY, *The Subject of Tragedy: Identity and Difference in Renaissance Drama*, London: Methuen, 1985.

WALTER BENJAMIN, 'On Some Motifs in Baudelaire', in *Illuminations*, trans, Harry Zohn, ed. Hannah Arendt, London: 1970.

TED BENTON, *The Rise and Fall of Structural Marxism: Althusser and his Influence*, London: Macmillan: 1984.

RICHARD CUST and ANN HUGHES, 'After Revisionism', in Richard Cust and Hughes, *Conflict in Early Stuart England: Studies in Religion and Politics, 1603–1642*, London: Longman, 1989.

NATALIE ZEMON DAVIS, *Fiction in the Archives*, Berkeley: University of California Press, 1988.

REGIS DEBRAY, *Le Scribe*, Paris: Grasset, 1980.

GILLES DELEUZE and FELIX GUATTARI, *L'anti-Oedipe*, Paris: Minuit, 1972.

JACQUES DERRIDA, 'The White Mythology: Metaphor In the Text of Philosophy', *New Literary History*, VI, i, 1974, 7–74.

UMBERTO ECO, 'Language, Power, Force', in *Faith in Fakes: Essays*, trans. William Weaver, London: Secker and Warburg: 1986.

MICHEL FOUCAULT, 'The Order of Discourse: Inaugural Lecture, Collège de France', trans, Ian McLeod, in *Untying the Text: Post- Structuralist Reader*, ed. Robert Young, London: Routledge & Kegan Paul, 1981a.

— *The History of Sexuality: Volume I: an Introduction*, trans. Robert Hurley, Harmondsworth: Penguin, 1981b.

ANDRÉ GLÜCKSMANN, *Les Maîtres Penseurs*, Paris: Grasset, 1977.

D. J. GORDON, *The Renaissance Imagination: essays and lectures*, ed. Stephen Orgel, Berkeley: University of California Press, 1975.

GERALD GRAFF, 'Co-optation', in H. Aram Veeser (ed.), *The New Historicism*, London: Roulege & Kegan Paul, 1989, 168–81.

ANTONIO GRAMSCI, *Selections from the Prison Notebooks*, ed. and trans. Quintin Hoare and Geoffrey Nowell Smith, London: Lawrence and Wishart: 1971.

STEPHEN GREENBLATT, *Renaissance Self-Fashioning: from More to Shakespeare*, Chicago: Chicago University Press, 1980.

— *Shakespearean Negotiations: the Circulation of Social Energy in Renaissance England*, Oxford: Oxford University Press 1988.

— 'Towards a Poetics of Culture', in *The New Historicism*, ed. H. Aram Veeser, London: Routledge: 1989, 1–14.

MICHAEL IGNATIEFF, 'Michel Foucault', *University Publishing*, 13, Summer 1984, Berkeley: University of California Press.

FREDRIC JAMESON,'Postmodernism and the Market', *Socialist Register:* 1990, London, 1990, 95–110.

ALAN LIU, *Wordsworth: the Sense of History*, Stanford: Stanford University Press, 1989.

GEORG LUKÁCS, *The Meaning of Contemporary Realism*, trans. John and Necke Mander, London: Merlin Press, 1963.

HERBERT MARCUSE, *One-Dimensional Man*, Boston: Beacon Press, 1964.

MARSHALL MCLUHAN, *Understanding Media: the Extensions of Man*, New York: McGrawHill, Inc., 1964.

STEPHEN ORGEL, *The Illusion of Power: Political Theater in the English Renaissance,* Berkeley: University of California Press, 1975.

MARK POSTMAN, *Amusing Ourselves to Death: Public Discourse in Age of Show Business*, London: William Heinemann, 1986.

EDWARD SAID, *Orientalism*, New York: Pantheon, 1978.

MARK SELTZER, *Henry James and the Art of Power,* Ithaca: Cornell University Press, 1984.

SUSAN SONTAG, *A Barthes Reader*, London: Jonathan Cape, 1982.

TZVETAN TODOROV, *The Conquest of America: the Question of the Other*, New York: Harper and Row, 1982.

LIONEL TRILLING, *Beyond Culture: Essays on Literature and Learning*, New York: Viking Press, 1968.

H. ARAM VEESER (ed.), *The New Historicism*, London: Routledge, 1989.

HAYDEN WHITE, *Metahistory: the Historical Imagination in Nineteenth–Century Europe*, Baltimore: The Johns Hopkins University Press, 1973.

1   The New Historicism in Renaissance Studies[*]

JEAN E. HOWARD

In 1986 the American journal ELR (*English Literary Renaissance*) devoted a special edition to New Historicism, and this effectively consolidated the movement for a 'return of history' in literary studies into a recognised school of criticism. Jean Howard's contribution provided an overview of the theoretical issues at stake, and defined New Historicism from a sympathetic, though not uncritical perspective. Surveying the work in progress, Howard explains the movement in terms of the critique of **essentialist humanism** in wider contemporary theory: the assault on the concept of a universal and transhistorical 'human nature'. It is as a consequence of this philosophical **decentring**, she suggests, that the New Historicist critics are drawn first and foremost to Renaissance literature, where the modern idea of an essential 'Man' was initially constituted. New Historicism is therefore committed to the premise that instead of passively reflecting history, Renaissance texts assisted in making it intelligible. This is a cautious formulation, and Howard is careful not to imply that art constructs the reality it represents. We reproduce here only the opening, more generalised sections of this essay.

A new kind of activity is gaining prominence in Renaissance studies: a sustained attempt to read literary texts of the English Renaissance in relationship to other aspects of the social formation in the sixteenth and early seventeenth centuries. This development, loosely called the 'new history' and flourishing both in Europe and America, involves figures such as Stephen Greenblatt, Jonathan Dollimore, Alan Sinfield, Kiernan Ryan, Lisa Jardine, Leah Marcus, Louis Montrose, Jonathan Goldberg, Stephen Orgel, Steven Mullaney, Don E. Wayne, Leonard Tennenhouse, Arthur Marotti, and others. Journals such as *ELH, English Literary Renaissance, Representations,* and *LTP: Journal of Literature Teaching Politics* regularly

[*] Reprinted from *ELR*, 16 (1986), pp. 13–20.

publish 'new history' pieces. In short, a critical movement is emerging, and in this essay I want to look at the new historicism both to account for its popularity and to try to define what, if anything, is new about its approach to the historical study of texts and then to examine some instances of new historical criticism.

1

Historical scholarship linking Renaissance literary works to various non-literary historical contexts is not, of course, in and of itself, new, although in the last thirty years in particular, formalist approaches have been in the ascendency in some quarters of Renaissance studies. This is partly due to the importance of lyric and partly due to the importance of Shakespeare in the English curriculum. For quite different reasons, formalism has dominated the study of both. In America, the lyric poems of the Renaissance provided many of the set texts, the verbal icons, used by New Critics to demonstrate their critical methods, and several generations of students trained in the New Criticism now teach today's students. And in both England and America, the plays of Shakespeare have often been treated not as products of a particular moment but as works for and of all times: universal masterpieces (Longhurst 1982). Consequently, until quite recently formalist studies of theme, genre, and structure dominated the criticism of these texts. History, when broached at all, usually meant the history of ideas, as in E.M.W. Tillyard's famous study of the importance to Renaissance literature of the 'Elizabethan world picture' (Tillyard 1943). In part, then, the new historicism is a reaction against formalism, though one must note that certain very contemporary formalisms – particularly structuralism and deconstruction – have not been enormously influential in Renaissance studies. The novel and the Romantic and modern periods have more often provided the exemplary texts for these movements. By contrast, the new historicism has been taken up with particular intensity, in part has been created, by Renaissance scholars.

Why is this so? In part, I believe, many teachers of Renaissance literature simply have grown weary, as I have, of teaching texts as ethereal entities floating above the urgencies and contradictions of history and of seeking in such texts the disinterested expression of a unified truth rather than some articulation of the discontinuities underlying any construction of reality. Yet a purely formalist pedagogy should be debilitating for those who teach *any* literature, not just that of the Renaissance. Why, then, is it critics of Renaissance texts who have found in a new historicism an answer to their dissatisfaction?

The answer, I believe, lies partly in the uncanny way in which, at *this* historical moment, an analysis of Renaissance culture can be made to speak to the concerns of late twentieth-century culture. For a long time the Renaissance as cultural epoch was constructed in the terms set forth by Jacob Burckhardt; it was the age of the discovery of man the individual,the age of the revival of classical culture, the age of the secularization of life. How enmeshed this picture was in nineteenth-century ideology is now clear, but it may be less clear what the *current* revival of interest in the Renaissance may have to do with twentieth-century concerns. Consider, for example, the work of Jonathan Dollimore, who is particularly interested in the way in which what he calls essentialist humanism has both dominated the study of English literature in the twentieth century and also has prevented recognition of the fact that man is not so much possessed of an essential nature as constructed by social and historical forces. Looking back at the seventeenth century, Dollimore sees it as a sort of privileged era lying between the Christian essentialism of the Middle Ages – which saw man as a unitary being who took his essence from God – and Enlightenment humanism – which first promulgated the idea of man the individual: a unified, separate, and whole entity with a core of identity emanating from within. For Dollimore, the late Renaissance was the age of skepticism in which in the drama in particular one finds recorded a recognition of the discontinuous nature of human identity and its social construction (Dollimore 1984). It is not hard to see affinities between this picture of the Renaissance and certain contemporary understandings of our own historical moment as the post-humanist epoch in which essentialist notions of selfhood are no longer viable.

I will return later to the theoretical issues raised by the fact that when a new historian looks at the past he or she is as likely as an old historian to seen an image of the seeing self, not an image of the other. But for the moment I want to continue to pursue further the way in which 'the Renaissance' is being reunderstood within that configuration of periods which constitutes the framework by which literary historians make the past intelligible. Within this framework the Renaissance has usually been assigned a transitional position between the Middle Ages – held to be encumbered with a monolithic Christian ideology and a static and essentially unhistorical view of itself – and the modern era – marked by the rise of capitalism with its attendant bourgeois ideology of humanism, progress and the all-important interiority and self-presence of the individual. Almost inevitably, this construction of the past has produced the question: just *how* modern and *how* medieval was this transitional period? Burckhardt, looking back at Renaissance Italy from mid-nineteenth-century Germany, stressed the modernity of the Renaissance, its sense of itself as definitively different from prior periods of history. Others have insisted on the fundamental continuity between the Renaissance and the Middle Ages. But now, as critics and historians sense the modern era slipping away and a new episteme inchoately emerging, the Renaissance is being appropriated in slightly different terms: as *neither* modern nor medieval, but as a boundary or liminal space between two more monolithic periods where one can see acted out a clash of paradigms and ideologies, a playfulness with signifying systems, a self-reflexivity, and a self-consciousness about the tenuous solidity of human identity which resonate with some of the dominant elements of postmodern culture.

In short, I would argue that the Renaissance, seen as the last refuge of preindustrial man, is of such interest to scholars of the postindustrial era because these scholars construe the period in terms reflecting their own sense of the exhilaration and fearfulness of living inside a gap in history, when the paradigms that structured the past seem facile and new paradigms uncertain. Clearly this emerging reading of the Renaissance is made possible by the traditional emphasis on the Renaissance as an age of transition. Previously critical emphasis was on continuity – on the way the period linked to the past or anticipated the future. Now the emphasis is on *dis*continuity, seen most clearly perhaps in Dollimore's insistence on the early seventeenth century as a kind of interperiod standing free of the orthodoxies of the Middle Ages and the Enlightenment. But the difference between prior and past conceptions of the Renaissance is also clear in the way the new historical critics so often make the period intelligible by narratives of rupture, tension, and contradictions, as, for example, when Greenblatt talks about the gap between the Renaissance ideology of human freedom and the actuality of Renaissance man as the subject of determining power relations (Greenblatt 1980) ,or, as we shall see, when Louis Montrose stresses the enormous contradictions in the social formation which Renaissance literature attempted to mediate. And, as I have been hinting, these narratives of discontinuity and contradiction are narratives which owe much to the way late twentieth-century man construes his own historical condition.

Having said this much, I hope it is clear that I don't find it odd or arbitrary that the new historical criticism has taken the Renaissance as one of its primary objects of study. And I hope it is clear that at least in one respect I find the 'new history' resembling older forms of historical inquiry in that both see the past at least in part through the terms made available by the present. This observation, moreover, raises a more fundamental question: in just what ways is the 'new' historical criticism new? Does its newness consist simply in its break with the formalism that has long been prominent in the study of Renaissance literature? Is its newness due mainly to the way it draws a somewhat different picture of the Renaissance than Burckhardt drew? Or are its methods and its understanding of what constitutes the historical investigation of texts in some fundamental way different from those which enabled an earlier historical criticism?

To answer these questions, I want to sketch what must of necessity be a simplified picture of some of the assumptions underlying the historical criticism of a figure such as Tillyard. These assumptions include the following: that history is knowable; and that historians and critics can see the facts of history objectively. (This last assumption is particularly paradoxical since it rests on the premise that while literature is implicated in history, historians and critics are not). The criticism resulting from these premises often led to the trivialization of literature: to its reduction to a mere reflection of something extrinsic to itself, and to the trivialization of criticism: its reduction to a mode for explaining (not reading) texts in terms of their relationship to a fixed ground, such as James I's monarchical practices, English imperialism, or Puritan theology. At its worst, such criticism reduced literary study to the search for topical references; at its best it illuminated particular texts in relationship to great men or events or ideas of a period, but its distinguishing mark was always the assumption that literature was a mirror reflecting something more real and more important than itself.

Contemporary theoretical work, it seems to me, has seriously put in question a number of these assumptions. For example much reception and reader-response criticism has directly challenged the idea that a reader/interpreter can ever escape his or her own historicity in order to encounter objectively the historical difference encoded in texts. Consequently, one must question the status of that 'knowledge' about the past produced either by the historian or the historically minded critic. Similarly, Saussurian linguistics has challenged the premise that language functions referentially. One mode of historical criticism assumes that literature is connected to history in that its representations are direct reflections of historical reality, but one must ask what happens to that assumption when the referentiality of language itself is questioned. If literature refers to no ground extrinsic to itself, what can be the nature of its relationship to an historical context or to material reality? In fact, if one accepts certain tendencies in poststructuralist thought, is the possibility of an historical criticism even conceivable?

It is only by addressing these and a number of other equally urgent theoretical issues that a new historical criticism can distinguish itself from an older, more positivistic critical practice. The new historicism may well turn out to be an important extension of the theoretical ferment of the past two decades, a movement which will fundamentally rethink how we study texts in history. On the other hand, there is a real danger that the emerging interest in history will be appropriated by those wishing to suppress or erase the theoretical revolution that has gone on in the last several decades. Ironically, the 'new history' may well turn out to be a backlash phenomenon: a flight from theory or simply a program for producing more 'new readings' suited to the twenty-five-page article and the sixty-minute class (Levin 1979). Readings remain, after all, the dominant form of scholarly production in the discipline, and as many are discovering, a cursory journey through Lawrence Stone or Keith Thomas can open up numerous possibilities for new readings based on the ostensible family structure, economic dilemmas, or political upheavals of the sixteenth and seventeenth centuries. There is nothing inherently wrong with doing readings, but if those readings are based on untenable or unexamined assumptions about literature and history, then they are merely a form of nostalgia and not a serious attempt to explore what it means to attempt an historical criticism in a postmodern era.

In order to evaluate just how new the historical work being done in regard to Renaissance literature really is, I want to do two things. First, I wish to examine in much greater detail some of the theoretical issues facing any historical criticism today and, second, to examine in some detail the work of two of the best practitioners of the new history – Stephen Greenblatt and Louis Montrose – in order to see how they engage or ignore the problematics of their undertaking. From this double examination I hope it will be possible to suggest some of the directions in which such criticism must move if its newness is to be fundamental and not cosmetic.

2

In order to understand what does, or might, constitute the core of a truly new historical criticism one must begin, I believe, with the basic issue of what one assumes to be the nature of man, the creature whose works, thought, and culture have been the focus of most historical inquiry. One of the most striking developments of contemporary thought is the widespread attack on the notion that man possesses a transhistorical core of being. Rather, everything from maternal 'instinct' to conceptions of the self are now seen to be the products of specific discourses and social processes (Foucault 1970). This is a much more radical view of just how thoroughly man is a creature of history than has obtained in the past. It is quite different to argue that man has no essential being and to argue that, while in different periods people display different customs and social arrangements, they nonetheless possess an unchanging core of human traits that makes them all part of 'the family of man' (Barthes 1972).

One can see the idea of a transhistorical human essence in Jonas Barish's very fine study of what he calls 'the anti-theatrical prejudice' in Western culture. For him, the prejudice, while taking slightly different forms from antiquity to the present, nonetheless reflects a fear or a distrust innate to or inherent in the human mind (Barish 1981). Barish does not really entertain the possibility that a phenomenon in one period, which *seems* analogous to a phenomenon in another, may arise amid such different social conditions and play such a different role in a culture's power relations and discursive systems that the two phenomena cannot be seen as continuous with one another or as the products of an underlying human nature.

By contrast, Jonathan Dollimore, in his study of seventeenth-century tragedy, takes as his point of departure the idea – which he sees inscribed within Renaissance texts – that man has no essential nature, no traits not the product of social forces at a particular historical juncture (Dollimore 1984). Consequently, while Barish assumes an essential core of humanness which history can modify or shape in various ways, Dollimore assumes that nothing exists before the human subject is *created* by history. Consequently, an historical criticism working from Dollimore's premises will find an enormous range of new topics open for historical investigation; topics such as the way emotions and what we call instincts – and not just economic structures or political beliefs – are produced in a particular, historically specific social formation, and the way, of course, in which literature variously participates in this process of construction.

While one may accept in theory that there is no shared human essence linking contemporary man to Renaissance man, however, that does not solve the problem of how one is to acknowledge or recognize the radical otherness of the past. As I suggested earlier, there is a powerful tendency to appropriate the past in terms of the present, and contemporary reader-response theorists have acutely drawn the attention of literary critics to the extent to which the interpreter and his or her historical moment are present in their interpretations of earlier literary works. Hayden White has been perhaps the most eloquent spokesperson for the view that the same is true for historians. For White, interpretation is a key part of each historian's work and consists largely of providing a 'plot structure for a sequence of events so that their nature as a comprehensible process is revealed by their figuration *as a story of a particular kind*', that is, as a narrative intelligible to the readers of a particular age (White 1978). White stresses how thoroughly the historical discipline differs from a pure descriptive science and how much it owes to literary art, as, through its dominant tropes and narrative structures, it gives to 'history' a shape owing as much to the patterns of intelligibility available to the historian from his own culture as to those that may have informed a prior age.

Similarly, Tzvetan Todorov in his book on the Spanish conquest of Central America takes as his primary concern the way the Spanish dealt with the otherness of the American Indians, either by construing them as nonhuman or bestial and, as such, fair game for any kind of genocidal treatment, or by construing them as embryonic Europeans needing only the help of a Spanish education and a Spanish religion to make them mirrors of their white 'brothers'. In neither case was the *difference* of the Indian tolerated or allowed to interrogate European ways. Instead, the Indians were either denied inclusion within the category of the human or assimilated utterly into the

Spanish idea of what the human was (Todorov 1984).

Recognizing in a fresh way the difficulty of escaping the prison of the present moment and present culture to realize historical and cultural otherness, how is a contemporary historical criticism to proceed? One of Michel Foucault's central contributions to contemporary historical studies has been to recognize and strive against the tendency to project the present into the past and so to construct narratives of continuity. He counters this tendency by postulating the notion of radical breaks between historical epistemes. He refuses to look for continuities, for precursors of one era in former eras, but by a massive study of the situated discourses of particular disciplines he attempts to let their strangeness, their difference, speak (Foucault 1977). Foucault's is a procedure of vigilance, and it produces some remarkable results. But it does not erase the fact that there is no transcendent space from which one can perceive the past 'objectively'. Our view is always informed by our present position; the objects we view available only in the slipperiness of their textualization. That does not seem to me to negate the project of historical investigation, but it does mandate a transformed attitude toward it. First of all, it seems necessary to abandon the myth of objectivity and to acknowledge that all historical knowledge is produced from a partial and a positioned vantage point. Further, instead of evoking a monolithic and repressive 'history' one must acknowledge the existence of 'histories' produced by subjects variously positioned within the present social formation and motivated by quite different senses of the *present* needs and *present* problems which it is hoped will be clarified or reconfigured through the study of the past.

The intellectual historian Dominick LaCapra captures something of the difficulty of contemporary historical criticism when he speaks of establishing a self-conscious 'dialogue' with the past. By using this term, he wishes to acknowledge, on the one hand, the impossibility of retrieving the 'objective facts' of history, and, on the other hand, the undesirability of a ' "presentist" quest for liberation from the "burden" of history through unrestrained fictionalizing and mythologizing' (La Capra 1983). La Capra deliberately evokes the language of psychoanalysis to explain his idea of this process of transference, a process in which past and present remain separate and yet merged, an understanding of the one proceeding only from self-conscious entanglement with the other. The goal of such a dialogue is not, certainly, the willful reproduction of the present in the mirror of the past, but it involves a steady acknowledgement that the past is not transparent and that the pursuit of history is neither objective nor disinterested.

I take, then, that as starting points a new historical literary criticism assumes two things: (1) the notion that man is a construct, not an essence; (2) that the historical investigator is likewise a product of his history and never able to recognize otherness in its pure form, but always in part through the frame work of the present. This last point leads one to what is perhaps the crux of any 'new' historical criticism, and that is to the issue of what one conceives history to be: a realm of retrievable fact or a *construct* made up of textualized traces assembled in various configurations by the historian/interpreter. Hayden White points to the central question in dispute when he argues that history is produced, not discovered, and when he shows how those synthesizing histories which attempt to describe a period are *someone's* historically–conditioned constructs. In doing so, he calls in question one of the ways literary critics have often used 'history', that is, as the realm of fact which can ground the seeming multiplicity or polysemous nature of the literary artifact. White writes: 'Nor is it unusual for literary theorists, when they are speaking about the 'context' of a literary work, to suppose that this context – the "historical milieu" – has a concreteness and an accessibility that the work itself can never have, as if it were easier to perceive the reality of a past world put together from a thousand historical documents than it is to probe the depths of a single literary work that is present to the critics studying it (White 1978).

More is at stake here, I think, than a simple naivete on the part of literature professors about what historians do. Rather, the notion of history as transparent and objectively knowable is *useful* to the literary critics, for it can serve as a means of unclouding the stubborn and troubling opacity of the literary text and of stabilizing its decentered language. A common way of speaking about literature and history is just that way: literature *and* history, text *and* context. In these binary oppositions, if one term is stable and transparent and the other in some way mirrors it, then that other term can be stabilized and clarified, too. This is particularly crucial at a time when the notion of textuality has challenged traditional ideas about a literary work's communicative clarity and mimetic nature. By explaining literature by a ground extrinsic to itself, the ground of history, which literature supposedly reflects, the critic makes the problem of opacity disappear. But at a price. One result of seeing literature and history in this particular way is the inevitable 'flattening' of the literary work. It is emptied of its rich signifying potentiality by being used as a springboard to something else, a mere pointer back to extratextual reality, as when Duke Vincentio is read simply as a representation of James I and the whole of *Measure for Measure* reduced to a comment on this monarch's beliefs and practices. Literature thus becomes, not something to be *read*, but to be *explained*. Second, such a procedure seldom stops to question why a particular historical context has been selected to align with the literary text, as if such choices were not often arbitrary in the extreme and inimical to seeing the full intertextual network in which a literary work exists. Third, the practice reduces literature to a merely mimetic object. I don't think any serious historical criticism can dodge the fact that undertaking such criticism raises the questions of some relationship between literature and what may be considered external to itself. The key question is: what is the nature of that relationship? Does the text absorb history into itself? Does it reflect an external reality? Does it produce the real?

It increasingly seems that in confronting these issues a new historical criticism has to accept, first, that 'history' is not objective, transparent, unified, or easily knowable and consequently is extremely problematic as a concept for grounding the meaning of a literary text; second, that the very binarism we casually reinforce every time we speak of literature and history, text and context, is unproductive and misleading. Literature is *part* of history, the literary text as much a context for other aspects of cultural and material life as they are for it. Rather than erasing the problem of textuality, one must enlarge it in order to see that *both* social and literary texts are opaque, self-divided, and porous, that is, open to the mutual intertextual influences of one another. This move means according literature real power. Rather than passively reflecting an external reality, literature is an agent in constructing a culture's sense of reality. It is part of a much larger symbolic order through which the world at a particular historical moment is conceptualized and through which a culture imagines its relationship to the actual conditions of its existence. In short, instead of a hierarchical relationship in which literature figures as the parasitic reflector of historical fact, one imagines a complex textualized universe in which literature participates in historical processes and in the political management of reality.

I take as an exemplary brief example of these assumptions Don Wayne's work on the way Ben Jonson's plays help to produce an ideology for a pre-capitalist age. Wayne argues that while Jonson seemingly remained an apologist for an older feudal ideology which stressed the importance of the social collectivity over the individual, plays such as *The Alchemist* and *Bartholomew Fair* find him paradoxically promulgating contractual rights by which the prerogatives of the individual are secured, including the rights of individual authorship (Wayne 1982). Clearly Jonson is responding to something in the social formation around him – to the emerging possibilities for printing texts as individual enterprises, to the breakdown of a national sense of community under the Stuarts, to the allure of the entrepreneurial spirit released by Puritanism and by the growth of the London merchant and professional class. Yet Wayne's chief point is that Jonson is also – through his dramatic texts – *producing* the modes of thought that encouraged and to some extent created these other changes so that it becomes nearly impossible to pinpoint an origin or single cause for social change. Many aspects of the social formation, including literary texts, work in a variety of ways and at a variety of speeds to produce the variegated entity we call history.

A major feature of a new historical criticism, therefore, must be a suspicion about an unproblematic binarism between literature and history and a willingness to explore the ways in which literature does more than reflect a context outside itself and instead constitutes one of the creative forces of history. In fact, until one truly banishes a mimetic theory of literature, several problems which have characteristically bedeviled the historical study of literature will continue to rear their heads. It is always interesting, for example, to watch what happens when people read Lawrence Stone on the Renaissance family and then try to relate what they find there to, say, Shakespeare's romantic comedies. Stone argues that marriages, at least among the middle and upper classes, were made late, were arranged by parents, were made largely for economic convenience, not love, and resulted in conjugal and parent-child relationships often lacking in warmth and intimacy (Stone 1977). What has all this to do with the picture of romantic love and rebellion against parental authority we see in Shakespeare's comedies? On the surface, not much; but what does this discrepancy mean: that Stone got things wrong? That literature is autonomous from the social realm? That Shakespeare is a universal genius who got at the enduring truths of life rather than at the anomalies of a particular historical moment? That literature is, after all, something to be read on a bus, a pure escape from the real? It is when faced with just these sorts of problems that one realizes the need for more than a simple mimetic theory of literature. A culture's discourse about love and the family need not, and probably seldom does, correspond exactly to how people live. (One could say the same about politics, economics, or personal identity.) One of the great strengths of Foucault, in my view, is his recognition that the discursive practices of an age, while producing or enabling certain behaviors, never coincide with them exactly. There is always some gap between what discourse authorizes and what people do, though 'history' may never be able to disclose that gap precisely. What is important is how and why cultures produce and naturalize particular constructions of reality: what contradictions such constructions neutralize or expose, what economic and political ends they advance, what kinds of power relations they display. Literature is one of many elements participating in a culture's representation of reality to itself, helping to form its discourse on the family, the state, the individual, helping to make the world intelligible, though not necessarily helping to represent it 'accurately'.

In any particular instance, to see how a text functions in the construal of reality means seeing it in an intertextual network of considerable historical specificity. For example, to understand how women were made intelligible in the Renaissance, one cannot look only to social 'facts', such as how many children they had, or of what diseases and at what ages they died. One must also consider how the medical, legal, and religious spheres functioned to provide a discourse about women which may have represented them in ways quite at odds with what we see as the apparent 'facts' of their situation. The whole point is to grasp the terms of the

discourse which made it possible to see the 'facts' in a particular way –
indeed, made it possible to see certain phenomena as facts at all. Only then
will we begin to grasp how another period shaped individuals as historical
subjects; and to see literature's role in this process one must place literary
representations in a much broader differential field in which *how* they
correspond to or challenge other constructions of reality and *how* they take
their place in a particular configuration of discursive practices and power
relations can be observed.

In this rethinking of the place of literature *in* history, it seems to me that
much of the historically based literary criticism can benefit from recent
developments in Marxist thought. It used to be that Marxism, while
providing one of the few theoretically coherent approaches to an historical
criticism, suffered from its own version of the history/literature binarism
in that it saw in literature and other elements of 'the superstructure' a
reflection of the dominant economic mode of production and of the class
struggle it spawned. In other words, a particular privilege was given to the
economic realm as the determining factor in every sort of cultural
production and in the shaping of human consciousness. This assumption
has been challenged, perhaps most influentially, by Louis Althusser, who
argues for the *relative* autonomy of the superstructure from the material
base and for the importance of the educational apparatus, the institution of
literature, and other factors, in the shaping of human consciousness. In
short, he acknowledges that there is not an homologous relationship
between all levels of culture such that the ideologies of the superstructure
can in any simple way be related to an economic base. Consequently, one
finds the question of cause and effect relationship more complicated than
was formerly thought, as I have already noted in regard to Wayne's work
on Jonson; and one must take more seriously than before the role of
literature in changing human consciousness and so, eventually, in affecting
other material practices – not merely being affected by them (Althusser
1971).

Furthermore, while it has always been Marxist criticism which has most
insistently probed the question of literature's relationship to ideology,
contemporary Marxism has developed more complex ways of approaching
that question than it formerly possessed. While ideology is a vexed term
with a complex history, it may be useful to distinguish two of its most
common definitions: first, as a false consciousness foisted on the working
classes by a dominant class; second, as any of those practices by which one
imagines one's relations to the actual conditions of one's existence. This
second, Althusserian definition of ideology denies that the ideological is
simply the product of a conspiratorial power group. Rather, the ideological
is omnipresent; it inheres in every representation of reality and every social
practice, as all of these inevitably confirm or naturalize a particular
construction(s) of reality. Consequently, there is no way in which ideology

can ever be absent from literature, any more than it can be absent from *any* discursive practice. Jonathan Dollimore argues, and I agree with him, that it may be useful to retain both understandings of ideology: to retain the option of seeing some literature as the conscious and direct product of one power group or classes attempts to control another group or class by the misrepresentation of their historical condition; and at the same time to recognize that in most instances power groups or classes are both less self-conscious and less monolithic than such a formulation implies and that a more complex approach to the problem of ideology requires a recognition of the pervasive, masterless (in the sense of acknowledging no one origin), and often heterogeneous nature of the ideological.

This being so, that the ideological is everywhere and traverses literature as surely as other modes of representation, the question becomes: does literature have a special way of treating the ideological? This, of course, has been an issue that has bedeviled Marxism for some time. In the 1960s Pierre Macherey contended that literature, separate both from science and ideology, inevitably produced a *parody* of ideology, a treatment of it which inevitably distanced the reader from the ideological matter being treated, exposing its contradictions and laying bare the artifice surrounding its production (Macherey 1978,pp. 51–65). But does literature really handle the ideological in this way? I think not, at least not in every instance. First, as Tony Bennett has recently shown, such a view rests on the premise (deriving most centrally in the twentieth century from Russian Formalism) that literature is a special and unique form of writing with its own inherent and universal properties, one of which is the way it acquires internal distance from the ideological material which traverses it (Bennett 1979,pp. 18–43). But as any historian of literature can show, the literary canon is a social construct, not an empirical given. As a number of boundary cases make clear today, some texts are regularly treated as literature and as something else. For example, are Bacon's essays literature or philosophy? Are diaries literature or something else? Is travel literature really literature or history or even philosophy? While it is quite possible in practical terms to speak of a literary canon, it seems quite another matter to assume that the texts in that canon are there by virtue of some mysterious inner property which they all share. They are all there for a variety of reasons having to do with the privileging of certain artifacts by powerful groups, and their 'properties' are in large measure the result of the operations performed upon them by generations of critics (Bennett 1979,p.9). Hence, while it may be useful for strategic or practical purposes to retain the category 'literature' it seems wrong to assign to the texts gathered under that rubric a single, universal stance toward the ideological.

In fact, I would argue that a new historical criticism attempting to talk about the ideological function of literature in a specific period can most usefully do so only by seeing a specific work relationally – that is, by seeing how its representations stand in regard to those of other specific works and discourses. A work can only be said to contest, subvert, recuperate, or reproduce dominant ideologies (and it may do any of these) if one can place the work – at least provisionally and strategically – in relation to others. And, as I have argued above, the most illuminating field of reference may not be just other literary works. To return to the example of the representation of women: in order to understand the ideological function of, say, certain plays for the public theater, it may be important to see their representations of women in the light of the representations offered in masques, in conduct manuals, in medical treatises, and in Puritan polemics all written at approximately the same time.

Moreover, it seems important to entertain the possibility that neither literary texts nor other cultural productions are monologic, organically unified wholes. Only when their heterogeneity is suppressed by a criticism committed to the idea of organic unity do they seem to reveal a unitary ideological perspective or generic code. It may be more productive to see them as sites where many voices of culture and many systems of intelligibility interact. Dominick LaCapra makes this point, and in doing so he draws both on the work of Jacques Derrida and on that of Mikhail Bakhtin, thus uniting deconstruction and Marxist demystification in the project of fracturing the unified surface of the text to let the multiplicity of its social voices be heard. In this project he finds two of Bakhtin's concepts, *heteroglossia* and *carnivalization* (in Michael Holquist's translation), to be particularly useful in that the first suggests that novelized discourse is polyvalent, riddled with 'unofficial' voices contesting, subverting, and parodying dominant discourses, while the second suggests that the emergence in writing of these 'unofficial' voices has the revolutionary potential to expose the arbitrary nature of official constructions of the real (LaCapra 1983,pp. 52–61; Bakhtin 1981). But it is important to remember that for Bakhtin not all literature performs a carnivalizing function or is dialogic and polyvalent. There are no inherent laws governing the functioning of those texts we call literature. Consequently, one of the greatest challenges facing a new historical criticism is to find a way to talk about and discriminate among the many *different* ways in which literature is traversed by – and produces – the ideologies of its time.

2 Literature, History, Politics*

CATHERINE BELSEY

While the New Historicism was emerging among American Renaissance scholars, an energetic debate was taking place in England about the function of English in education and the social ramifications of the **canon** or 'great tradition' of literature. Catherine Belsey's essay was an intervention in this debate, and she argued that the advent of linguistics had so altered the concept of meaning that writing and reading could no longer be taken for granted as unmediated or innocent exercises. Crucially, the notion of an unproblematic 'history' had been displaced by Michel Foucault's researches into the discontinuous **histories** of different groups and institutions. His theory that **discourse** is tied to **power** demands that literary critics turn their attention to the political reasons why certain texts (such as Shakespeare's) have been made valuable since the Renaissance. Written before the name 'New Historicism' had become general among American critics, this article showed that English Renaissance specialists were also engaged in a 'return to history', but with a more pragmatic cultural agenda.

To bring these three terms together is hardly to do anything new. *Literature and History* has been doing it since its inception; the Essex Conference volumes do it (Barker 1981); Raymond Williams has spent his life doing it; historians like E.P. Thompson and Christopher Hill, glancing sideways at literature, have frequently done it; a venerable tradition of Marxist criticism all over Europe does it. Less marginally, as far as the institution of literary criticism in Britain is concerned, T.S. Eliot, F.R. Leavis and E.M.W. Tillyard did it when they constructed between them a lost Elizabethan utopia where thought and feeling were one, where the native rhythms of speech expressed in poetry the intuitive consciousness of an organic

*Reprinted from *Literature and History*, 9 (1983),pp. 17–26.

community, and every one recognised in the principle of order the necessity of submission to the proper authorities, social and divine.

And yet paradoxically to bring these three terms together *explicitly* is still to scandalise the institution of literary criticism, because it is to propose a relationship between the transcendent (literature), the contingent (history) and the merely strategic (politics). The institution is dedicated to the infinite repetition of the best that has been thought and said in the world, and this luminous heritage, however shaded by the Discarded Image of medieval ideas, or the Victorian Frame of Mind, stands ready to be released from history by the apparatus criticus which the academic profession supplies, and to reappear resplendent before every new generation of student-critics. The model for the institution's conception of history as a kind of perpetual present, and its conviction of the vulgarity of politics, is Arnold's essay, 'The Study of Poetry', where it is clear from the 'touchstones' Arnold invokes that great poetry from Homer to Milton, despite minor differences of language and setting, has always taught the same elegiac truth, that this world is inevitably a place of sorrow and that the only heroism is a solitary resignation of the spirit.

The sole inhabitant of the universe of literature is Eternal Man (and the masculine form is appropriate), whose brooding, feeling presence precedes, determines and transcends history as it precedes and determines the truths inscribed in the English Syllabus, the truths examination candidates are required to reproduce. "'When we read Chaucer's early poems we feel the author's awareness of how complex and involved the events and circumstances of life are, of how they defy any single interpretation". Discuss' (Oxford Honour School of English Language and Literature, 'Chaucer and Langland ', 1980). Miraculously, Chaucer's awareness of the complexity of it all precisely resembles mine, ours, everyone's. Every liberal's, that is, in the twentieth century: a modern 'recognition' is rendered eternal by literary criticism. Examination questions, the ultimate location of institutional power, identify the boundaries of the discipline, and define what it is permissible to 'discuss', as they so invitingly and misleadingly put it (Davies 1982, p.39). "'The sense of a peculiarly heightened personal dignity is at the centre of Donne's work" (Alvarez). *Either* discuss with reference to Donne *or* describe the sense of personal dignity in any other writer of the period' (Oxford Honour School ... 'English Literature from 1600 to 1740', 1980). Or any other writer of any other period, perhaps, because it is a reading from the present, from a position of liberal humanism, which finds the sense of personal dignity at issue wherever it looks.

Historians have been quite clear, at least since Eric Hobsbawm's seminal articles were published in *Past and Present* in 1954, that the seventeenth century was a period of general crisis. That general crisis has apparently no repercussions whatever for the literature of the period as it is defined in the broad run of examinations at O Level, at A Level and in the universities. Where the crisis is glimpsed, it is instantly depoliticised: '"Courtly poetry without a court." What do the Cavalier poets gain or lose by the decline and final absence of a Court? Discuss one or more poets.'(Cambridge English Tripos, Part II, 'Special Period, 1616–60', 1981). Had the question asked what was gained or lost from the collapse of the Court by agricultural labourers, by an emerging feminism or by radical politics, the answer might have mattered. But that would be history. What matters in English is the implications of the Revolution of the 1640s for the Cavalier poets. Alternatively, the crisis is personalised as the idiosyncratic interest of an individual: '"Throughout *Paradise Lost* Milton's concern is to present and investigate a crisis of authority."Discuss' (Oxford Honour School ...'Spenser and Milton', 1980). What it is not possible to say in answer to that question is how a crisis of authority is at the heart of *Paradise Lost*, not as a matter for the author's investigation, but as a source of fragmentation within the poem and the writing of the poem. It is precisely the location of authority – in God and in the human will, in the subjectivity of the narrator and in a signification which is outside the narrator and appeals to all human cultures – or rather, it is these contradictory locations of authority which insist on the inadequacy of any reading of the poem that looks for 'Milton's concern' as a guide to its possible meanings. And among these possible meanings are the limits of what can be said about authority in a period when authority is in crisis.

When the institution of literary criticism in Britain invokes history, whether as world picture or as long-lost organic community, it is ultimately in order to suppress it, by showing that *in essence* things are as they have always been. The function of scholarship, as of coventional criticism, is finally to reinstate the continuity of felt life which the ignorance of a trivialising society obscures. No history: no politics. Because if there has never been change at a fundamental level, there are no rational grounds for commitment to change. No politics – or rather, no overt politics, since there is, of course, no political neutrality in the assertion of an unchanging essential human nature.

The radical theoretical work of the last twenty years has not always confronted the suppression of history and politics in literary criticism. Structuralism, widely regarded, when it began to appear in Britain in the sixties and early seventies, as the beginning of the end of civilisation as we know it, quite failed to challenge the institution on this central issue. Saussure's *Course in General Linguistics* is a remarkably plural text. Insofar as its readers confined themselves to its discovery of an opposition which precisely replicated the classic liberal opposition between the individual and society, structuralism offered no threat to the equilibrium of the free West. Freed by the concept of the difference between *langue* and *parole*, which permitted utterance within the permutations already authorised by the language-system, the structuralists set off in quest of similar timeless enabling systems in other spheres, the form of all societies, the pattern of all narrative, the key to all mythologies. It was the signifying system itself which was held to lay down, long before the drama of history was inscribed in it, the elementary structures of culture and of subjectivity (Lacan 1977, p, 148). Structuralism thus proclaimed Eternal Man and the suppression of history with a new and resounding authority. Ironically, Saussure's analysis of language as a system of differences was invoked to initiate the elimination of all difference.

But it was also Saussure's work, in conjunction with the Marxist analysis of ideology, which permitted Roland Barthes on behalf of anarchism to identify Eternal Man as the product and pivot of bourgeois mythology (Barthes 1972, p. 140), and subsequently to repudiate the structuralist equalisation of all narrative 'under the scrutiny of an in-different science' (Barthes 1975, p. 3). This was possible because one of the effects of the *Course in General Linguistics* was to relativise meaning by detaching it from the world outside language. Insofar as language is the condition of meaning and thought, meaning and thought differ from one language to another, one culture to another. As linguistic habits alter, cultures are transformed. Difference, history, change reappear.

They disappear again, however, in American deconstructionism, which nails its colours to the free play of the eternal signifier. Here all writing and all speech is fiction in a timeless present without presence, and the subject celebrates its own non-being in an infinite space where there is no room for politics. Deconstructionism has nothing to say about the relationship between literature and history, or the political implications of either. Nothing explicit, that is.

What is at stake is the elision of the signified. Saussure distinguished three terms or orders – the signifier (the sound or written image), the signified (the meaning) and the referent (the thing in the world). A certain elusiveness in Saussure's theory concerning the relationship between meaning and *intention* prompted Derrida's deconstruction of Saussure's phono-centrism, and in the interests of contesting the notion of a pure, conceptual intelligibility, a 'truth in the soul' which precedes the signifier (Derrida 1976, p. 15). Derrida in that context treats as suspect, as he puts it, the difference between signifier and the signified (p. 14). The order of the signified is subsumed under 'presence', which is understood indiscriminately as concept, intention or referent, so that meaning, being and truth are collapsed together. Elsewhere Derrida's notion of *differance* does not eliminate the possibility of signification. Meaning exists, neither as being nor as truth, but as linguistic difference, textually produced, contextually deferred (Derrida 1973, pp. 129–60). But the opening pages of *Grammatology* invite vulgar deconstructionists to take it that there is no such thing as meaning, and in consequence, since meaningless language is literally unthinkable, that words mean whatever you want them to mean. This *Looking-Glass* reasoning leads at best to an anarchic scepticism, the celebration of undecidability as an end in itself, and at worst to the reinstatement of the mirror phase, where the critic-subject at play rejoices in its own linguistic plenitude. In the constant and repeated assertion of the evaporation of meaning there is no place to analyse the contest for meaning, and therefore no politics, and there is no possibility of tracing changes of meaning, the sliding of the signified, in history.

It was at this point in the debate that political post-structuralism began to turn more insistently to the work of Foucault. (It was also, perhaps, at this point in the debate that Foucault's own work became more explicitly political). Foucault goes beyond Derridean scepticism to the extent that he identifies the relationship between meaning (or discourse-as-knowledge) and power. Conceding that language does not map the world, but distinguishing signified from referent and intention, knowledge from what is true (because guaranteed by being or by things), Foucault reinstates politics in a post-structuralist world which, despite the heroic efforts of Althusser, could not support the concept of science. *I, Pierre Rivière* ... documents Pierre Rivière's murder in 1835 of his mother, his sister and his brother. It is made clear that the meaning of Pierre's memoir exceeds any single reading of it, since reading always takes place from a position and on behalf of a position. The question is not, 'what is the *truth* of Pierre Rivière's behaviour?', 'was he *really* mad?' but 'from what positions, inscribed in what knowledge, did the contest between the legal and the medical professions for control of Pierre Rivière take place? And in addition, 'what possibilities of a reading of these documents are available now which were not available in the 1830s? From the perspective of the present, the records of Pierre Rivière's act of unauthorised resistance can be read as a part of the history of the present, because they demonstrate the social and discursive construction of a deviant and at the same time permit him to speak. The 'humanitarian' practice which confines the criminally insane for life silences them even more effectively than execution, since whatever they say is rendered inaudible, 'mad'.

Foucault's work politicises the polyphony of the signified. The plurality of meaning is not exclusively a matter of infinite play, as recent history demonstrates. Meanings produce practices and generate behaviour. It was explicitly in a contest for the meaning of 'aggression' – as colonialism, as theft, or as violence – that British and Argentine soldiers killed and mutilated each other in the South Atlantic, both sides using might to establish that might is not right. In this as in all other just wars it was evident that the letter kills. While the American deconstructionists play, Reagan is preparing to reduce us all to radioactive rubble to preserve our freedom. The control of meanings – of freedom, democracy, the American way of life – the control of these meanings is political power, but it is a mistake to suppose that the abolition of the signified is the abolition of power. On the contrary, deconstructionism collaborates with the operations of meaning-as-power precisely insofar as it protests that there is no such thing.

Foucault's work brings together two of my three terms, history and politics, in its analysis of the ways in which power produces new knowledges. It is a history of ideas in which ideas are understood as generating practices, a history of discourses in which discourses define and are reproduced in institutions. It offers a challenge to classical Marxist politics to the extent that it refuses to find a central and determining locus of power in the mode of production, and a challenge to empiricist history in its refusal to treat documents as transparent. In a sense we needed both challenges. Whatever the inadequacies of Althusserian Marxism, it was impossible for a post-structuralist politics subsequently to retreat from the decentring concept of overdetermination. To attribute a relative autonomy to ideology was to open up the possibility of a history of the forms in which people become conscious of their differences and begin to fight them out. These forms are precisely the classical superstructural forms of law, metaphysics, aesthetics, and so on, but with the addition of those areas where struggle has become increasingly pressing in the twentieth century–sexuality, the family, subjectivity. The theory of relative autonomy, however vulnerable in itself, permitted attention within Marxism to these areas as sites of struggle.

But if post-structural politics implied the dispersal of history into new areas, it also implied historiography which was both more and less than the transcription of lost experience. To take a single example of the problem, Lawrence Stone's book, *The Family, Sex and Marriage in England, 1500–1800*, published in 1977, is extremely welcome insofar as it tackles precisely one of those areas which politics (specifically, in this instance, feminist politics) had brought to prominence. But Stone's vocabulary of 'evidence', 'source'. 'documents'and 'sampling' define the historian's quarry, however elusive, as something anterior to textuality, revealed through its expression in the mass of diaries, memoirs, autobiographies and letters cited. History is seen as the recovered presence of pure, extra-discursive, representative experience, 'how it (usually) felt'. What Stone produces in consequence is a smooth, homogeneous evolution, with overlapping strata for enhanced verisimilitude, from the open lineage family of the late Middle Ages to the affective nuclear family in the seventeenth and eighteenth centuries. But the affective nuclear family begins to be glimpsed in discourse in the mid-sixteenth century, and there is evidence (if evidence is what is at stake) that this concept of a private realm, in which power is exercised invisibly for the public good, defines itself in this period in opposition to a control of marriage exercised directly but precariously by the sovereign as head of the church. What

Stone's quest for the representative experience behind the documents eliminates is the *politics* of the history of the family, precisely the issue which put it on the feminist map, the contest for power, which is also a contest for meaning in its materiality, the struggle about the meaning and practice of family life.

Representative experience is understood to be whatever a lot of people said they felt, and it is held to be the origin of, and to issue in, representative behaviour. This notion of the 'fit' between documented feelings and recorded behaviour relegates to the margins of history any feelings or behaviour which were not dominant. Struggle thus becomes marginal, always the province, except in periods of general struggle, of the idiosyncratic few. But more important, modes of resistance to what was dominant are ignored if they could not be formulated in so many words, were not allowed a voice, were not experienced as resistance or can be defined as deviant. Stone makes no space, for instance for a consideration of witchcraft as a practice offering women a form of power which was forbidden precisely by orthodox concepts of the family.

The point is worth dwelling on because Stone is by no means an isolated case. Among those radical historians for whom struggle is heroic, if still idiosyncratic, the quest for experience and the belief that documents are ultimately transparent remain common. But documents do not merely transcribe experience: to the extent that they inevitably come from a context where power is a stake, they are worth analysis not as access to something beyond them, not as evidence of how it felt, but as themselves locations of power and resistance to power.

A post-structuralist history needs to re-examine Stone's mass of documents (and perhaps others), and to address to them a different series of questions. These include the following (borrowed, in modified form, from Foucault):

What are the modes and conditions of these texts?
Where do they come from; who controls them; on behalf of whom?
What possible subject positions are inscribed in them?
What meanings and what contests for meaning do they display?

(cf. Foucault 1977 p. 138)

The answers to these questions give us a different history of the family, sex and marriage. This is the history not of an irrecoverable experience, but of meanings, of the signified in its plurality, not the referent in its singular but imaginary presence. It is, therefore, a history of struggle and, in consequence, a political history.

Such a history is not offered as objective, authoritative, neutral or true. It is not outside history itself, or outside the present. On the contrary, it is part of history, part of the present. It is irreducibly textual, offering no place outside discourse from which to interpret or judge. It is explicitly partial, from a position and on behalf of a position. It is not culturally relative in so far as relativism is determinist and therefore a- political: 'I think like this because my society thinks like this'. But its effect is to relativise the present, to locate the present in history and in process.

Foucault's work gives us a methodology for producing our own history and politics, a history which is simultaneously a politics, but it has little to say about my third term, literature. Literature is not a knowledge. Literary criticism is a knowledge, produced in and reproducing an institution. Some of the most important and radical work of the last decade has been devoted to analysis of the institution of literary criticism, challenging its assumptions, exposing its ideological implications and relativising its claims to universality and timelessness. One of the central concerns of this work has been the interrogation of the idea of literature itself as 'the central co-ordinating concept of the discourse of literary criticism, supplying the point of reference to which relationships of difference and similarity within the field of writing are articulated' (Bennett 1981, p. 139). Tony Bennett's point here is an important one. 'Literature' signifies as an element in a system of differences. It is that which is *not* minor, popular, ephemeral or trivial, as well as that which is not medicine, economics, history or, of course, politics. 'Literature' designates a value and a category.

That conjunction – of value and category – issues in English departments as we know them, and generates, I have argued, the continuous production and reproduction of hierarchies of subjectivity (Belsey, 1982). We need, therefore, as Tony Bennett argues, to call into question both the category– the autonomy of literary studies – and the value – Literature as distinct from its residue, popular fiction. We need to replace the quest for value by an 'analysis of the social contestation of value' (Bennett 1981, p. 143).

Work on the institution of literary criticism is centrally concerned with the reception of literary texts, with the text as site of the range of possible meanings that may be produced during the course of its history, and with the knowledges inscribed in both dominant and radical discourses. Its importance seems to me to be established beyond question. Here is a field of operations which brings together literature, history and politics in crucial ways, undermining the power of the institution and challenging the category of Literature.

The effect of this project, in other words, is to decentre literary criticism, to displace 'the text', the 'primary material', from its authoritative position at the heart of the syllabus, to dislodge the belief in the close reading of the text as the critic's essential and indispensable skill. Quite whether we can afford to dispose of the literary text altogether is not usually made clear, but it seems implicit in the project that we can do without it for most of the time. What is to be read closely is criticism, official reports on the teaching of English, examination papers, and all the other discursive displays of institutional power.

But before we throw out the Arden Shakespeares and the Penguin English Library (in order to make a space for the Critical Heritage and the Newbolt Report), I want to propose a way of recycling the texts, on the grounds that work on the institution is not the only way of bringing together literature, history and politics, of undermining literary studies as currently constituted, or of challenging the category of Literature. I want to argue in favour of at least one additional way of doing all those things (in the hope of forestalling one of those fierce bouts of either-orism which periodically dissipate the energies of the left).

Literature (or fiction: the fields defined by the two words are not necessarily co-extensive: what about Bacon's *Essays*, Donne's sermons, the 'Epistle to Dr Arbuthnot', *The Prelude*? But perhaps we read these texts as fiction now, so the term will perhaps serve to modify the ideological implications of Literature) – literature or fiction is not a knowledge, but it is not only a site where knowledge is produced. It is also the location of a range of knowledges. In this sense the text always exceeds the history of its reception. While on the one hand meaning is never single, eternally inscribed in the words on the page, on the other hand readings do not spring unilaterally out of the subjectivities (or the ideologies) of readers. The text is not an empty space, filled with meaning from outside itself, any more than it is the transcription of an authorial intention, filled with meaning from outside language. As a signifying practice, writing always offers raw material for the production of meanings, the signified in its plurality, on the understanding, of course, that the signified is distinct from the intention of the author (pure concept) or the referent (a world already constituted and re-presented).

The intertextual relations of the text are never purely literary. Fiction draws not only on other fiction but on the knowledges of its period, discourses in circulation which are themselves sites of power and the contest for power. In the case of *Macbeth*, for instance, the Victorian fable of vaulting ambition and its attendant remorse and punishment is also a repository of Reformation Christianity, morbid, demonic, apocalyptic; of the Jacobean law of sovereignty and succession; of Renaissance medicine; and of Stuart history. Equally, since narrative fiction depends on impediments (where there are no obstacles to be overcome there's no story), *Macbeth* depends on resistance to those knowledges, on what refuses or escapes them: on witchcraft seen as a knowledge which repudiates Christian knowledge, on regicide, madness, suicide, as evasions of a control which is thereby shown to be precarious. A political and historical reading of *Macbeth* might analyse these discourses, not in the manner of Tillyard, as a means of a deeper understanding of the text, and at the same time a lost golden world where nature itself rose up to punish resistance to the existing order, but on the contrary, as a way of encountering the discourses themselves in their uncertainty, their instability, their relativity.

Narrative necessarily depends on the establishment within the story of fictional forms of control and resistance to control, norms and the repudiation of norms. And in the period to which English departments are centrally committed, from the Renaissance to the present, the criterion of verisimilitude, towards or against which fiction has consistently pressed, has necessitated that these concepts of control and normality be intelligible outside fiction itself. Thus, sovereignty, the family, subjectivity are defined and redefined in narrative fiction, problematised and reproblematised. *Macbeth* (again) offers, in the scene with Lady Macduff, an early instance of the emerging concept of the affective nuclear family – a private realm of domestic harmony shown as vulnerable to crisis in a public and political world which is beginning to be perceived as distinct from it. It presents, on the other hand, the fragmentation of the subject, Macbeth, under the pressure of a crisis in which the personal and the political are still perceived as continuous.

In *Critical Practice* I tried to distinguish between three kinds of texts, which I identified as declarative, imperative and interrogative. The declarative text imparts 'knowledge' (fictional or not) to the reader, the imperative text (propaganda) exhorts, instructs or orders the reader, and the interrogative text poses questions by enlisting the reader in contradiction (Belsey 1980, pp 90ff.). It now seems to me that this classification may have been excessively formalistic, implying that texts can unilaterally determine their reception by the reader. As we know, a reading practice which actively seeks out contradiction can *produce* as interrogative a text which has conventionally been read as declarative. Nonetheless, the categories may be useful if they enable us to attribute a certain kind of specificity to literary/fictional texts. The danger of formalism is to be set against the structuralist danger of collapsing all difference. That there is a formal indeterminacy does not mean that we can never speak of form, any more than the polyphony of 'freedom' prevents us from condemning police states. In the period of *Macbeth* many of the available written texts are imperative – sermons, tracts, pamphlets, marked as referring to a given external reality, and offering the reader a position of alignment with one set of values and practices and opposition to others (divorce, for instance, or patriarchal sovereignty). Fictional (declarative or interrogative) texts, by contrast, marked as alluding only indirectly to 'reality', informing without directly exhorting, offer a space for the problematisation of the knowledges they invoke in ways which imperative texts cannot risk. Radically contradictory definitions of marriage in a divorce pamphlet inevitably reduce its propaganda-value: plays, on the contrary, can problematise marriage without affecting the coherence of the story.

To say this is not, I hope, to privilege literature (and certainly not Literature) but only to allow it a certain specificity which identifies its use-value in the construction of the history of the present. A vest is not a sock, but it is not in consequence obvious that one is better than the other. On the basis of this specificity which is neither privilege nor autonomy, I want to urge that lyric poetry, read as fiction, is also worth recycling. Sexuality and subjectivity are the twin themes of the lyric, and since any text longer than, say, an imagist poem, moves towards argument or narrative, and therefore towards crisis, similar definitions and problematisations of these areas of our history offer themselves for analysis here. Sexuality, gender, the subjects are not fixed but slide in history, and this sliding is available to an analysis which repudiates both the quarry of an empiricist history (experience, the world) and the quarry of conventional criticism (consciousness, the author).

The quest is for, say, the subject in its meanings. The word, 'I', the fixed centre of liberal humanism, may always *designate* the speaker, but it means something new in the late sixteenth century, and something new again in the early nineteenth century. Equally, sexuality is not given but socially produced. We don't have access to the eighteenth-century experience of sexuality, but we can analyse the contest in that period for its meaning. It may be the case that the size of household in Britain has not changed much since the Middle Ages, but the meaning of the family, institutionally and in practice, has changed fundamentally – and can therefore change again. This kind of analysis is a stake through the heart of Eternal Man, and the world of practice as well as theory is consequently laid open to effective radical political action.

The reading practice implied by this enterprise – the production of a political history from the raw material of literary texts – is a result of all that post-structuralism has urged about meaning: its often marginal location, its disunity and discontinuity, as well as its plurality. In this way the text reappears, but not as it 'really was'. On the contrary, this is the text as it never was, though it was never anything else – dispersed, fragmented, produced, politicised. The text is no longer the centre of a self–contained exercise called literary criticism. It is one of the places to begin to assemble the political history of the present.

I say 'to begin' because it is immediately apparent that such a history is not bounded by the boundaries of Literature or literature. Literary value becomes irrelevant: political assassination is problematised in Pickering's play, *Horestes* (1567) as well as in *Hamlet*. Equally, the subject is a legal and a psychoanalytic category just as much as a literary one; the family is defined by medical and religious discourses as well as by classic realist texts. And so the autonomy of literature begins to dissolve, its boundaries to waver as the enterprise unfolds. The text does not disappear, though the canon does; and fiction is put to work for substantial political ends which replace the mysterious objectives of aesthetic satisfaction and moral enrichment.

Two projects, related but distinct, immediately present themselves. The first is the synchronic analysis of a historical moment, starting possibly but not inevitably from literary texts. This has perhaps been the project of the Essex conferences, focussed on a series of crises (1848, 1936, 1642, 1789), and subtitled, 'the Sociology of Literature'. The Essex volumes have made available some excellent work, but if the projected archaeology did not materialise in its entirety, there are reasons for this which have little to do with the value or the practicality of the project itself. I suspect that one of these reasons was that the project was not shared by all participants. (There is no reason why it should have been: it makes no exclusive claims). Ideally the project is a collective one, but it's not easy to work collectively if you meet only once a year. It's also a long-term project involving deliberate and patient analysis, and it may be that the conference paper is not an ideal place for its presentation and discussion.

But if the Essex conferences have not achieved everything that was hoped for, they have produced work which in various ways suggests important directions for the future (Barker 1981). And in addition, there is a second and analogous project – what Foucault sporadically calls a genealogy because it traces change without invoking a single point of origin (Foucault 1977, pp. 139–64, etc.). This is a diachronic analysis of specific discontinuities – in sovereignty, gender, the subject, for instance. And where else should we begin this analysis but by looking at fiction, poetry, autobiography? If we start with the texts on the syllabus – because they are available and for no other very specific reason – we shall not end with them, because the enquiry inevitably transgresses the boundaries of the existing discipline.

The proposal is to reverse the Leavisian enterprise of constructing (inventing) a lost organic world of unfallen orality, undissociated sensibility and uncontested order. In fact, in so far as it concerns the sixteenth and seventeenth centuries, the kind of archaeology I have in mind uncovers a world of violence, disorder and fragmentation. The history of the present is not a history of a fall from grace but of the transformations of power and resistances to power. The claim is not that such a history, or such a reading of literary texts, is more accurate, but only that it is more radical. No less partial, it produces the past not in order to present an ideal of hierarchy, but to relativise the present, to demonstrate that since change has occurred in those areas which seem most intimate and most inevitable, change in those areas is possible for us.

According to Foucault, who invents the verb 'to fiction' in order to undermine his own use of the word 'truth', 'one "fictions" a history starting from a political reality that renders it true, one "fictions" a politics that doesn't as yet exist starting from a historical truth' (Foucault 1979, pp. 74–5). I want to add this: the literary institution has 'fictioned' a criticism which uncritically protests its own truth; we must instead 'fiction' a literature which renders up our true history in the interests of a politics of change.

3 Shakespeare, Cultural Materialism and the New Historicism*

JONATHAN DOLLIMORE

The 'return to history' in the study of Renaissance literature proceeded on different tracks in America and England in the 1980s, and Jonathan Dollimore's essay was a discussion of these divergences, as well as an account of why it was that in both cases historicist criticism was focusing on Shakespearean culture. Critics were divided, he considered, between those who believed that culture makes history and those who affirmed that history makes culture. In particular, interpretation of Renaissance drama polarised in a debate about whether texts tended to subvert or reinforce order. This **subversion/containment** dispute was important in relation to the institutional role of intellectuals, and Dollimore argued for an 'oppositional criticism' alive to the material force of culture and therefore explicit about its own political position. He termed this, after the English radical theorist, Raymond Williams, and in contradistinction to New Historicism, **Cultural Materialism**.

One of the most important achievements of 'theory' in English studies has been the making possible a truly interdisciplinary approach to – some might say exit from – the subject. Actually, such an objective had been around for a long time, though largely unrealised outside of individual and often outstanding studies. With the various structuralisms, Marxism, psychoanalysis, semiotics and post-structuralism, there occurred a significant dismantling of barriers (barriers of exclusion as well as of containment) and many critics discovered what they had wanted to know for some time – how, for example, history and philosophy could be retrieved from their 'background' status and become part of both the content and the perspective of criticism. At the same time this was possible only because quite new conceptions of philosophy and history were involved. In utilising theory in the field of literary studies we find that it has made possible far

*Reprinted from *Political Shakespeare: New Essays in Cultural Materialism*, ed. Jonathan Dollimore and Alan Sinfield (Manchester University Press, 1985), pp. 2–18.

more than it has actually introduced. By this criterion alone it proves a major intellectual contribution. But not everyone approves, as the anti-theoretical invective of recent years has shown. We don't propose to dwell on this reaction, nor on the much vaunted 'crisis' in English studies, except to remark that if there is a crisis it has more to do with this reaction than with theory itself.

But of course 'theory' is as erroneous a title as was 'structuralism', both giving a misleading impression of unity where there is in fact enormous diversity. We are concerned here with one development of recent years, cultural materialism; it preceded the advent of theory but also derived a considerable impetus from it.

The term 'cultural materialism' is borrowed from its recent use by Raymond Williams; its practice grows from an eclectic body of work in Britain in the post-war period which can be broadly characterised as cultural analysis. That work includes the considerable output of Williams himself, and, more generally, the convergence of history, sociology and English in cultural studies, some of the major developments in feminism, as well as continental Marxist-structuralist and post-structuralist theory, especially that of Althusser, Macherey, Gramsci and Foucault.

The development of cultural materialism in relation to Renaissance litera-ture has been fairly recent although there is already a diverse and developing field of work relating literary texts to, for example the following: enclosures and the oppression of the rural poor (Williams 1973); state power and resis-tance to it (Lever 1971); reassessments of what actually were the dominant ideologies of the period and the radical countertendencies to these (Aers 1981, Heinemann 1981, Sinfield 1982, Dollimore 1984); witchcraft; the chal-lenge and containment of the carnivalesque (Stallybrass 1986); a feminist recovery of the actual conditions of women and the altered understanding of their literary representations which this generates (Jardine 1983, Shepherd 1981); conflict between class fractions within the State and, correspondingly, the importance of a non-monolithic conception of power (Dollimore and Sinfield 1985b).

Much of this work is explicitly concerned with the operations of power. But it is in the United States that most attention has been given to the representations of power in Renaissance literature. This work is part of an important perspective which has come to be called the new historicism, a perspective concerned generally with the interaction in this period between State power and cultural forms and, more specifically, with those genres and practices where State and culture most visibly merge. An analysis by the new historicism of power in early modern England as itself deeply theatrical – and therefore of the theatre as a prime location for the representation and legitimation of power – has led to some remarkable studies of the Renaissance theatre as well as of individual plays, Shakespeare's included.

According to Marx, men and women make their own history but not in conditions of their own choosing. Perhaps the most significant divergence within cultural analysis is that between those who concentrate on culture as this making of history, and those who concentrate on the unchosen conditions which constrain and inform that process of making. The former allows much to human agency, and tends to privilege human experience; the latter concentrates on the formative power of social and ideological structures which are both prior to experience and in some sense determining of it, and so opens up the whole question of autonomy.

A similar divergence is acknowledged in Stephen Greenblatt's *Renaissance Self-Fashioning*, an outstanding instance of the new historicism. In an epilogue Greenblatt tells how he began with an intention to explore 'the role of human autonomy in the construction of identity'. But as the work progressed the emphasis fell more and more on cultural institutions - family, religion and the State – and 'the human subject itself began to seem remarkably unfree; the ideological product of the relations of power in a particular society' (Greenblatt 1980, p.256).

History versus the human condition

Materialist criticism refuses to privilege 'literature' in the way that literary criticism has done hitherto; as Raymond Williams argued in an important essay, 'we cannot separate literature and art from other kinds of social practice, in such a way as to make them subject to quite special and distinct laws'. This approach necessitates a radical contextualising of literature which eliminates the old divisions between literature and its 'background', text and context. The arts 'may have quite specific features as practices, but they cannot be separated from the general social process' (Williams 1980, p.44). This attention to social process has far-reaching consequences. To begin with it leads us beyond idealist literary criticism – that preoccupied with supposedly universal truths which find their counterpart in 'man's' essential nature; the criticism in which history, if acknowledged at all, is seen as inessential or a constraint transcended in the affirmation of a transhistorical human condition.

It would be wrong to represent idealist criticism as still confidently dominant in Shakespeare studies; in fact it is a vision which has been failing for some time, and certainly before the advent of theory. In recent decades its advocates have tended to gesture towards this vision rather than confidently affirm it; have hesitated over its apparent absence, often then to become preoccupied with the tragic sense of life as one which recuperated the vision as absence, which celebrated not man's transcendent consciousness but his will to endure and to know why transcendence was itself an illusion. In short, an existentialist-tragic sense of life was in tension with a more explicitly spiritual one, the former trying to break with the latter but being unable to because it had nowhere to go; a diminished metaphysic, aetiolation became the condition of its survival.

Materialist criticism also refuses what Stephen Greenblatt calls the monological approach of historical scholarship of the past, one 'concerned with discovering a single political vision, usually identical to that said to be held by the entire literate class or indeed the entire population' (Greenblatt 1982, p.5). E. M. W. Tillyard's very influential *The Elizabethan World Picture*, first published in 1943 and still being reprinted, is perhaps the most notorious instance. Tillyard was concerned to expound an idea of cosmic order ' so taken for granted, so much part of the collective mind of the people, that it is hardly mentioned except in explicitly didactic passages' (Tillyard 1943, p.18).

The objection to this is not that Tillyard was mistaken in identifying a metaphysic of order in the period, nor even that it had ceased to exist by the turn of the century (two criticisms subsequently directed at him). The error, from a materialist perspective, is falsely to unify history and social process in the name of 'the collective mind of the people'. And such a perspective would construe the 'didactic passages' referred to by Tillyard in quite different terms: didacticism was not the occasional surfacing, the occasional articulation, of the collective mind but a strategy of ideological struggle. In other words, the didactic stress on order was in part an anxious reaction to emergent and (in)-subordinate social forces which were perceived as threatening. Tillyard's world picture, to the extent that it did still exist, was not shared by all; it was an ideological legitimation of an existing social order, one rendered the more necessary by the apparent instability, actual *and* imagined, of that order. If this sounds too extreme then we need only recall Bacon's remark to some circuit judges in 1617: 'There will be a perpetual defection, except you keep men in by preaching, as well as law doth by punishing'. Sermons were not simply the occasion for the collective mind to celebrate its most cherished beliefs but an attempt to tell sectors of an unruly populace what to think 'in order' to keep them in their place.

Historians who have examined the effects of social change and reactions to it present a picture quite opposite to Tillyard's:

> In the late sixteenth and early seventeenth centuries … this almost hysterical demand for order at all costs was caused by a collapse of most of the props of the medieval world picture. The unified dogma and organization of the Catholic Church found itself challenged by a number of rival creeds and institutional structures … the reliance upon the intellectual authority of the Ancients was threatened by new scientific discoveries. Moreover in England there occurred a phase of

unprecedented social and geographical mobility which at the higher
levels transformed the composition and size of the gentry and
professional classes, and at the lower levels tore hundreds of thousands
of individuals loose from their traditional kinship and neighbourhood
backgrounds.

(Stone 1977, pp.653-4).

In making sense of a period in such rapid transition, and of the
contradictory interpretations of that transition from within the period
itself, we might have recourse to Raymond Williams's very important
distinction between residual, dominant, and emergent aspects of culture
(Williams 1977, pp.121-7). Tillyard's world picture can then be seen as in
some respects a dominant ideology, in others a residual one, with one or
both of these perhaps being confronted and displaced by new, emergent
cultural forms. Nor is this threefold distinction exhaustive of cultural
diversity: there will also be levels of culture appropriately described as
subordinate, repressed and marginal. Non-dominant elements interact with
the dominant forms, sometimes coexisting with, or being absorbed or even
destroyed by them, but also challenging, modifying or even displacing
them. Culture is not by any stretch of the imagination – not even the
literary imagination – a unity.

Tillyard was not entirely unaware of this, though it is presumably with
unwitting irony that he writes of 'the educated nucleus that *dictated* the
current beliefs of the Elizabethan Age' and of cosmic order as 'one of the
genuine *ruling* ideas of the age' (Tillyard 1943, pp.22, 7). Because, for
Tillyard, the process of ideological legitimation was itself more or less
legitimate, it is a process which in his book – and much more so than his
claims about the Elizabethan world picture itself – is accepted to the point
of being barely recognised. Further, because Tillyard revered the period
('the "real" Elizabethan age – the quarter century from 1580–1605 – was after
all the great age', p. 130) what he discerned as its representative literature
is presented as the legitimate object of study. And those literary forms
wherein can be glimpsed the transgression of the world picture – where, that
is, we glimpse subordinate cultures resisting or contesting the dominant –
these are dismissed as unworthy of study because unrepresentative:
'[Hooker] represents far more truly the background of Elizabethan
literature than do the coney-catching pamphlets or the novel of low-life'
(p.22). But whose literature, and whose background?

There are several ways of deploying the concept of ideology, and these
correspond to its complex history. One which in particular concerns
materialist criticism traces the cultural connections between signification
and legitimation: the way that beliefs, practices and institutions legitimate
the dominant social order or *status quo* - the existing relations of
domination and subordination. Such legitimation is found (for example) in

the representation of sectional interests as universal ones. Those who rule may in fact be serving their own interests and those of their class, but they, together with the institutions and practices through which they exercise and maintain power, are understood as working in the interests of the community as a whole. Secondly, through legitimation the existing social order – that is, existing social relations – are 'naturalised', thus appearing to have the unalterable character of natural law. History also tends to be invested with a law of development (teleology) which acts as the counterpart of natural law, a development leading 'inevitably' to the present order and thereby doubly ratifying it. Legitimation further works to efface the fact of social contradiction, dissent and struggle. Where these things present themselves unavoidably they are often demonised as attempts to subvert the social order. Therefore, if the very conflicts which the existing order generates from within itself are construed as attempts to subvert it from without (by the 'alien'), that order strengthens itself by simultaneously repressing dissenting elements and eliciting consent for their action: the protection of society from subversion.

This combined emphasis on universal interests, society as a 'reflection' of the 'natural' order of things, history as a 'lawful' development leading up to and justifying the present, the demonising of dissent and otherness, was central to the age of Shakespeare.

The politics of Renaissance theatre

I want to consider next why the socio-political perspective of materialist criticism is especially appropriate for recovering the political dimension of Renaissance drama. This entails a consideration of the theatre as an institution and, more generally, literature as a practice.

Analysts of literature in the Renaissance were much concerned with its effect. The almost exclusive preoccupation in traditional English studies with the intrinsic meaning of texts leads us to miss, ignore or underestimate the importance of this fact. Effect was considered not at the level of the individual reader in abstraction, but of actual readers - and, of course, audiences. Rulers and preachers were only two groups especially concerned to determine, regulate, and perhaps exploit these effects.

As regards the theatre there were two opposed views of its effectiveness. The one view stressed its capacity to instruct the populace - often, and quite explicitly, to keep them obedient. Thus Heywood, in an *Apology for Actors*, claimed that plays were written and performed to teach 'subjects obedience to their king' by showing them 'the untimely end of such as have moved tumults, commotions and insurrections'. The other view claimed virtually the opposite, stressing the theatre's power to demystify authority and even to subvert it; in 1605 Samuel Calvert had complained that plays were representing 'the present Time, not sparing either King, State or Religion, in so great Absurdity, and with such Liberty, that any would be afraid to hear them'. In an often cited passage from *Basilikon Doron* James I likened the king to 'one set on a stage, whose smallest actions and gestures, all the people gazingly do behold'; any 'dissolute' behaviour on his part breeds contempt in his subjects and contempt is 'the mother of rebellion and disorder'. The theatre could encourage such contempt by, as one contemporary put it in a description of Shakespeare's *Henry VIII*, making 'greatness very familiar, if not ridiculous'. A year after *Basilikon Doron* appeared, a French ambassador recorded in a despatch home that James was being held in just the contempt that he feared and, moreover, that the theatre was encouraging it.

A famous attempt to use the theatre to subvert authority was of course the staging of a play called *Richard II* (probably Shakespeare's) just before the Essex rising in 1601; Queen Elizabeth afterwards anxiously acknowledged the implied identification between her and Richard II, complaining also that 'this tragedy was played 40 times in open streets and houses'. As Stephen Greenblatt points out, what was really worrying for the Queen was both the repeatability of the representation - and hence the multiplying numbers of people witnessing it - and the locations of these repetitions: '*open* streets and houses'. In such places the 'conventional containment' of the playhouses is blurred and perhaps relinquished altogether with the consequence that the 'safe' distinction between illusion and reality itself blurs: 'are the "houses" to which Elizabeth refers public theatres or private dwellings where her enemies plot her overthrow? Can "tragedy" be a strictly literary term when the Queen's own life is endangered by the play?' (Greenblatt 1982, p. 4).

Jane P. Tompkins has argued that the Renaissance inherited from the classical period a virtually complete disregard of literature's meaning and a correspondingly almost exclusive emphasis on its effect: what mattered, ultimately, was action not signification, behaviour not discourse. In a sense yes: Tompkins's emphasis on effect is both correct and important, especially as she goes on to show that this pragmatic view of literature made its socio-political dimension *obviously* significant at the time (Tompkins 1980, pp. 201-10). But Tompkins draws a distinction between effect and signification which is too extreme, even for this period: effectivity is both decided and assessed in the practice of signification. If we ignore this then we are likely to ignore also the fact that socio-political effects of literature are in part achieved in and through the practice of appropriation. Thus what made Elizabeth I so anxious was not so much a retrospectively and clearly ascertained effect of the staging of *Richard II* (the uprising was, after all, abortive and Essex was executed) but the fact of the play having been appropriated - been given significance for a particular cause and in certain 'open' contexts. This period's pragmatic conception of literature meant that such appropriations were not a perversion of true literary reception, they were its reception.

This applies especially to tragedy, that genre traditionally thought to be most capable of transcending the historical moment of inception and of representing universal truths. Contemporary formulations of the tragic certainly made reference to universals but they were also resolutely political, especially those which defined it as a representation of tyranny. Such accounts, and of course the plays themselves, were appropriated as both defences of and challenges to authority.

Thomas Elyot, in *The Governor*, asserted that, in reading tragedies, a man shall be led to 'execrate and abhor the intolerable life of tyrants', and for Sidney tragedy made 'Kings fear to be tyrants'. Puttenham in *The Art* of *English Poesy* had said that tragedy revealed tyranny to 'all the world', while the downfall of the tyrant disclosed (perhaps incongruously) both historical vicissitude ('the mutability of fortune') and God's providential order (his 'just punishment'). In contrast Fulke Greville explicitly disavowed that his own tragedies exemplified God's law in the form of providential retribution. Rather, they were concerned to 'trace out the high ways of ambitious governors'. He further stressed that the 'true stage' for his plays was not the theatre but the reader's own life and times - 'even the state he lives in'. This led Greville actually to destroy one of his tragedies for fear of incrimination - it could, he said, have been construed as 'personating...vices in the present Governors, and government'. (It seems he had in mind the events of the Essex rebellion.) Raleigh, in his *History of the World*, warns of the danger of writing in general when the subject is contemporary history: if the writer follows it too closely 'it may happily strike out his teeth'. Those like Greville and Raleigh knew then that the idea of literature passively reflecting history was erroneous; literature was a practice which intervened in contemporary history in the very act of representing it.

Consolidation, subversion, containment

Three aspects of historical and cultural process figure prominently in materialist criticism; consolidation, subversion and containment. The first refers, typically, to the ideological means whereby a dominant order seeks to perpetuate itself; the second to the subversion of that order, the third to the containment of ostensibly subversive pressures.

The metaphysic of order in the Elizabethan period has already been briefly considered. Those of Tillyard's persuasion saw it as consolidating, that is socially cohesive in the positive sense of transcending sectional interests and articulating a genuinely shared culture and cosmology, characterised by harmony, stability and unity. In contrast, materialist criticism is likely to consider the ideological dimension of consolidation - the way, for example, that this world picture reinforces particular class and gender interests by presenting the existing social order as natural and God-given (and therefore immutable). Interestingly, ideas approximating to these contrasting positions circulated in the period. Those Elizabethan sermons which sought to explain social hierarchy as a manifestation of Divine Law, and which drew analogies between hierarchy in the different levels of cosmos, nature and society, would be an example of the first, and the assertion in Ben Jonson's *Sejanus* that "'tis place, /Not blood, discerns the noble, and the base' of the second.

Important differences exist within materialist criticism of Renaissance literature between those who emphasise the process of consolidation and those who discover resistances to it. Here the disagreement tends to be at distinct but overlapping levels: actual historical process and its discursive representation in literature. So, for example, within feminist criticism of the period, there are those who insist on its increasing patriarchal oppressiveness, and, moreover, insist that the limiting structures of patriarchy are also Shakespeare's. Kathleen McLuskie summarises this perspective as follows: 'Shakespeare … gave voice to the social views of his age. His thoughts on women were necessarily bounded by the parameters of hagiography and misogyny'(McLuskie 1983). Conversely, other feminist critics want to allow that there were those in the period, including Shakespeare, who could and did think beyond these parameters, and participated in significant resistance to such constructions of women (Shepherd 1981, Dusinberre 1975, Kahn 1981). But this second perspective, at least in its materialist version, is united with the first in rejecting a third position, namely that which sees Shakespeare's women as exemplifying the transhistorical (universal) qualities of 'women', with Shakespeare's ability to represent these being another aspect of a genius who transcends not only his time but also his sex. A materialist feminism, rather than simply co-opting or writing off Shakespeare, follows the unstable constructions of, for example, gender and patriarchy back to the contradictions of their historical moment. Only thus can the authority of the patriarchal bard be understood and effectively challenged.

In considering in that same historical moment certain representations of authority, along with those which ostensibly subvert it, we discover not a straightforward opposition but a process much more complex. Subversiveness may for example be apparent only, the dominant order not only containing it but, paradoxical as it may seem, actually producing it for its own ends.

To some extent the paradox disappears when we speak not of a monolithic power structure producing its effects but of one made up of different, often competing elements, and these not merely producing culture but producing it through appropriations. The importance of this concept of appropriation is that it indicates a process of making or transforming. If we talk only of power producing the discourse of subversion we not only hypostatise power but also efface the cultural differences - and context – which the very process of containment presupposes. Resistance to that process may be there from the outset or itself produced by it. Further, although subversion may indeed be appropriated by authority for its own purpose, once installed it can be used against authority as well as used by it. Thus the demonised elements in Elizabethan culture - for example, masterless men – are, quite precisely, identified as such in order to ratify the exercise of power, but once identified they are also there as a force to be self-identified. But this didn't make them a power in their own right; on the contrary, for masterless men to constitute a threat to order it was usually - though not always - necessary that they first be mobilised or exploited by a counter-faction within the dominant.

But appropriation could also work the other way: subordinate, marginal or dissident elements could appropriate dominant discourses and likewise transform them in the process. I have already suggested what Essex may have been trying to do with *Richard II*: another recently rediscovered instance is recounted in Carlo Ginzburg's *The Cheese and the Worms* (Ginzburg 1980). This book relates how Menocchio, an Italian miller and isolated heretic, interpreted seemingly very orthodox texts in a highly challenging way - construing from them, for example, a quite radical materialist view of the universe. Ginzburg emphasises the 'one-sided and arbitrary' nature of Menocchio's reading, and sees its source as being in a peasant culture, oral, widespread and at once sceptical, materialist and rationalist. It is this culture and not at all the intrinsic nature of the texts which leads Menocchio to appropriate them in a way subversive enough to incur torture and eventually death by burning for heresy.

The subversion-containment debate is important for other reasons. It is in part a conceptual or theoretical question: what, for example, are the criteria for distinguishing between, say, that which subverts and that which effects change? Stephen Greenblatt provides a useful working definition here: radical subversiveness is defined as not merely the attempt to seize existing authority, but as a challenge to the principles upon which authority is based (Greenblatt 1985, p.41). But we are still faced with the need for interpretation simply in making this very distinction: theoretical clarification of necessity involves historical enquiry and vice versa. And the kind of enquiry at issue is inextricably bound up with the question of perspective: which one, and whose? How else for example can we explain why what is experienced as subversive at the time may retrospectively be construed as a crucial step towards progress? More extremely still, how is it that the same subversive act may be later interpreted as having contributed to either revolutionary change or anarchic disintegration?

Nothing can be intrinsically or essentially subversive in the sense that prior to the event subversiveness can be more than potential; in other words it cannot be guaranteed *a priori*, independent of articulation, context and reception. Likewise the mere thinking of a radical idea is not what makes it subversive: typically it is the context of its articulation: to whom, how many and in what circumstances; one might go further and suggest that not only does the idea have to be conveyed, it has also actually to be used to refuse authority *or* be seen by authority as capable and likely of being so used. It is, then, somewhat misleading to speak freely and only of 'subversive thought'; what we are concerned with (once again) is a *social process*. Thus the 'Machiavellian' demystification of religion was circulating for centuries before Machiavelli; what made it actually subversive in the Renaissance was its being taken up by many more than the initiated few. Even here interpretation and perspective come into play: we need to explain why it was taken up, and in so doing we will almost certainly have to make judgements about the historical changes it helped precipitate. Explicitness about one's own perspective and methodology become unavoidable in materialist criticism and around this issue especially: as textual, historical, sociological and theoretical analysis are drawn together, the politics of the practice emerges.

'Ruling culture does not define the whole of culture, though it tries to, and it is the task of the oppositional critic to re-read culture so as to amplify and strategically position the marginalised voices of the ruled, exploited, oppressed, and excluded' (Lentricchia 1983, p.15). Frank Lentricchia, here quoting Raymond Williams, rightly insists that cultural domination is not a static unalterable thing; it is rather a *process*, one always being contested, always having to be renewed. As Williams puts it: 'alternative political and cultural emphases, and the many forms of opposition and struggle, are important not only in themselves but as indicative features of what the hegemonic process has in practice had to work to control' (Williams 1977, p. 13). At the same time, 'the mere pluralization of voices and traditions (a currently fashionable and sentimental gesture) is inadequate to the ultimate problem of linking repressed and master voices as the agon of history, their abiding relation of class conflict' (Lentricchia 1983, p.131). Arguably an oppositional criticism will always be deficient, always liable to despairing collapse, if it underestimates the extent, strategies and flexible complexity of domination. Of course one can, sometimes, recover history from below. But to piece together its fragments may be eventually to disclose not the self-authenticating other, but the self-division intrinsic to (and which thereby perpetuates) subordination. At other times we will listen in vain for voices from the past or search for their traces in a 'history' they never officially entered. But even to be receptive to that fact involves a radical shift in awareness which is historically quite recent. And it is a shift which means that if we feel the need to disclose the effectiveness and complexity of the ideological process of containment, this by no means implies a fatalistic acceptance that it is somehow inevitable and that all opposition is hopeless. On the contrary the very desire to disclose that process is itself oppositional and motivated by the knowledge that, formidable though it be, it is a process which is historically contingent and partial - never necessary or total. It did not, and still does not, have to be so.

4 Marlowe and the Will to Absolute Play*

STEPHEN GREENBLATT

The automatic assumption that a human being is a self-creating, free and unique individual has been central to modern culture, but in the Renaissance was still contentious and problematic. A key issue for the historicist criticism that was written in the 1980s was therefore the artful fabrication of the sovereign self in texts of the Renaissance period. Stephen Greenblatt's *Renaissance Self-Fashioning* was one of the earliest and most influential books to address this question of **subjectivity**. The chapter on the plays of Christopher Marlowe describes the way that dramatic characters such as Tamburlaine and Faustus struggle to invent identities for themselves but are overwhelmed by social circumstances. They express Marlowe's own anarchic self-destructiveness, but also the violence with which the new selfhood tore against the old collective orthodoxies. Though Greenblatt quotes Marx's aphorism that 'men and women do make their own history, if not in circumstances of their making', the debt here is to Nietzsche, for whom history is an endless **spectacle** of the **will to power**, like a play without a plot.

On 26 June 1586 a small fleet, financed by the Earl of Cumberland, set out from Gravesend for the South Seas. It sailed down the West African coast, sighting Sierra Leone in October, and at this point we may let one of those on board, the merchant John Sarracoll, tell his own story:

> The fourth of November we went on shore to a town of the Negroes... which we found to be but lately built: it was of about two hundred houses, and walled about with mighty great trees, and stakes so thick, that a rat could hardly get in or out. But as it chanced, we came directly upon a port which was not shut up, where we entered with such

---

*Reprinted from *Renaissance Self-Fashioning: from More to Shakespeare* (University of Chicago Press, 1980), pp. 193–221.

fierceness, that the people fled all out of the town, which we found to
be finely built after their fashion, and the streets of it so intricate that it
was difficult for us to find the way out that we came in at. We found
their houses and streets so finely and cleanly kept that it was an
admiration to us all, for that neither in the houses nor streets was so
much dust to be found as would fill an egg shell. We found little in
their houses, except some mats, gourds, and some earthen pots. Our
men at their departure set the town on fire, and it was burnt (for the
most part of it) in a quarter of an hour, the houses being covered with
reed and straw.

This passage is atypical, for it lacks the blood bath that usually climaxes
these incidents, but it will serve as a reminder of what until recently was
called one of the glorious achievements of Renaissance civilization, and it
will serve as a convenient bridge from the world of Edmund Spenser to the
world of Christopher Marlowe.

What is most striking in Sarracoll's account, of course, is the casual,
unexplained violence. Does the merchant feel that the firing of the town
needs no explanation? If asked, would he have had one to give? Why does
he take care to tell us why the town burned so quickly, but not why it was
burned? Is there an aesthetic element in his admiration of the town, so finely
built, so intricate, so cleanly kept? And does this admiration conflict with or
somehow fuel the destructiveness? If he feels no uneasiness at all why does
he suddenly shift and write not *we* but *our men* set the town on fire? Was
there an order or not? And, when he recalls the invasion, why does he think
of rats? The questions are all met by the moral blankness that rests like thick
snow on Sarracoll's sentences: 'The 17th day of November we departed from
Sierra Leona, directing our course for the Straits of Magellan'.

If, on returning to England in 1587, the merchant and his associates had
gone to see the Lord Admiral's Men perform a new play, *Tamburlaine the
Great*, they would have seen an extraordinary meditation on the roots of
their own behavior. For despite all the exoticism in Marlowe – Scythian
shepherds, Maltese Jews, German magicians – it is his own countrymen
that he broods upon and depicts. As in Spenser, though to radically
different effect, the 'other world' becomes a mirror. If we want to
understand the historical matrix of Marlowe's achievement, the analogue
to Tamburlaine's restlessness, aesthetic sensitivity, appetite, and violence,
we might look not at the playwright's literary sources, not even at the
relentless power-hunger of Tudor absolutism, but at the acquisitive
energies of English merchants, entrepreneurs, and adventurers, promoters
alike of trading companies and theatrical companies.

But what bearing does Marlowe actually have on a passage like the one
with which I opened? He is, for a start, fascinated by the idea of the
stranger in a strange land. Almost all of his heroes are aliens or

wanderers, from Aeneas in Carthage to Barabas in Malta, from Tamburlaine's endless campaigns to Faustus's demonic flights. From his first play to his last, Marlowe is drawn to the idea of physical movement, to the problem of its representation within the narrow confines of the theater. Tamburlaine almost ceaselessly traverses the stage, and when he is not actually on the move he is imagining campaigns or hearing reports of grueling marches. The obvious effect is to enact the hero's vision of a nature that'Doth teach us all to have aspiring minds' and of the soul that 'Wills us to wear ourselves and never rest' (1 *Tam*, II,vi 871,877 [*The Works of Christopher Marlowe*, ed. C Tucker Brooke, Oxford 1910]). But as always in Marlowe, this enactment, this realization on the level of the body in time and space, complicates, qualifies, exposes, and even mocks the abstract conception. For the cumulative effect of this restlessness is not so much heroic as grotesquely comic, if we accept Bergson's classic definition of the comic as the mechanical imposed upon the living. Tamburlaine *is* a machine, a desiring machine that produces violence and death. Menaphon's admiring description begins by making him sound like Leonardo's Vitruvian Man or Michelangelo's David and ends by making him sound like an expensive mechanical device, one of those curious inventions that courtiers gave to the queen at New Year's: a huge, straight, strongly jointed creature with a costly pearl placed between his shoulders, the pearl inscribed with celestial symbols. Once set in motion, this *thing* cannot slow down or change course; it moves at the same frenzied pace until it finally stops.

One further effect of this unvarying movement is that, paradoxically, very little progress seems to be made, despite fervent declarations to the contrary. To be sure, the scenes change, so quickly at times that Marlowe seems to be battering against the boundaries of his own medium: at one moment the stage represents a vast space, then suddenly contracts to a bed, then turns in quick succession into an imperial camp, a burning town, a besieged fortress, a battlefield, a tent. But then all of those spaces seem curiously alike. The relevant contrast is *Antony and Cleopatra* where the restless movement is organized around the deep structural opposition of Rome and Egypt, or 1 *Henry IV* where the tavern, the court, and the country are perceived as diversely shaped spaces, spaces that elicit and echo different tones, energies, and even realities. In *Tamburlaine* Marlowe contrives to efface all such differences, as if to insist upon the essential meaninglessness of theatrical space, the vacancy that is the dark side of its power to imitate any place. This vacancy – quite literally, this absence of scenery – is the equivalent in the medium of the theater to the secularization of space, the abolition of qualitative up and down, which for Cassirer is one of the greatest achievements of Renaissance philosophy, the equivalent then to the reduction of the universe to the coordinates of a map (Cassirer 1968, Chapter 1).

Give me a Map, then let me see how much
Is left for me to conquer all the world,
That these my boys may finish all my wants.

(2 *Tam*,V, iii, 4516–18)

Space is transformed into an abstraction, then fed to the appetitive machine. This is the voice of conquest, but it is also the voice of wants never finished and of transcendental homelessness. And though the characters and situations change, that voice is never entirely absent in Marlowe. Barabas does not leave Malta, but he is the quintessential alien: at one point his house is seized and turned into a nunnery, at another he is thrown over the walls of the city, only to rise with the words, 'What, all alone?' Edward II should be the very opposite; he is, by his role, the embodiment of the land and its people, but without Gaveston he lives in his own country like an exile. Only in *Doctor Faustus* does there seem to be a significant difference: having signed away his soul and body, Faustus begins a course of restless wandering, but at the close of the twenty-four years, he feels a compulsion to return to Wittenberg. Of course, it is ironic that when a meaningful sense of place finally emerges in Marlowe, it does so only as a place to die. But the irony runs deeper still. For nothing in the covenant or in any of the devil's speeches requires that Faustus has to pay his life where he originally contracted to sell it; the urge is apparently in Faustus, as if he felt there were a fatality in the place he had undertaken his studies, felt it appropriate and even necessary to die there and nowhere else. 'O would I had never seen Wittenberg', he despairingly tells his friends. But the play has long before this exposed such a sense of place to radical questioning. To Faustus's insistent demands to know the 'where about' of hell, Mephistophilis replies,

Hell hath no limits, nor is circumscrib'd
In one self place, for where we are is hell,
And where hell is, must we ever be

(II,i, 567–69)

By implication, Faustus's feeling about Wittenberg is an illusion, one of a network of fictions by which he constitutes his identity and his world. Typically, he refuses to accept the account of a limitless, inner hell, countering with the extraordinary, and in the circumstances, ludicrous 'I think hell's a fable.' Mephistophilis's quiet response slides from parodic agreement to devastating irony: 'Aye, think so still, till experience change thy mind.' The experience of which the devil speaks can refer not only to torment after death but to Faustus's life in the remainder of the play: the half-trivial, half-daring exploits, the alternating states of bliss and despair, the questions that are not answered and the answers that bring no real satisfaction, the wanderings that lead nowhere. The chilling line may carry a further suggestion: 'Yes, continue to think that hell's a fable, until experience *transforms* your mind.' At the heart of this mental transformation is the anguished perception of time as inexorable, space as abstract. In his final soliloquy, Faustus's frenzied invocation to time to stop or slow itself gives way to horrified clarity: ' The stars move still, time runs, the clock will strike' (1460). And his appeal to nature – earth, stars, air, ocean – at once to shield him and destroy him is met by silence: space is neutral and unresponsive.

Doctor Faustus then does not contradict but rather realizes intimations about space and time in Marlowe's other plays. That man is homeless, that all places are alike, is linked to man's inner state, to the uncircumscribed hell he carries within him. And this insight returns us to the violence with which we began, the violence of Tamburlaine and of the English merchant and his men. It is not enough to say that their actions are the expression of brute power, though they are certainly that, nor even that they bespeak a compulsive suspicion and hatred that one Elizabethan voyager saw as characteristic of the military mind. For experiencing this limitlessness, this transformation of space and time into abstractions, men do violence as a means of marking boundaries, effecting transformation, signaling closure. To burn a town or to kill all of its inhabitants is to make an end and, in so doing, to give life a shape and certainty that it would otherwise lack. The great fear, in Barabas's words, is 'That I may vanish o'er the earth in air, / And leave no memory that e'er I was ' (*J of M*, I.ii, 499–500). As the town where Zenocrate dies burns at his command, Tamburlaine proclaims his identity, fixed forever in the heavens by his acts of violence:

> Over my Zenith hang a blazing star,
> That may endure till heaven be dissolv'd,
> Fed with the fresh supply of earthly dregs,
> Threat'ning a death and famine to this land

> (2 *Tam*, III,ii,3196–99)

In this charred soil and the blazing star, Tamburlaine seeks literally to make an enduring mark in the world, to stamp his image on time and space. Similarly, Faustus, by violence not on others but on himself, seeks to give his life a clear fixed shape. To be sure, he speaks of attaining 'a world of profit and delight, / Of power, of honor, of omnipotence' (83–4), but perhaps the hidden core of what he seeks is the limit of twenty-four years to live, a limit he himself sets and reiterates. Time so marked out should have a quality different from other time, should possess its end: 'Now will I make an end immediately,' he says, writing with his blood.

But in Marlowe's ironic world, these desperate attempts at boundary and closure produce the opposite effect, reinforcing the condition they are meant to efface. Tamburlaine's violence does not transform space from the abstract to the human, but rather further reduces the world to a map, the very emblem of abstraction:

> I will confute those blind Geographers
> That make a triple region in the world,
> Excluding Regions which I mean to trace,
> And with this pen reduce them to a Map,
> Calling the Provinces, Cities and towns
> After my name and thine *Zenocrate*.
>
> (1 *Tam*, IV,iv, 1715–20)

At Tamburlaine's death, the map still stretches out before him, and nothing bears his name save Marlowe's play (the crucial exception to which we will return). Likewise at his death, pleading for 'some end to my incessant pain,' Faustus is haunted by eternity: 'O no end is limited to damned souls' (1458).

The reasons why attempts at making a mark or an end fail are complex and vary significantly with each play, but one critical link is the feeling in almost all Marlowe's protagonists that they are *using up* experience. This feeling extends to our merchant, John Sarracoll, and his men: they not only visit Sierra Leone, they consume it. Tamburlaine exults in just this power to 'Conquer, sack, and utterly consume / Your cities' (2 *Tam*, IV, iii, 3867–8). He even contrives to use up his defeated enemies, transforming Bajazeth into his footstool, the kings of Trebizon and Soria into horses to be discarded, when they are broken-winded, for 'fresh horse' (2 *Tam*,V, i, 4242). In a bizarrely comic moment, Tamburlaine's son suggests that the kings just captured be released to resume the fight, but Tamburlaine replies, in the language of consumption, 'Cherish thy valor still with fresh supplies: / And glut it not with stale and daunted foes' (2 *Tam* IV,i, 3761–2). Valor, like any appetite, always demands new food.

Faustus's relationship to knowledge is strikingly similar; in his opening soliloquy he bids farewell to each of his studies in turn as something he has used up. He needs to cherish his mind with fresh supplies, for nothing can be accumulated, nothing saved or savored. And as the remainder of the play makes clear, each of these farewells is an act of destruction: logic, medicine, law, and divinity are not so much rejected as violated. The violence arises not only from the desire to mark boundaries but from the feeling that what one leaves behind, turns away from, *must* no longer exist; that objects endure only for the moment of the act of attention and then are effaced; that the next moment cannot be fully grasped until the last is destroyed. Marlowe writes in the period in which European man embarked on his extraordinary career of consumption, his eager pursuit of knowledge, with one intellectual model after another seized, squeezed dry, and discarded, and his frenzied exhaustion of the world's resources:

> Lo here my sons are all the golden Mines,
> Inestimable drugs and precious stones,
> More worth than *Asia* and the world beside,
> And from th'Antarctic Pole, Eastward behold
> As much more land which never was descried,
> Wherein are rocks of Pearl that shine as bright
> As all the Lamps that beautify the Sky,
> And shall I die, and this unconquered?
>
> (2 *Tam*, V, iii, 4544–51)

So fully do we inhabit this construction of reality that most often we see beyond it only in accounts of cultures immensely distant from our own:

> 'The Nuer [writes Evans-Pritchard] have no expression equivalent to 'time' in our language, and they cannot, therefore, as we can, speak of time as though it were something actual, which passes, can be wasted, can be saved, and so forth. I do not think that they ever experience the same feeling of fighting against time or of having to co-ordinate activities with an abstract passage of time because their points of reference are mainly the activities themselves, which are generally of a leisurely character ... Nuer are fortunate.
>
> (Evans-Pritchard 1940, p. 103)

Of course, such a conception of time and activity had vanished from Europe long before the sixteenth century, but English Renaissance works, and Marlowe's plays in particular, give voice to a radically intensified sense that time is abstract, uniform, and inhuman. The origins of this sense of time are difficult to locate with any certainty. Puritans in the late sixteenth century were already campaigning vigorously against the medieval doctrine of the unevenness of time, a doctrine that had survived largely intact in the Elizabethan church calendar. They sought, in effect, to desacramentalize time, to discredit and sweep away the dense web of saints' days, 'dismal days', seasonal taboos, mystic observances, and folk festivals that gave time a distinct, irregular shape; in its place, they urged a simple, flat routine of six days work and a sabbath rest. Moreover, there seem, in this period, to have been subtle changes in what we may call family time. At one end of the life cycle, traditional youth groups were suppressed or fell into neglect, customs that had allowed adolescents considerable autonomy were overturned, and children were brought under the stricter discipline of the immediate family. At the other end, the

Protestant rejection of the doctrine of purgatory eliminated the dead as an 'age group,' cutting off the living from ritualized communion with their deceased parents and relatives. Such changes might well have contributed to a sense in Marlowe and some of his contemporaries that time is alien, profoundly indifferent to human longing and anxiety. Whatever the case, we certainly find in Marlowe's plays a powerful feeling that time is something to be resisted and a related fear that fulfillment or fruition is impossible. 'Why waste you thus the time away?' an impatient Leicester asks Edward II, whose crown he has come to fetch. 'Stay a while,' Edward replies, 'let me be king till night' (2045), whereupon, like Faustus, he struggles vainly to arrest time with incantation. At such moments, Marlowe's celebrated line is itself rich with irony: the rhythms intended to slow time only consume it, magnificent words are spoken and disappear into a void. But it is precisely this sense of the void that compels the characters to speak so powerfully, as if to struggle the more insistently against the enveloping silence.

That the moments of intensest time-consciousness all occur at or near the close of these plays has the effect of making the heroes seem to struggle against theatrical time. As Marlowe uses the vacancy of theatrical space to suggest his characters' homelessness, so he uses the curve of *theatrical* time to suggest their struggle against extinction, in effect against the nothingness into which all characters fall at the end of a play. The pressure of the dramatic medium itself likewise underlies what we may call the *repetition compulsion* of Marlowe's heroes. Tambulaine no sooner annihilates one army than he sets out to annihilate another, no sooner unharnesses two kings than he hitches up two more. Barabas gains and loses, regains and reloses his wealth, while pursuing a seemingly endless string of revenges and politic murders, including, characteristically, two suitors, two friars, two rulers, and, in effect, two children. In *Edward II* the plot is less overtly episodic, yet even here, after spending the first half of the play alternately embracing and parting from Gaveston, Edward immediately replaces the slain favorite with Spencer Junior and thereby resumes the same pattern, the willful courting of disaster that is finally 'rewarded' in the castle cesspool. Finally, as C. L. Barber observes, 'Faustus repeatedly moves through a circular pattern, from thinking of the joys of heaven, through despairing of ever possessing them, to embracing magical dominion as a blasphemous substitute' (Barber 1964, p.99). The pattern of action and the complex psychological structure embodied in it vary with each play, but at the deepest level of the medium itself the motivation is the same: the renewal of existence through repetition of the self-constituting act. The character repeats himself in order to continue to be that same character on the stage. Identity is a theatrical invention that must be reiterated if it is to endure.

To grasp the full import of this notion of repetition as self fashioning, we must understand its relation to the culturally dominant notion of repetition as a warning or memorial, an instrument of civility. In this view recurrent patterns exist in the history of individuals or nations in order to inculcate crucial moral values, passing them from generation to generation. Men are notoriously slow learners and, in their inherent sinfulness, resistant to virtue, but gradually, through repetition, the paradigms may sink in and responsible, God-fearing, obedient subjects may be formed. Accordingly, Tudor monarchs ordered the formal reiteration of the central tenets of the religious and social orthodoxy, carefully specifying the minimum number of times a year these tenets were to be read aloud from the pulpit. Similarly, the punishment of criminals was public, so that the state's power to inflict torment and death could act upon the people as an edifying caution. The high number of such executions reflects not only judicial 'massacres' but the attempt to teach through reiterated terror. Each branding or hanging or disemboweling was theatrical in conception and performance, a repeatable admonitory drama enacted on a scaffold before a rapt audience. Those who threatened order, those on whose nature nurture could never stick – the traitor, the vagabond, the homosexual, the thief – were identified and punished accordingly. This idea of the 'notable spectacle', the 'theater of God's judgment,' extended quite naturally to the drama itself, and, indeed, to all of literature which thus takes its rightful place as part of a vast, interlocking system of repetitions, embracing homilies and hangings, royal progresses and rote learning. It is by no means only timeservers who are involved here; a great artist like Spenser embraces his participation in this system, though, of course, that participation is more complex than most. In Spenser's rich and subtle version of the civilizing process, the apparent repetitions within each book and in The *Faerie Queene* as a whole serve to initiate hero and reader alike into the nuances of each of the virtues, the complex discriminations that a humane moral sensibility entails, while the shifting resolutions of analogous problems help to shore up values that are threatened by the shape of a prior resolution. The heroes' names and the virtues they embody both exist prior to the experiences chronicled in their books and are fully established by means of those experiences; Spenserian repetition expresses that which is already in some sense real, given by the power that exists outside the poem and that the poem celebrates.

Marlowe seems to have regarded the drama's participation in such a system – an admonitory fiction upholding a moral order – with a blend of obsessive fascination and contemptuous loathing. *Tamburlaine* repeatedly teases its audience with the *form* of the cautionary tale, only to violate the convention. All of the signals of the tragic are produced, but the play stubbornly, radically, refuses to become a tragedy. 'The Gods, defenders of the innocent, /Will never prosper your intended drifts' (1 *Tam*, I,ii,264–65), declares Zenocrate in Act I and then promptly falls in love with her captor. With his dying breath, Cosroe curses Tamburlaine – a sure prelude to disaster – but the disaster never occurs. Bajazeth, the king of Arabia, and even Theridamas and Zenocrate have powerful premonitions of the hero's downfall, but he passes from success to success. Tamburlaine is proud, arrogant, and blasphemous; he lusts for power, betrays his allies, overthrows legitimate authority, and threatens the gods; he rises to the top of the wheel of fortune and then steadfastly refuses to budge. Since the dominant ideology no longer insists that rise-and-decline and pride-goes-before-a-fall are unvarying, universal rhythms, we undoubtedly miss some of the shock of Tamburlaine's career, but the play itself invokes those rhythms often enough to surprise us with their failure to materialize.

Having undermined the notion of the cautionary tale in *Tamburlaine*, Part 1, Marlowe demolishes it in Part 2 in the most unexpected way – by suddenly invoking it. The slaughter of thousands, the murder of his own son, the torture of his royal captives are all without apparent consequence; then Tamburlaine falls ill, and when? When he burns the Koran! The one action which Elizabethan churchmen themselves might have applauded seems to bring down divine vengeance. The effect is not to celebrate the transcendent power of Mohammed but to challenge the habit of mind that looks to heaven for rewards and punishments, that imagines human evil as 'the scourge of God.' Similarly, in *Doctor Faustus*, as Max Bluestone observes, the homiletical tradition is continually introduced only to be undermined by dramatic spectacle (Bluestone 1969, p.82), while in *Edward II* Marlowe uses the emblematic method of admonitory drama, but uses it to such devastating effect that the audience recoils from it in disgust. Edward's grisly execution is, as orthodox interpreters of the play have correctly insisted, iconographically 'appropriate,' but this appropriateness can only be established *at the expense* of every complex, sympathetic human feeling evoked by the play. The audience is forced to confront its insistence upon coherence, and the result is a profound questioning of the way audiences constitute meaning in the theater and in life.

There is a questioning too of the way *individuals* are constituted in the theater and in life. Marlowe's heroes fashion themselves not in loving submission to an absolute authority but in self-conscious opposition: Tamburlaine against hierarchy, Barabas against Christianity, Faustus against God, Edward against the sanctified rites and responsibilities of kingship, marriage, and manhood. And where identity in More, Tyndale, Wyatt, and Spenser had been achieved through an attack upon something perceived as alien and threatening, in Marlowe it is achieved through a subversive identification with the alien. Marlowe's strategy of subversion is seen most clearly in *The Jew of Malta*, which, for this reason, I propose to consider in some detail. For Marlowe, as for Shakespeare, the figure of the Jew is useful as a powerful rhetorical device, an embodiment for a Christian audience of all they loathe and fear, all that appears stubbornly, irreducibly different. Introduced by Machiavel, the stock type of demonic villainy, Barabas enters already trailing clouds of ignominy, already a 'marked case'. But while never relinquishing the anti-Semitic stereotype and the conventional motif of the villain-undone-by-his-villainy, Marlowe quickly suggests that the Jew is not the exception to but rather the true representative of his society. Though he begins with a paean to liquid assets, Barabas is not primarily a usurer, set off by his hated occupation from the rest of the community, but a great merchant, sending his argosies around the world exactly as Shakespeare's much loved Antonio does. His pursuit of wealth does not mark him out but rather establishes him – if anything, rather respectably – in the midst of all the other forces in the play: the Turks exacting tribute from the Christians, the Christians expropriating money from the Jews, the convent profiting from these expropriations, religious orders competing for wealthy converts, the prostitute plying her trade and the blackmailer his. When the Governor of Malta asks the Turkish 'Bashaw,' 'What wind drives you thus into *Malta* road?' the latter replies with perfect frankness, 'The wind that bloweth all the world besides, / Desire of gold' (III, 1421–3). Barabas's own desire of gold, so eloquently voiced at the start and vividly enacted in the scene in which he hugs his money bags, is the glowing core of that passion which fires all the characters. To be sure, other values are expressed – love, faith, and honor – but as private values these are revealed to be hopelessly fragile, while as public values they are revealed to be mere screens for powerful economic forces. Thus on the one hand, Abigail, Don Mathias, and the nuns are killed off with remarkable ease and, in effect, with the complicity of the laughing audience. (The audience at the Royal Shakespeare Company's brilliant 1964 production roared with delight when the poisoned nuns came tumbling out of the house). On the other hand, the public invocation of Christian ethics or knightly honor is always linked by Marlowe to baser motives. The knights concern themselves with Barabas's 'inherent sin' only at the moment when they are about to preach him out of his possessions, while the decision to resist the 'barbarous misbelieving *Turks*' facilitates all too easily the sale into slavery of a shipload of Turkish captives. The religious and political ideology that seems at first to govern Christian attitudes toward infidels in fact does nothing of the sort; this ideology is clearly subordinated to considerations of profit.

It is because of the primacy of money that Barabas, for all the contempt heaped upon him, is seen as the dominant spirit of the play, its most energetic and inventive force. A victim at the level of religion and political power, he is, in effect, emancipated at the level of civil society, emancipated in Marx's contemptuous sense of the word in his essay *On the Jewish Question*:

The Jew has emancipated himself in a Jewish manner, not only by acquiring the power of money, but also because *money* has become, through him and also apart from him, a world power, while the practical Jewish spirit has become the practical spirit of the Christian nations. The Jews have emancipated themselves in so far as the Christians have become Jews.

(Marx 1963, p.35)

Barabas's avarice, egotism, duplicity, and murderous cunning do not signal his exclusion from the world of Malta but his central place within it. His 'Judaism' is, again in Marx's word, 'a universal *antisocial* element of the *present time*' (ibid., p.34)

For neither Marlowe nor Marx does this recognition signal a turning away from Jew-baiting; if anything, Jew-baiting is intensified even as the hostility it excites is directed as well against Christian society. Thus Marlowe never discredits anti-Semitism, but he does discredit early in the play a 'Christian' social concern that might otherwise have been used to counter a specifically Jewish antisocial element. When the Governor of Malta seizes the wealth of the Jews on the ground that it is 'better one want for a common good, / Then many perish for a private man'(I, 331– 2), an audience at all familiar with the New Testament will hear in these words echoes not of Christ but of Caiaphas and, a few lines further on, of Pilate. There are, to be sure, moments of social solidarity – as when the Jews gather around Barabas to comfort him or when Ferneze and Katherine together mourn the death of their sons – but they are brief and ineffectual. The true emblem of the society of the play is the slave market, where 'Every one's price is written on his back' (II, 274). Here in the marketplace men are literally turned, in Marx's phrase,'into *alienable*, saleable objects, in thrall to egoistic need and huckstering' (ibid., p.39). And at this level of society, the religious and political barriers fall away: the Jew buys a Turk at the Christian slave market. Such is the triumph of civil society.

For Marlowe the dominant mode of perceiving the world, in a society hag-ridden by the power of money and given over to the slave market, is contempt, *contempt* aroused in the beholders of such a society and, as important, governing the behavior of those who bring it into being and function within it. This is Barabas's constant attitude, virtually his signature; his withering scorn lights not only on the Christian rulers of Malta ('thus slaves will learn', he sneers, when the defeated Governor is forced into submission [V, 2150]), but on his daughter's suitor ('the slave looks like a hog's cheek new sing'd' [II, 803]), his daughter ('An *Hebrew* born, and would become a Christian. / *Cazzo, diabolo*' [IV, 1527– 28]), his slave Ithamore ('Thus every villain ambles after wealth/ Although he ne'er be richer than in hope' [III, 1354–5]), the Turks ('How the slave jeers at him' observes the Governor of Barabas greeting Calymath [V, 2339]), the pimp, Pilia-Borza ('a shaggy, totter'd staring slave ' [IV,1858]), his fellow Jews ('See the simplicity of these base slaves' [I, 448]), and even, when he has blundered by making the poison too weak, himself ('What a damn'd slave was I' [V,2025]). Barabas's frequent asides assure us that he is feeling contempt even when he is not openly expressing it, and the reiteration of the derogatory epithet *slave* firmly anchors this contempt in the structure of relations that governs the play. Barabas's liberality in bestowing this epithet – from the Governor to the pimp – reflects the extraordinary unity of the structure, its intricate series of mirror images: Pilia-Borza's extortion racket is repeated at the 'national' level in the extortion of the Jewish community's wealth and at the international level in the Turkish extortion of the Christian tribute. The play depicts Renaissance international relations as a kind of glorified gangsterism, a vast 'protection' racket.

At all levels of society in Marlowe's play, behind each version of the racket (and making it possible) is violence or the threat of violence, and so here too Barabas's murderousness is presented as at once a characteristic of his accursed tribe and the expression of a universal phenomenon. This expression, to be sure, is extravagant – he is responsible, directly or indirectly, for the deaths of Mathias, Lodowick, Abigail, Pilia-Borza, Bellamira, Ithamore, Friar Barnadine, and innumerable poisoned nuns and massacred soldiers – and, as we shall see, this extravagance helps to account for the fact that in the last analysis Barabas cannot be assimilated to his world. But if Marlowe ultimately veers away from so entirely sociological a conception, it is important to grasp the extent to which Barabas expresses in extreme, unmediated form the motives that have been partially disguised by the spiritual humbug of Christianity, indeed the extent to which Barabas is *brought into being* by the Christian society around him. His actions are always responses to the initiatives of others : not only is the plot of the whole play set in motion by the Governor's expropriation of his wealth, but each of Barabas's particular plots is a reaction to what he perceives as a provocation or a threat. Only his final stratagem – the betrayal of the Turks – seems an exception, since the Jew is for once in power, but even this fatal blunder is a response to his perfectly sound perception that '*Malta* hates me, and in hating me / My life's in danger' (V, 2131–32).

Barabas's apparent passivity sits strangely with his entire domination of the spirit of the play, and once again, we may turn to Marx for an explication of Marlowe's rhetorical strategy: 'Judaism could not create a new world. It could only bring the new creations and conditions of the world within its own sphere of activity, because practical need, the spirit of which is self–interest, is always passive, cannot expand at will, but *finds* itself extended as a result of the continued development of society'(ibid., p.38). Though the Jew is identified here with the spirit of egotism and selfish need, his success is credited to the triumph of Christianity which 'objectifies' and hence alienates all national, natural, moral, and theoretical relationships, dissolving 'the human world into a world of atomistic, antagonistic individuals' (ibid., p.39). The concrete emblem of this alienation in Marlowe is the slave market; its ideological expression is the religious chauvinism that sees Jews as inherently sinful, Turks as barbarous misbelievers.

The Jew of Malta ends on a powerfully ironic note of this 'spiritual egotism' (to use Marx's phrase) when the Governor celebrates the treacherous destruction of Barabas and the Turks by giving due praise 'Neither to Fate nor Fortune, but to Heaven' (V, 2410). (Once again, the Royal Shakespeare Company's audience guffawed at this bit of hypocritical sententiousness.) But we do not have to wait until the closing moments of the play to witness the Christian practice of alienation. It is, as I have suggested, present throughout, and nowhere more powerfully than in the figure of Barabas himself. For not only are Barabas's actions called forth by Christian actions, but his identity itself is to a great extent the product of the Christian conception of a Jew's identity. This is not entirely the case: Marlowe invokes an 'indigenous' Judaism in the wicked parody of the materialism of Job and in Barabas's repeated invocation of Hebraic exclusivism ('these swine-eating Christians,' etc.). Nevertheless Barabas's sense of himself, his characteristic response to the world, and his self-presentation are very largely constructed out of the materials of the dominant, Christian culture. This is nowhere more evident than in his speech, which is virtually composed of hard little aphorisms, cynical adages, worldly maxims – all the neatly packaged nastiness of his society. Where Shylock is differentiated from the Christians even in his use of the common language, Barabas is inscribed at the center of the society of the play, a society whose speech is a tissue of aphorisms. Whole speeches are little more than strings of sayings: maxims are exchanged, inverted, employed as weapons; the characters enact and even deliberately 'stage' proverbs (with all of the manic energy of Breughel's 'Netherlandish Proverbs'). When Barabas, intent upon poisoning the nuns, calls for the pot of rice porridge, Ithamore carries it to him along with a ladle, explaining that since 'the proverb says, he that eats with the devil had need of a long spoon, I have brought you a ladle' (III,1360–62). And when Barabas and Ithamore together strangle Friar Barnadine, to whom Abigail has revealed their crimes in confession, the Jew explains, 'Blame not us but the proverb, Confess and be hang'd' (IV, 1655).

Proverbs in *The Jew of Malta* are a kind of currency, the compressed ideological wealth of society, the money of the mind. Their terseness corresponds to that concentration of material wealth that Barabas celebrates: 'Infinite riches in a little room'. Barabas's own store of these ideological riches comprises the most cynical and self-serving portion:

Who is honor'd now but for his wealth?

(I,151)

Ego mihimet sum semper proximus.

(I,228)

A reaching thought will search his deepest wits
And cast with cunning for the time to come.

(I,455–6)

         ... in extremity
We ought to make bar of no policy

(I,507–8)

         ... Religion
Hides many mischiefs from suspicion.

(I,519–20)

Now will I show my self to have more of the Serpent
Than the Dove; that is, more knave than fool.

(II,797–8)

Faith is not to be held with Heretics.

(I,1076)

For he that liveth in Authority,
And neither gets him friends, nor fills his bags,
Lives like the Ass that *Aesop* speaketh of,
That labors with a load of bread and wine,
And leaves it off to snap on Thistle tops.

(V,2139–43)

For so I live, perish may all the world.

(V,2292)

This is not the exotic language of the Jews but the product of the whole
society, indeed, its most familiar and ordinary face. And as the essence of
proverbs is their anonymity, the effect of their recurrent use by Barabas is
to render him more and more typical, to *de-individualize* him. This is, of
course, the opposite of the usual process. Most dramatic characters –
Shylock is the appropriate example – accumulate identity in the course of
their play; Barabas loses it. He is never again as distinct and unique an
individual as he in the first moments:

Go tell 'em the Jew of *Malta* sent thee, man:
Tush, who amongst 'em knows not *Barabas*?

(I,i, 102–3)

Even his account of his past – killing sick people or poisoning wells –
tends to make him more vague and unreal, accommodating him to an
abstract, anti-Semitic fantasy of a Jew's past.

71

In this effacement of Barabas's identity, Marlowe reflects not only upon his culture's bad faith, its insistence upon the otherness of what is in fact its own essence, but also upon the tragic limitations of rebellion against this culture. Like all of Marlowe's heroes, Barabas defines himself by negating cherished values, but his identity is itself, as we have seen, a social construction, a fiction composed of the sleaziest materials in his culture. If Marlowe questions the notion of literature as cautionary tale, if his very use of admonitory fictions subverts them, he cannot dismiss the immense power of the social system in which such fictions play their part. Indeed the attempts to challenge this system – Tamburlaine's world conquest, Barabas's Machiavellianism, Edward's homosexuality, and Faustus's skepticism – are subjected to relentless probing and exposed as unwitting tributes to that social construction of identity against which they struggle. For if the heart of Renaissance orthodoxy is a vast system of repetitions in which disciplinary paradigms are established and men gradually learn what to desire and what to fear, the Marlovian rebels and skeptics remain embedded within this orthodoxy: they simply reverse the paradigms and embrace what the society brands as evil. In so doing, they imagine themselves set in diametrical opposition to their society where in fact they have unwittingly accepted its crucial structural elements. For the crucial issue is not man's power to disobey, but the characteristic modes of desire and fear produced by a given society, and the rebellious heroes never depart from those modes. With their passionate insistence on will, Marlowe's protagonists anticipate the perception that human history is the product of men themselves, but they also anticipate the perception that this product is shaped, in Lukács phrase, by forces that arise from their relations with each other and which have escaped their control (Lukács 1971, p.15). As Marx writes in a famous passage in *The Eighteenth Brumaire of Louis Bonaparte:*

> Men make their own history, but they do not make it just as they please; they do not make it under circumstances chosen by themselves, but under circumstances directly found, given and transmitted from the past. The tradition of all the dead generations weighs like a nightmare on the brain of the living. And just when they seem engaged in revolutionising themselves and things, in creating something entirely new, precisely in such epochs of revolutionary crisis they anxiously conjure up the spirits of the past.
>
> (Marx 1972, p.437)

Marlowe's protagonists rebel against orthodoxy, but they do not do so just as they please; their acts of negation not only conjure up the order they would destroy but seem at times to be themselves conjured up by that very order. *The Jew of Malta* continually demonstrates, as we have seen, how close Barabas is to the Gentile world against which he is set; if this demonstration exposes the hypocrisy of that world, it cuts against the Jew as well, for his loathing must be repeatedly directed against a version of himself, until at the close he boils in the pot he has prepared for his enemy. Similarly, Faustus's whole career binds him ever more closely to that Christian conception of the body and the mind, that divinity, he thought he was decisively rejecting. He dreams of living 'in all voluptuousness' (337), but his pleasures are parodic versions of Holy Communion.

Of all Marlowe's heroes, only Tamburlaine comes close to defining himself in genuinely radical opposition to the order against which he wars; he does so by virtue of a powerful if sporadic materialism that Marlowe seems to have compounded out of a strange blend of scholarly and popular heterodox elements in his culture. From academic life, Marlowe could draw upon Lucretian naturalism, with its vision of a cosmos formed by the restless clash of opposing elements; from popular culture – the culture we glimpse fleetingly in ballads, trial records, and the like – he could draw upon an unillusioned reduction of ideology to power and of power to violence. From both he could derive the remarkable centrality of the body that is the play's obsessive preoccupation. The action of *Tamburlaine* – endless stabbing, chaining, drowning, lancing, hanging – is almost entirely directed toward what we may call a theatrical proof of the body's existence. In what seems a zany parody of Christ and Doubting Thomas, Tamburlaine at one point wounds himself for the edification of his sons: 'Come boys, and with your fingers search my wound, / And in my blood wash all your hands at once' (2 *Tam*, III, ii, 3316–17). Likewise, the dying in the play – and they are legion – speak of themselves in an oddly detailed, almost clinical language, as if to insist upon the corporeal reality of their experience:

> I feel my liver pierced, and all my veins,
> That there begin and nourish every part,
> Mangled and torn, and all my entrails bathed
> In blood that straineth from their orifex.

> (2 *Tam*, IV, 3417–20)

Yet even here, I would argue, the movement toward a truly radical alternative is thwarted by the orthodoxy against which it struggles. The materialist rejection of transcendence is belied by Tamburlaine's single-minded commitment of 'princely deeds' of violence. The body is affirmed only in wounding and destroying it, and this aggression ironically generates the odd note of detachment – bodilessness – that characterizes even those lines I have just quoted. A different attitude toward the flesh – sensual enjoyment, self-protection, tolerant acceptance, ease – is explicitly attacked and killed in the figure of Tamburlaine's 'cowardly' (and remarkably sympathetic) son Calyphas. Tamburlaine stabs Calyphas because the 'effeminate brat' possesses

> A form not meet to give that subject essence
> Whose matter is the flesh of Tamburlaine,
> Wherein an incorporeal spirit moves.

(2 Tam,IV,i,3786–8)

The Aristotelian language of the Schoolmen here signals the operation, within the bizarre and barbaric scene, of precisely those conservative principles against which Tamburlaine had seemed to be set, just as moments later the former Scythian shepherd can speak of plaguing 'such peasants as resist in me/The power of heaven's eternal majesty' (2 *Tam*, IV, i, 3831–2)

Tamburlaine rebels against hierarchy, legitimacy, the whole established order of things, and to what end? To reach, as he declares, 'The sweet fruition of an earthly crown.' *Earthly* tantalizingly suggests a materialist alternative to the transcendental authority upon which all the 'legitimate' kings in the play base their power, but the suggestion is not realized. Theridamas's response to Tamburlaine's declaration of purpose sounds for an instant as if it were about to confirm such an alternative, but then by a trick of syntax it veers away:

> And that made me to join with Tamburlaine,
> For he is gross and like the massy earth
> That moves not upwards, nor by princely deeds,
> Doth mean to soar above the highest sort.

(1 Tam, II,vi, 881–4)

Tamburlaine's will is immeasurably stronger, but its object is essentially the same as that of Mycetes, Cosroe, Bajazeth, or any of the other princelings who strut around the stage. Part 1 ends not in an act of revolt but in the supreme gesture of legitimacy, a proper marriage, with the Scourge of God earnestly assuring his father-in-law of Zenocrate's unblemished chastity. The close of Part 2 may seem closer to an act of radical freedom –

> Come, let us march against the powers of heaven
> And set black streamers in the firmament
> To signify the slaughter of the gods –

(2 Tam, V, iii, 4440–2)

but, as in *Faustus*, the blasphemy pays homage to the power it insults. In just this way, several years after Marlowe wrote his play, an illiterate visionary, condemned to death for claiming to be Christ come in judgment upon the queen and her councillors, demanded on the scaffold that God deliver him from his enemies: 'If not, I will fire the heavens, and tear thee from thy throne with my hands.' Such acts of aggression are spectacular, but they are ultimately bound in by the orthodoxy against which they revolt.

Marlowe stands apart then from both orthodoxy and skepticism; he calls into question the theory of literature and history as repeatable moral lessons, and he calls into question his age's characteristic mode of rejecting those lessons. But how does he himself understand his characters' motivation, the force that compels them to repeat the same actions again and again? The answer, as I have already suggested, lies in their will to self-fashioning. Marlowe's heroes struggle to invent themselves; they stand, in Coriolanus's phrase, 'As if a man were author of himself/ And knew no other kin' (V,iii, 36–37). Shakespeare characteristically forces his very Marlovian hero to reach out and grasp his mother's hand; in Marlowe's plays with the exception of *Dido Queen of Carthage*, we never see and scarcely even hear of the hero's parents. Tamburlaine is the son of nameless 'paltry' Scythians, Faustus of 'parents base of stock' (12), and Barabas, so far as we can tell, of no one at all. (Even in *Edward II*, where an emphasis on parentage would seem unavoidable, there is scant mention of Edward I). The family is at the center of most Elizabethan and Jacobean drama as it is at the center of the period's economic and social structure; in Marlowe it is something to be neglected, despised, or violated. Two of Marlowe's heroes kill their children without a trace of remorse; most prefer male friendships to marriage or kinship bonds; all insist upon free choice in determining their intimate relations. Upon his father's death, Edward immediately sends for Gaveston; Barabas adopts Ithamore in place of Abigail; Faustus cleaves to his sweet Mephistophilis; and, in a more passionate love scene than any with Zenocrate, Tamburlaine wins the ardent loyalty of Theridamas.

The effect is to dissolve the structure of sacramental and blood relations that normally determine identity in this period and to render the heroes virtually autochthonous, their names and identities given by no one but themselves. Indeed self-naming is a major enterprise in these plays, repeated over and over again as if the hero continues to exist only by virtue of constantly renewed acts of will. Augustine had written in *The City of God* that 'if God were to withdraw what we may call his "constructive power" from existing things, they would cease to exist, just as they did not exist before they were made.' In the neutrality of time and space that characterizes Marlowe's world, this 'constructive power' must exist within the hero himself; if it should fail for an instant he would fall into nothingness, become, in Barabas's words, 'a senseless lump of clay / That will with every water wash to dirt' (I, 450–1). Hence the hero's compulsion to repeat his name and his actions, a compulsion Marlowe links to the drama itself. The hero's re-presentations fade into the reiterated performances of the play.

If Marlowe's protagonists fashion themselves, they are, as we have seen, compelled to use only those forms and materials produced by the structure of relations in their particular, quite distinct worlds. We watch Tamburlaine construct himself out of phrases picked up or overheard: 'And ride in triumph through Persepolis' (1 *Tam*, II,v, 754) or 'I that am term'd the Scourge and Wrath of God' (1 *Tam*, III, iii, 1142). Like the gold taken from unwary travelers or the troops lured away from other princes, Tamburlaine's identity is something *appropriated*, seized from others. Even Edward II, with his greater psychological complexity, can only clothe himself in the metaphors available to this station, though these metaphors – the 'Imperial Lion', for example – often seem little applicable. And the most haunting instance in Marlowe of this self-fashioning by quotation or appropriation occurs in *Doctor Faustus*, when the hero concludes the signing of the fatal deed with the words 'Consummatum est' (515).

To unfold the significance of this repetition of Christ's dying words, we must restore them to their context in the Gospel of John:

> After this, Jesus knowing that all things were now ac-complished, that the Scripture might be fulfilled, saith, I thirst. Now there was set a vessel full of vinegar; and they filled a sponge with vinegar, and put it upon hys-sop, and put it to his mouth. When Jesus therefore had received the vinegar, he said, It is finished [Consum-matum est]: and he bowed his head, and gave up the ghost.
>
> (John 19: 28–30)

As it is written in Psalm 69, 'and in my thirst they gave me vinegar to drink', so it is fulfilled; Christ's thirst is not identical to the body's normal longing for drink, but an *enactment* of that longing so that he may fully accomplish the role darkly prefigured in the Old Testament. The drink of vinegar is the final structural element in the realization of his identity. Faustus's use of Christ's words then evokes the archetypal act of role-taking; by reenacting the moment in which Christ acknowledges the fulfillment of his being, the magician hopes to touch upon the primal springs of identity itself. But whatever identity Faustus can thereby achieve is limited to the status of brilliant parody. His blasphemy is the uncanny expression of a perverse, despairing faith, an appropriation to himself of the most solemn and momentous words available in his culture to mark the decisive boundary in his life, an ambiguous equation of himself with Christ, first as God, then as dying man.

'*Consummatum est*' is the culmination of Faustus's fantasies of making an end, and hence a suicide that demonically parodies Christ's self-sacrifice. But in the Gospels, as we have seen, the words are a true end; they are spoken at the moment of fulfillment and death. In *Doctor Faustus* they are rather a beginning, spoken at the moment Faustus is embarking on his bargain. Unlike Christ, who is his own transcendent object, and whose career is precisely the realization of himself, Faustus, and all of Marlowe's self fashioning heroes, must posit an object in order to exist. Naming oneself is not enough; one must also name and pursue a goal. And if both the self and object so constituted are tragically bounded by the dominant ideology against which they vainly struggle, Marlowe's heroes nevertheless manifest a theatrical energy that distinguishes their words as well as their actions from the surrounding society. If the audience's perception of radical difference gives way to a perception of subversive identity, that too in its turn gives way: in the *excessive* quality of Marlowe's heroes, in their histrionic extremism, lies that which distinguishes their self-fashioning acts from the society around them. The Turks, friars, and Christian knights may all be driven by acquisitive desire, but only Barabas can speak of 'Infinite riches in a little room', only he has the capacity for what one must call aesthetic experience:

Bags of fiery *Opals, Sapphires, Amethysts,*
Jacinths, hard *Topaz,* grass-green *Emeralds,*
Beauteous *Rubies,* sparkling *Diamonds,*
And seld-seen costly stones ....

(I, 60–3)

Similarly, Theridamas may declare that 'A God is not so glorious as a King,' but when he is asked if he himself would be a king, he replies, 'Nay, though I praise it, I can live without it' (1 *Tam*,II,v,771). Tamberlaine cannot live without it, and his reward is not only 'The sweet fruition of an earthly crown' but what Plato's rival Gorgias conceives as 'the magic violence of speech'.

It is this Gorgian conception of rhetoric, and not the Platonic or Aristotelian, that is borne out in Marlowe's heroes. For Gorgias man is forever cut off from the knowledge of being, forever locked in the partial, the contradictory, and the irrational. If anything exists, he writes, it is both incomprehensible and incommunicable, for 'that which we communicate is speech, and speech is not the same thing as the things that exist.' This tragic epistemological distance is never bridged; instead, through the power of language men construct deceptions in which and for which they live. Gorgias held that deception – *apate* – is the very essence of the creative imagination: the tragic artist exceeds his peers in the power to deceive. Such a conception of art does not preclude its claim to strip away fraud,

since tragedy 'with its myths and emotions has created a deception such
that its successful practitioner is nearer to reality than the unsuccessful,
and the man who lets himself be deceived is wiser than he who does not.'
In *The Jew of Malta* Barabas the deceiver gives us his own version of this
aesthetic:'A counterfeit profession,' he tells his daughter, 'is better / Than
unseen hypocrisy' (I,531–2). In the long run, the play challenges this
conviction, at least from the point of view of survival: the Governor, who is
the very embodiment of 'unseen hypocrisy' eventually triumphs over the
Jew's 'counterfeit profession.' But Marlowe uses the distinction to direct
the audience's allegiance toward Barabas; to lie and to know that one is
lying seems more attractive, more aesthetically pleasing, and more moral
even, than to lie and believe that one is telling the truth.

The ethical basis of such a discrimination does not bear scrutiny; what
matters is that the audience becomes Barabas's accomplice. And the pact is
affirmed over and over again in Barabas's frequent, malevolently comic
asides:

> *Lodowick* Good *Barabas*, glance not at our holy Nuns.
> *Barabas*   No, but I do it through a burning zeal,
> *Hoping ere long to set the house a fire* [Aside]

> (II,iii,849–51)

Years ago, in Naples, I watched a deft pickpocket lifting a camera from a
tourist's shoulder-bag and replacing it instantaneously with a rock of equal
weight. The thief spotted me watching but did not run away – instead he
winked, and I was frozen in mute complicity. The audience's conventional
silence becomes in *The Jew of Malta* the silence of the passive accomplice,
winked at by his fellow criminal. Such a relationship is, of course, itself
conventional. The Jew has for the audience something of the attractiveness
of the wily, misused slave in Roman comedy, always on the brink of
disaster, always revealed to have a trick or two up his sleeve. The mythic
core of this character's endless resourcefulness is what Nashe calls 'stage-
like resurrection,' and, though Barabas is destined for a darker end, he is
granted at least one such moment: thrown over the city walls and left for
dead, he springs up full of scheming energy. At this moment, as elsewhere
in the play, the audience waits expectantly for Barabas's recovery, *wills* his
continued existence, and hence identifies with him.

Barabas first wins the audience to him by means of the incantatory
power of his language, and it is through this power too that Faustus
conjures up the Prince of Deceptions and that Tamburlaine makes his
entire life into a project, transforming himself into an elemental,
destructive force, driving irresistibly forward: 'For Will and Shall best
fitteth Tamburlaine' (1 *Tam*, III,iii, 1139). He collapses all the senses of these
verbs – intention, command, prophecy, resolution, and simple futurity – into

his monomaniacal project. All of Marlowe's heroes seem similarly obsessed, and the result of their passionate willing, their insistent, reiterated naming of themselves and their objects, is that they become more intensely real to us, more present, than any of the other characters. This is only to say that they are the protagonists, but once again Marlowe relates the shape of the medium itself to the central experience of the plays; his heroes seem determined to realize the Idea of themselves as dramatic heroes. There is a parallel in Spenser's Malbecco who is so completely what he is – in this case, so fanatically jealous – that he becomes the allegorical incarnation of Jealousy itself. But where this self-realization in Spenser is Platonic, in Marlowe it is Gorgian – that is, Platonism is undermined by the presence of the theater itself, the unavoidable distance between the particular actor and his role, the insistent awareness in audience and players alike of illusion.

Within the plays this awareness is intensified by the difficulties the characters experience in sustaining their lives as projects, by that constant reiteration to which, as we have seen, they are bound. For even as no two performances or readings of a text are exactly the same, so the repeated acts of self-fashioning are never absolutely identical; indeed as Gilles Deleuze has recently observed, we can only speak of repetition by reference to the difference or change that it causes in the mind that contemplates it (Deleuze 1968, p.96). The result is that the objects of desire, at first so clearly defined, so avidly pursued, gradually lose their sharp outlines and become more and more like mirages. Faustus speaks endlessly of his appetite, his desire to be glutted, ravished, consumed, but what is it exactly that he wants? By the end of the play it is clear that knowledge, voluptuousness, and power are each mere approximations of the goal for which he sells his soul and body; what that goal is remains maddeningly unclear. 'Mine own fantasy / ... will receive no object' (136–7), he tells Valdes and Cornelius, in a phrase that could stand as the play's epigraph. At first Barabas seems a simpler case: he wants wealth, though there is an unsettling equivocation between the desire for wealth as power and security and desire for wealth as an aesthetic, even metaphysical gratification. But the rest of the play does not bear out this desire as the center of Barabas's being: money is not finally the jealous God of the Jew of Malta. He seeks rather, at any cost, to revenge himself on the Christians. Or so we think until he plots to destroy the Turks and restore the Christians to power. Well then, he wants always to serve his own self-interest: *Ego mihimet sum semper proximus* (I, 228). But where exactly is the self whose interests he serves? Even the Latin tag betrays an ominous self-distance: 'I am always my own neighbor,' or even, 'I am always *next* to myself.' Edward II is no clearer. He loves Gaveston, but why? 'Because he loves me more than all the world'(372). The desire returns from its object, out there in the world, to the self, a self that is nonetheless exceedingly unstable. When Gaveston is killed, Edward has within seconds adopted someone else; the will exists, but the object of the will is little more than an illusion. Even Tamburlaine, with his firm declaration of a goal, becomes ever more equivocal. 'The sweet fruition of an earthly crown' turns out not to be what it first appears – the acquisition of kingship – for Tamburlaine continues his restless pursuit long after his acquisition. His goal then is power which is graphically depicted as the ability to transform virgins with blubbered cheeks into slaughtered carcasses. But when Tamburlaine views the corpses he has made and defines this object for himself, it immediately becomes something else, a mirror reflecting yet another goal:

> All sights of power to grace my victory:
> And such are objects fit for *Tamburlaine,*
> Wherein as in a mirror may be seen,
> His honor, that consists in shedding blood.

(1 Tam, V,ii, 2256–9)

It is Tamburlaine, in his celebrated speech 'What is beauty sayeth my sufferings then?' (1 *Tam*, V, ii, 1941ff.), who gives the whole problem of reaching a desired end its clearest formal expression in Marlowe: beauty, like all the goals pursued by the playwright's heroes, always hovers just beyond the reach of human thought and expression. The problem of exclusiveness is one of the major preoccupations of Renaissance thinkers from the most moderate to the most radical, from the judicious Hooker to the splendidly injudicious Bruno. Marlowe is deeply influenced by this contemporary thought, but he subtly shifts the emphasis from the infinity that draws men beyond what they possess to the problem of the human will, the difficulty men experience in truly wanting anything. It is a commonplace that for Saint Augustine the essence of evil is that anything should be 'sought for itself, whereas things should be sought only in terms of the search for God.' Marlowe's heroes seem at first to embrace such evil: they freely proclaim their immense hunger for something which takes on the status of a personal absolute, and they relentlessly pursue this absolute. The more threatening an obstacle in their path, the more determined they are to obliterate or overreach it: I long for, I burn, I will. But, as we have seen, we are never fully convinced by these noisy demonstrations of single-minded appetite. It is as if Marlowe's heroes wanted to be wholly perverse, in Augustine's sense, but were incapable of such perversity, as if they could not finally desire anything for itself. For Hooker and Bruno alike, this inability arises from the existence of transcendent goals – it is a proof of the existence of God; for Marlowe it springs from the suspicion that all objects of desire are fictions, theatrical illusions shaped by human subjects. And those subjects are themselves fictions, fashioned in reiterated acts of self-naming. The problem is already understood in its full complexity by

Montaigne, but, as Auerbach observes, 'his irony, his dislike of big words, his calm way of being profoundly at ease with himself, prevent him from pushing on beyond the limits of the problematic and into the realm of the tragic' (Auerbach 1968,p.311). Marlowe, whose life suggests the very opposite of that 'peculiar equilibrium' that distinguishes Montaigne, rushes to embrace the tragic with a strange eagerness.

Man can only exist in the world by fashioning for himself a name and an object, but these, as Marlowe and Montaigne understood, are both fictions. No particular name or object can entirely satisfy one's inner energy demanding to be expressed or fill so completely the potential of one's consciousness that all longings are quelled, all intimations of unreality silenced. As we have seen in the controversy between More and Tyndale, Protestant and Catholic polemicists demonstrated brilliantly how each other's religion – the very anchor of reality for millions of souls – was a cunning theatrical illusion, a demonic fantasy, a piece of poetry. Each conducted his unmasking, of course, in the name of the *real* religious truth, but the collective effect upon a skeptical intellect like Marlowe's seems to have been devastating. And it was not only the religious dismantling of reality to which the playwright was responding. On the distant shores of Africa and America and at home, in their 'rediscovered' classical texts, Renaissance Europeans were daily confronting evidence that their accustomed reality was only one solution, among many others, of perennial human problems. Though they often tried to destroy the alien cultures they encountered, or to absorb them into their ideology, they could not always destroy the testimony of their own consciousness. 'The wonder is not that things are,' writes Valéry, 'but that they are *what* they are and not something else.' Each of Marlowe's plays constitutes reality in a manner radically different from the plays that preceded it, just as his work as a whole marks a startling departure from the drama of his time. Each of his heroes makes a different leap from inchoate appetite to the all-consuming project: what is necessary in one play is accidental or absent in the next. Only the leap itself is always necessary, at once necessary and absurd, for it is the embracing of a fiction rendered desirable by the intoxication of language, by the will to play.

Marlowe's heroes *must* live their lives as projects, but they do so in the midst of intimations that the projects are illusions. Their strength is not sapped by these intimations: they do not withdraw into stoical resignation or contemplative solitude, nor do they endure for the sake of isolated moments of grace in which they are in touch with a wholeness otherwise absent in their lives. Rather they take courage from the absurdity of their enterprise, a murderous, self-destructive, supremely eloquent, playful courage. This playfulness in Marlowe's works manifests itself as cruel humor, murderous practical jokes, a penchant for the outlandish and absurd, delight in role-playing, entire absorption in the game at hand and consequent indifference to what lies outside the boundaries of the game, radical insensitivity to human complexity and suffering, extreme but disciplined aggression, hostility to transcendence.

There is some evidence, apart from the cruel, aggressive plays themselves, for a similar dark playfulness in Marlowe's own career, with the comic (and extremely dangerous) blasphemies, the nearly overt (and equally dangerous) homosexuality – tokens of a courting of disaster as reckless as that depicted in Edward or Faustus. In the life, as in the plays, the categories by which we normally organize experience are insistently called into question – is this a man whose recklessness suggests that he is out of control or rather that he is supremely in control, control so coolly mocking that he can, to recall Wyatt, calcu'.;te his own excesses? What little we know about Marlowe's mysterious stint as a double agent in Walsingham's secret service – it seems that he went to Rheims in 1587, perhaps posing as a Catholic in order to ferret out incriminating evidence against English Catholic seminarians – and what little we can gather from the contents of the Baines libel suggests, beyond estrangement from ideology, a fathomless and eerily playful self-estrangement. The will to play flaunts society's cherished orthodoxies, embraces what the culture finds loathsome or frightening, transforms the serious into the joke and then unsettles the category of the joke by taking it seriously, courts self-destruction in the interest of the anarchic discharge of its energy. This is play on the brinks of an abyss, *absolute* play.

In his turbulent life and, more important, in his writing, Marlowe is deeply implicated in his heroes, though he is far more intelligent and self-aware than any of them. Cutting himself off from the comforting doctrine of repetition, he writes plays that spurn and subvert his culture's metaphysical and ethical certainties. We who have lived after Nietzsche and Flaubert may find it difficult to grasp how strong, how recklessly courageous Marlowe must have been: to write as if the admonitory purpose of literature were a lie, to invent fictions only to create and not to serve God or the state, to fashion lines that echo in the void, that echo more powerfully because there is nothing but a void. Hence Marlowe's implication in the lives of his protagonists and hence too his surmounting of this implication in the creation of enduring works of art. For the one true goal of all these heroes is to be characters in Marlowe's plays; it is only for this, ultimately, that they manifest both their playful energy and their haunting sense of unsatisfied longing.

5 Invisible Bullets: Renaissance Authority and its Subversion, *Henry IV* and *Henry V**

STEPHEN GREENBLATT

The greatest single intellectual stimulus to New Historicism has been Foucault's demolition of the **repressive hypothesis** or social-control model of authority, and his proposition that power operates through the desires it produces rather than those it forbids. Stephen Greenblatt's widely circulated essay on Shakespeare's Henry IV plays sets a pattern for the application of Foucault's pessimistic ideas to literary texts. As in *Renaissance Self-Fashioning* (Chapter 4), Greenblatt's method is to examine Western culture anthropologically, starting from a colonial anecdote that exposes European values as social constructs. He then adduces game theory to suggest that Prince Hal's career as an agent provocateur in the London underworld is typical of the theatricality with which the modern **state** incites **subversion**, the better to contain it. This interpretation is a striking reversal of the idealisation of **carnival** (or art) as liberation in both humanist and Marxist criticism. By viewing culture as a game, the study of history itself becomes a branch of literary criticism, which Greenblatt calls **Cultural Poetics**.

In his notorious police report of 1593 on Christopher Marlowe, the Elizabethan spy Richard Baines informed his superiors that Marlowe had declared, among other monstrous opinions, that 'Moses was but a juggler, and that one Heriots, being Sir Walter Ralegh's man, can do more than he.' The 'Heriots' cast for a moment in this lurid light is Thomas Harriot, the most profound Elizabethan mathematician, an expert in cartography, optics, and navigational science, an adherent of atomism, the first Englishman to make a telescope and turn it on the heavens, the author of the first original book about the first English colony in America, and the

---

*Reprinted from *Political Shakespeare: New Essays in Cultural Materialism*, ed. Jonathan Dollimore and Alan Sinfield (Manchester University Press, 1985).

possessor throughout his career of a dangerous reputation for atheism. In all of his extant writings, private correspondence as well as public discourse, Harriot professes the most reassuringly orthodox religious faith, but the suspicion persisted. When he died of cancer in 1621, one of his contemporaries, persuaded that Harriot had challenged the doctrinal account of creation *ex nihilo*, remarked gleefully that 'a *nihilum* killed him at last: for in the top of his nose came a little red speck (exceeding small), which grew bigger and bigger, and at last killed him'.

Charges of atheism levelled at Harriot or anyone else in this period are extremely difficult to assess, for such accusations were smear tactics, used with reckless abandon against anyone whom the accuser happened to dislike. At a dinner party one summer evening in 1593, Sir Walter Ralegh teased an irascible country parson named Ralph Ironside and found himself the subject of a state investigation; at the other end of the social scale, in the same Dorsetshire parish, a drunken servant named Oliver complained that in the Sunday sermon the preacher had praised Moses excessively but had neglected to mention his fifty-two concubines, and Oliver too found himself under official scrutiny. Few if any of these investigations turned up what we would call atheists, even muddled or shallow ones; the stance that seems to come naturally to the greenest college freshman in late twentieth-century America seems to have been almost unthinkable to the most daring philosophical minds of late sixteenth-century England.

The historical evidence, of course, is unreliable; even in the absence of substantial social pressure, people lie quite readily about their most intimate beliefs. How much more must they have lied in an atmosphere of unembarrassed repression. Still, there is probably more than politic concealment involved here. After all, treason was punished as harshly as atheism, and yet, while the period abounds in documented instances of treason in word and deed, there are virtually no professed atheists. If ever there were a place to confirm the proposition that within a given social construction of reality certain interpretations of experience are sanctioned and others excluded, it is here, in the boundaries that contained sixteenth-century scepticism. Like Machiavelli and Montaigne, Thomas Harriot professed belief in God, and there is no justification, in any of these cases, for a simple dismissal of the profession of faith as mere hypocrisy.

I am not, of course, arguing that atheism was literally unthinkable in the late sixteenth century; rather that it was almost always thinkable only as the thought of another. This is, in fact, one of its attractions as a smear; atheism is one of the characteristic marks of otherness. Hence the ease with which Catholics can call Protestant martyrs atheists, and Protestants routinely make similar charges against the Pope. The pervasiveness and frequency of these charges then does not signal the probable existence of a secret society of freethinkers, a School of Night, but rather registers the operation of a religious authority that, whether Catholic or Protestant, characteristically confirms its power in this period by disclosing the threat of atheism. The authority is secular as well as religious; hence at Ralegh's 1603 treason trial, Justice Popham solemnly warned the accused not to let 'Harriot, nor any such Doctor, persuade you there is no eternity in Heaven, lest you find an eternity of hell-torments'. Nothing in Harriot's writings suggests that he held the position attributed to him here, but of course the charge does not depend upon evidence; Harriot is invoked as the archetypal corrupter, Achitophel seducing his glittering Absolom. If he did not exist, he would have to be invented.

Yet atheism is not the only mode of subversive religious doubt, and we cannot entirely discount the persistent rumors of Harriot's heterodoxy by pointing to his perfectly conventional professions of faith and to the equal conventionality of the attacks upon him. Indeed I want to suggest that if we look closely at A *Brief and True Report of the New Found Land of Virginia,* the only work Harriot published in his lifetime and hence the work in which he was presumably the most cautious, we can find traces of exactly the kind of material that could lead to the remark attributed to Marlowe, that 'Moses was but a juggler, and that one Heriots, being Sir Walter Ralegh's man, can do more than he.' Further, Shakespeare's Henry plays, like Harriot in the New World, can be seen to confirm the Machievellian hypothesis of the origin of princely power in force and fraud even as they draw their audience irresistibly toward the celebration of that power.

The apparently feeble wisecrack attributed to Marlowe finds its way into a police file because it seems to bear out one of the Machiavellian arguments about religion that most excited the wrath of sixteenth-century authorities: Old Testament religion, the argument goes, and by extension the whole Judeo-Christian tradition, originated in a series of clever tricks, fraudulent illusions perpetrated by Moses, who had been trained in Egyptian magic, upon the 'rude and gross' (and hence credulous) Hebrews. This argument is not actually to be found in Machiavelli, nor does it originate in the sixteenth century; it is already fully formulated in early pagan polemics against Christianity. But it seems to acquire a special force and currency in the Renaissance as an aspect of a heightened consciousness, fuelled by the period's prolonged crises of doctrine and church governance, of the social function of religious belief.

Here Machiavelli's writings are important, for *The Prince* observes in its bland way that if Moses's particular actions and methods are examined closely, they do not appear very different from those employed by the great pagan princes, while the *Discourses* treat religion as if its primary function were not salvation but the achievement of civic discipline and hence as if its primary justification were not truth but expediency. Thus Romulus's successor, Numa Pompilius, 'finding a very savage people, and wishing to reduce them to civil obedience by the arts of peace, had recourse to religion as the most necessary and assured support of any civil society'. For although 'Romulus could organize the Senate and establish other civil and military institutions without the aid of divine authority, yet it was very necessary for Numa, who feigned that he held converse with a nymph, who dictated to him all that he wished to persuade the people to.' In truth, continues Machiavelli, 'there never was any remarkable lawgiver amongst any people who did not resort to divine authority, as otherwise his laws would not have been accepted by the people'.

From here it was only a short step, in the minds of Renaissance authorities, to the monstrous opinions attributed to the likes of Marlowe and Harriot. Kyd, under torture, testified that Marlowe had affirmed that 'things esteemed to be done by divine power might have as well been done by observation of men', and the Jesuit Robert Parsons claimed that in Ralegh's 'school of Atheism', 'both Moses and our Saviour, the Old and the New Testament, are jested at'. On the eve of Ralegh's treason trial, some 'hellish verses' were lifted from an anonymous tragedy written ten years earlier and circulated as Ralegh's own confession of atheism. (The movement here is instructive: the fictional text returns to circulation as the missing confessional language of real life). At first the earth was held in common, the verses declare, but this golden age gave way to war, kingship, and property:

> Then some sage man, above the vulgar wise,
> Knowing that laws could not in quiet dwell,
> Unless they were observed, did first devise
> The names of Gods, religion, heaven, and hell ...
> Only bug-bears to keep the world in fear.

Now Harriot does not give voice to any of these speculations, but if we look attentively at his account of the first Virginia colony, we find a mind that seems interested in the same set of problems, a mind indeed that seems to be virtually testing the Machiavellian hypotheses. Sent by Ralegh to keep a record of the colony and to compile a description of the resources and inhabitants of the area, Harriot took care to learn the North Carolina Algonkian dialect and to achieve what he calls a 'special familiarity with some of the priests'. The Indians believe, he writes, in the immortality of the soul and in otherworldly punishments and rewards for behaviour in this world: 'What subtlety soever be in the *Wiroances* and Priests, this opinion worketh so much in many of the common and simple sort of people that it maketh them have great respect to their Governors, and also great care what they do, to avoid torment after death and to enjoy bliss'. The split between the priests and the people implied here is glimpsed as well in the description of the votive images: 'They think that all the gods are of human shape, and therefore they represent them by images in the forms of men, which they call Kewasowak... The common sort think them to be also gods.'

We have then, as in Machiavelli, a sense of religion as a set of beliefs manipulated by the subtlety of the priests to help ensure social order and cohesion. To this we may add a still more telling observation not of the internal function of native religion but of the impact of European culture upon the Indians:

> Most things they saw with us [Harriot writes] as mathematical instruments, sea compasses, the virtue of the loadstone in drawing iron, a perspective glass whereby was showed many strange sights, burning glasses, wildfire works, guns, books, writing and reading, spring clocks that seem to go of themselves, and many other things that we had, were so strange unto them, and so far exceeded their capacities to comprehend the reason and means how they should be made and done, that they thought they were rather the works of gods then of men, or at the leastwise they had been given and taught us of the gods.

The effect of this delusion, born of what Harriot supposes to be the vast technological superiority of the European, is that the savages began to doubt that they possessed the truth of God and religion and to suspect that such truth 'was rather to be had from us, whom God so specially loved than from a people that were so simple, as they found themselves to be in comparison of us'.

What we have here, I suggest, is the very core of the Machiavellian anthropology that posited the origin of religion in a cunning imposition of socially coercive doctrines by an educated and sophisticated lawgiver upon a simple people. And in Harriot's list of the marvels - from wildfire to reading - with which he undermined the Indians' confidence in their native understanding of the universe, we have the core of the claim attributed to Marlowe: that Moses was but a juggler and that Ralegh's man Harriot could do more than he. It was, we may add, supremely appropriate that this hypothesis should be tested in the encounter of the Old World and the New, for though vulgar Machiavellianism implied that all religion was a sophisticated confidence trick, Machiavelli himself saw that trick as possible only at a radical point of origin: 'if any one wanted to establish a republic at the present time', he writes, 'he would find it much easier with the simple mountaineers, who are almost without any civilization, than with such as are accustomed to live in cities'.

In Harriot then we have one of the earliest instances of a highly significant phenomenon: the testing upon the bodies and minds of non-Europeans or, more generally, the non-civilised, of a hypothesis about the origin and nature of European culture and belief. Such testing could best occur in this privileged anthropological moment, for the comparable situations in Europe itself tended to be already contaminated by prior contact. Only in the forest, with a people ignorant of Christianity and startled by its bearers' technological potency, could one hope to reproduce accurately, with live subjects, the relation imagined between Numa and the primitive Romans, Moses and the Hebrews. And the testing that could then take place could only happen once, for it entails not detached observation but radical change, the change Harriot begins to observe in the priests who 'were not so sure grounded, nor gave such credit to their traditions and stories, but through conversing with us they were brought into great doubts of their own'. I should emphasise that I am speaking here of events as reported by Harriot. The history of subsequent English–Algonkian relations casts doubts upon the depth, extent, and irreversibility of the supposed Indian crisis of belief. In the *Brief and True Report*, however, the tribe's stories begin to *collapse* in the minds of their traditional guardians, and the coercive power of the European beliefs begins to show itself almost at once in the Indians' behaviour:

> On a time also when their corn began to wither by reason of a drought which happened extra-ordinarily, fearing that it had come to pass by reason that in some thing they had displeased us, many would come to us and desire us to pray to our God in England, that he would preserve their corn, promising that when it was ripe we also should be partakers of the fruit.

If we remember that, like virtually all sixteenth-century Europeans in the New World, the English resisted or were incapable of provisioning themselves and were in consequence dependent upon the Indians for food, we may grasp the central importance for the colonists of this dawning Indian fear of the Christian God. As Machiavelli understood, physical compulsion is essential but never sufficient; the survival of the rulers depends upon a supplement of coercive belief.

The Indians must be persuaded that the Christian God is all-powerful and committed to the survival of his chosen people, that he will wither the corn and destroy the lives of savages who displease him by disobeying or plotting against the English. We have then a strange paradox: Harriot tests and seems to confirm the most radically subversive hypothesis in his culture about the origin and function of religion by imposing his religion – with all of its most intense claims to transcendence, unique truth, inescapable coercive force – upon others. Not only the official purpose but the survival of the English colony depends upon this imposition. This crucial circumstance is what has licensed the testing in the first place; it is only as an agent of the English colony, dependent upon its purposes and committed to its survival, that Harriot is in a position to disclose the power of human achievements – reading, writing, gunpowder and the like – to appear to the ignorant as divine and hence to promote belief and compel obedience.

Thus the subversiveness which is genuine and radical – sufficiently disturbing so that to be suspected of such beliefs could lead to imprisonment and torture – is at the same time contained by the power it would appear to threaten. Indeed the subversiveness is the very product of that power and furthers its ends. One may go still further and suggest that the power Harriot both serves and embodies not only produces its own subversion but is actively built upon it: in the Virginia colony, the radical undermining of Christian order is not the negative limit but the positive condition for the establishment of the order. And this paradox extends to the production of Harriot's text: *A Brief and True Report,* with its latent heterodoxy, is not a reflection upon the Virginia colony nor even a simple record of it – not, in other words, a privileged withdrawal into a critical zone set apart from power – but a continuation of the colonial enterprise.

By October 1586, there were rumours in England that there was little prospect of profit in Virginia, that the colony had been close to starvation, and that the Indians had turned hostile. Harriot accordingly begins with a descriptive catalogue in which the natural goods of the land are turned into social goods, that is, into 'merchantable commodities': 'Cedar, a very sweet wood and fine timber; whereof if nests of chests be there made, or timber thereof fitted for sweet and fine bedsteads, tables, desks, lutes, virginals, and many things else,.... [it] will yield profit.' The inventory of these commodities is followed by an inventory of edible plants and animals, to prove to readers that the colony need not starve, and then by the account of the Indians, to prove that the colony could impose its will upon them. The key to this imposition, as I have argued, is the coercive power of religious belief, and the source of this power is the impression made by advanced technology upon a 'backward' people.

Hence Harriot's text is committed to record what we have called his confirmation of the Machiavellian hypothesis, and hence too this confirmation is not only inaccessible as subversion to those on whom the religion is supposedly imposed but functionally inaccessible to most readers and quite possibly to Harriot himself. It may be that Harriot was demonically conscious of what he was doing - that he found himself situated exactly where he could test one of his culture's darkest fears about its own origins, that he used the Algonkians to do so, and that he wrote a report on his findings, a coded report, of course, since as he wrote to Kepler years later, 'our situation is such that I still may not philosophize freely'. But we do not need such a biographical romance to account for the phenomenon: the subversiveness, as I have argued, was produced by the colonial power in its own interest, and *A Brief and True Report* was, with perfect appropriateness, published by the great Elizabethan exponent of missionary colonialism, the Reverend Richard Hakluyt.

Yet it is misleading, I think, to conclude without qualification that the radical doubt implicit in Harriot's account is *entirely* contained. Harriot was, after all, hounded through his whole life by charges of atheism and, more tellingly, the remark attributed to Marlowe suggests that it was fully possible for a contemporary to draw the most dangerous conclusions from the Virginia report. Moreover, the 'Atlantic Republican Tradition', as Pocock has argued, does grow out of the 'Machiavellian moment' of the sixteenth century, and that tradition, with its transformation of subjects into citizens, its subordination of transcendent values to capital values, does ultimately undermine, in the interests of a new power, the religious and secular authorities that had licensed the American enterprise in the first place. What we have in Harriot's text is a relation between orthodoxy and subversion that seems, in the same interpretive moment, to be perfectly stable and dangerously volatile.

We can deepen our understanding of this apparent paradox if we consider a second mode of subversion and its containment in Harriot's account. Alongside the *testing* of a subversive interpretation of the dominant culture, we find the recording of alien voices or, more precisely, of alien interpretations. The occasion for this *recording* is another consequence of the English presence in the New World, not in this case the threatened extinction of the tribal religion but the threatened extinction of the tribe:

> There was no town where we had any subtle device practiced against us [Harriot writes] but that within a few days after our departure from every such town, the people began to die very fast, and many in short space; in some towns about twenty, in some forty, in some sixty and in one six score, which in truth was very many in respect of their numbers. The disease was so strange, that they neither knew what it was, nor how to cure it; the like by report of the oldest man in the country never happened before, time out of mind.

Harriot is writing, of course, about the effects of measles, smallpox, or perhaps simply the common cold upon people with no resistance to them, but a conception of the biological basis of epidemic disease lies far, far in the future. For the English the deaths must be a moral phenomenon – the notion is for them as irresistible as the notion of germs for ourselves – and hence the 'facts' as they are observed are already moralised: the deaths only occurred 'where they used some practice against us', that is, where the Indians conspired secretly against the English. And, with the wonderful self-validating circularity that characterises virtually all powerful constructions of reality, the evidence for these secret conspiracies is precisely the deaths of the Indians.

Now it is not surprising that Harriot seems to endorse the idea that God is protecting his chosen people by killing off untrustworthy Indians; what is surprising is that Harriot is interested in the Indians' own anxious speculations about the unintended but lethal biological warfare that was destroying them. Drawing upon his special familiarity with the priests, he records a remarkable series of conjectures, almost all of which assume – correctly, as we now know – that their misfortune was linked to the presence of the strangers. 'Some people', observing that the English remained healthy while the Indians died, 'could not tell', Harriot writes, 'whether to think us gods or men'; others, seeing that the members of the first colony were all male, concluded that they were not born of women and therefore must be spirits of the dead returned to mortal form (an Algonkian 'Night of the Living Dead'). Some medicine men learned in astrology blamed the disease on a recent eclipse of the sun and on a comet – a theory Harriot considers seriously and rejects – while others shared the prevailing English interpretation and said 'that it was the special work of God' on behalf of the colonists. And some who seem in historical hindsight eerily prescient prophesied 'that there were more of [the English] generation yet to come, to kill theirs and take their places'. The supporters of this theory even worked out a conception of the disease that in some features uncannily resembles our own: 'Those that were immediately to come after us [the first English colonists], they imagined to be in the air, yet invisible and without bodies, and that they by our entreaty and for the love of us did make the people to die ... by shooting invisible bullets into them.'

For a moment, as Harriot records these competing theories, it may seem to a reader as if there were no absolute assurance of God's national interest, as if the drive to displace and absorb the other had given way to conversation among equals, as if all meanings were provisional, as if the signification of events stood apart from power. This impression is intensified for us by our awareness that the theory that would ultimately triumph over the moral conception of epidemic disease was already at least metaphorically present in the conversation. In the very moment that the moral conception is busily authorising itself, it registers the possibility (indeed from our vantage point, the inevitability) of its own destruction.

But why, we must ask ourselves, should power record other voices, permit subversive inquiries, register at its very centre the transgressions that will ultimately violate it? The answer may be in part that power, even in a colonial situation, is not perfectly monolithic and hence may encounter and record in one of its functions materials that can threaten another of its functions; in part that power thrives on vigilance, and human beings are vigilant if they sense a threat; in part that power defines itself in relation to such threats or simply to that which is not identical with it. Harriot's text suggests an intensification of these observations: English power in the first Virginia colony *depends* upon the registering and even the production of such materials. 'These their opinions I have set down the more at large', Harriot tells the 'Adventurers, Favorers, and Wellwishers' of the colony to whom his report is addressed, 'that it may appear unto you that there is good hope they may be brought through discrete dealing and government to the embracing of the truth, and consequently to honor, obey, fear, and love us'. The recording of alien voices, their preservation in Harriot's text, is part of the process whereby Indian culture is constituted as a culture and thus brought into the light for study, discipline, correction, transformation. The momentary sense of instability or plenitude – the existence of other voices – is produced by the monological power that ultimately denies the possibility of plenitude, just as the subversive hypothesis about European religion is tested and confirmed only by the imposition of that religion.

We may add that the power of which we are speaking is in effect an allocation method – a way of distributing resources to some and denying them to others, critical resources (here primarily corn and game) that prolong life or, in their absence, extinguish it. In a remarkable study of how societies make 'tragic choices' in the allocation of scarce resources (e.g. kidney machines) or in the determination of high risks (e.g. the military draft), Guido Calabresi and Philip Bobbitt observe that by complex mixtures of approaches, societies attempt to avert 'tragic results, that is, results which imply the rejection of values which are proclaimed to be fundamental'. These approaches may succeed for a time, but it will eventually become apparent that some sacrifice of fundamental values has taken place, whereupon 'fresh mixtures of methods will be tried, structured ... by the shortcomings of the approaches they replace'. These too will in time give way to others in a 'strategy of successive moves' that comprises an 'intricate game', a game that reflects the simultaneous perception of an inherent flaw and the determination to 'forget' that perception in an illusory resolution (Calabresi and Bobbitt 1978, p. 195). Hence the simple operation of any systematic order, any allocation method, will inevitably run the risk of exposing its own limitations, even (or perhaps especially) as it asserts its underlying moral principle.

This exposure is at its most intense at moments in which a comfortably established ideology confronts unusual circumstances, moments when the moral value of a particular form of power is not merely assumed but explained. We may glimpse such a moment in Harriot's account of a visit from the colonists' principal Indian ally, the chief Wingina. Wingina was persuaded that the disease decimating his people was indeed the work of the Christian God and had come to request the English to ask their god to direct his lethal magic against an enemy tribe. The colonists tried to explain that such a prayer would be 'ungodly', that their God was indeed responsible for the disease but that, in this as in all things, he would only act 'according to his good pleasure as he had ordained'. Indeed if men asked God to make an epidemic he probably would not do it; the English could expect such providential help only if they made sincere 'petition for the contrary', that is, for harmony and good fellowship in the service of truth and righteousness.

The problem with these assertions is not that they are self-consciously wicked (in the manner of Richard III or Iago) but that they are highly moral and logically coherent; or rather, what is unsettling is one's experience of them, the nasty sense that they are at once irrefutable ethical propositions and pious humbug designed to conceal from the English themselves the rapacity and aggression that is implicit in their very presence. The explanatory moment manifests the self-validating, totalising character of Renaissance political theology – its ability to account for almost every occurrence, even (or above all) apparently perverse or contrary occurrences – and at the same time confirms for us the drastic disillusionment that extends from Machiavelli to its definitive expression in Hume and Voltaire. In his own way, Wingina himself clearly thought his lesson in Christian ethics was polite nonsense. When the disease had in fact spread to his enemies, as it did shortly thereafter, he returned to the English to thank them – I presume with the Algonkian equivalent of a sly wink – for their friendly help, for 'although we satisfied them not in promise, yet in deeds and effect we had fulfilled their desires'. For Harriot, this 'marvelous accident', as he calls it, is another sign of the colony's great expectations.

Once again a disturbing vista – a sceptical critique of the function of Christian morality in the New World – is glimpsed only to be immediately closed off. Indeed we may feel at this point that subversion scarcely exists and may legitimately ask ourselves how our perception of the subversive and orthodox is generated. The answer, I think, is that 'subversive' is for us a term used to designate those elements in Renaissance culture that contemporary authorities tried to contain or, when containment seemed impossible, to destroy, and that now conform to our own sense of truth and reality. That is, we locate as 'subversive' in the past precisely those things that are not subversive to ourselves, that pose no threat to the order by which we live and allocate resources: in Harriot's *Brief and True Report*, the function of illusion in the establishment of religion, the displacement of providential conception of disease by one focused on 'invisible bullets', the exposure of the psychological and material interests served by a certain conception of divine power. Conversely, we identify as the principle of order and authority in Renaissance texts things that we would, if we took them seriously, find subversive for ourselves: religious and political absolutism, aristocracy of birth, demonology, humoral psychology, and the like. That we do not find such notions subversive, that we complacently identify them as principles of aesthetic or political order, is a version of the process of containment that licensed what we call the subversive elements in Renaissance texts: that is, our own values are sufficiently strong for us to contain almost effortlessly alien forces. What we find then in Harriot's *Brief and True Report* can best be described by adapting a remark about the possibility of hope that Kafka once made to Max Brod: There is subversion, no end of subversion, only not for us.

I want now to consider the relevance of what I've been saying to our understanding of more complex literary works. It is tempting to focus such remarks on Shakespeare's *Tempest* where Caliban, Prospero's 'savage and deformed slave' enters cursing the expropriation of his island and exits declaring that he will 'be wise hereafter, / And seek for grace'. What better instance, in the light of Harriot's Virginia, of the containment of a subversive force by the authority that has created that force in the first place : 'This thing of darkness', Prospero says of Caliban at the close, 'I acknowledge mine.'

But I do not want to give the impression that the process I have been describing is applicable only to works that address themselves directly or allusively to the New World. Shakespeare's plays are centrally and repeatedly concerned with the production and containment of subversion and disorder, and the three modes that we have identified in Harriot's text – testing, recording, and explaining – all have their recurrent theatrical equivalents. I am speaking not solely of plays like *Measure for Measure* and *Macbeth*, where authority is obviously subjected to open, sustained, and radical questioning before it is reaffirmed, with ironic reservations, at the close, but of a play like *1 Henry IV* in which authority seems far less problematical. 'Who does not all along see', wrote Upton in the mid-eighteenth century, 'that when prince Henry comes to be king he will assume a character suitable to his dignity?' My point is not to dispute this interpretation of the prince as, in Maynard Mack's words, 'an ideal image of the potentialities of the English character' (Mack 1965, p. xxv), but to observe that such an ideal image involves as its positive condition the constant production of its own radical subversion and the powerful containment of that subversion.

We are continually reminded that Hal is a 'juggler', a conniving hypocrite, and that the power he both serves and comes to embody is glorified usurpation and theft; yet at the same time, we are drawn to the celebration of both the prince and his power. Thus, for example, the scheme of Hal's moral redemption is carefully laid out in his soliloquy at the close of the first tavern scene, but as in the act of *explaining* what we have examined in Harriot, Hal's justification of himself threatens to fall away at every moment into its antithesis. 'By how much better than my word I am', Hal declares, 'By so much shall I falsify men's hopes' (I, ii, 210–11). To falsify men's hopes is to exceed their expectations, and it is also to disappoint their expectations, to deceive men, to turn their hopes into fictions, to betray them. Not only are the competing claims of Bolingbroke and Falstaff at issue but our own hopes, the fantasies continually aroused by the play of absolute friendship and trust, limitless playfulness, innate grace, plenitude. But though all of this is in some sense at stake in Hal's soliloquy and though we can perceive at every point, through our own constantly shifting allegiances, the potential instability of the structure of power that has Henry IV at the pinnacle and Robin Ostler, who 'never joy'd since the price of oats rose' (II, i, 12), near the bottom, Hal's 'redemption' is as inescapable and inevitable as the outcome of those practical jokes the madcap prince is so fond of playing. Indeed, the play insists, this redemption is not something toward which the action moves but something that is happening at every moment of the theatrical representation.

The same yoking of the unstable and the inevitable may be seen in the play's acts of *recording*, that is, the moments in which we hear voices that seem to dwell in realms apart from that ruled by the potentates of the land. These voices exist and have their apotheosis in Falstaff, but their existence proves to be utterly bound up with Hal, contained politically by his purposes as they are justified aesthetically by his involvement. The perfect emblem of this containment is Falstaff's company, marching off to Shrewsbury: 'discarded unjust servingmen, younger sons to younger brothers, revolted tapsters, and ostlers trade-fall'n, the cankers of a calm world and a long peace' (IV, ii, 27–30). These are, as many a homily would tell us, the very types of Elizabethan subversion – masterless men, the natural enemies of social discipline – but they are here pressed into service as defenders of the established order, 'good enough to toss', as Falstaff tells Hal, 'food for powder, food for powder' (IV, ii, 65–6). For power as well as powder, and we may add that this food is produced as well as consumed by the great.

Shakespeare gives us a glimpse of this production in the odd little scene in which Hal, with the connivance of Poins, reduces the puny tapster Francis to the mechanical repetition of the word 'Anon':

Prince	Nay, but hark you, Francis: for the sugar thou gavest me, 'twas a pennyworth, was't not?
Francis	O Lord, I would it had been two!
Prince	I will give thee for it a thousand pound. Ask me when thou wilt, and thou shalt have it.
Poins	[*Within*] Francis!
Francis	Anon, anon.
Prince	Anon, Francis? No Francis; but tomorrow, Francis; or, Francis, a' Thursday; or indeed, Francis, when thou wilt.

(II, iv, 58–67)

The Bergsonian comedy in such a moment resides in Hal's exposing a drastic reduction of human possibility: 'That ever this fellow should have fewer words than a parrot', he says at the scene's end, 'and yet the son of a woman!' (II, iv, 98). But the chief interest for us resides in the fact that Hal has himself produced the reduction he exposes. The fact of this production, its theatrical demonstration, implicates Hal not only in the linguistic poverty upon which he plays but in the poverty of the five years of apprenticeship Francis has yet to serve: 'Five year!' Hal exclaims, 'by'r lady, a long lease for the clinking of pewter' (II, iv, 45–6). And as the Prince is implicated in the production of this oppressive order, so is he implicated in the impulse to abrogate it: 'But, Francis, darest thou be so valiant as to play the coward with thy indenture, and show it a fair pair of heels and run from it?' (II, iv, 46–8). It is tempting to think of this peculiar moment – the Prince awakening the apprentice's discontent – as linked darkly with some supposed uneasiness in Hal about his own apprenticeship, but if so the momentary glimpse of a revolt against authority is closed off at once with a few words of calculated obscurity designed to return Francis to his trade without enabling him to understand why he must do so:

> *Prince*   Why then your brown bastard is your only drink! for look you, Francis, your white canvas doublet will sully. In Barbary, sir, it cannot come to so much.
>
> *Francis*   What, sir?
>
> *Poins*   [*Within*] Francis!
>
> *Prince*   Away, you rogue, dost thou not hear them call?
>
> (II, iv, 73–9)

If Francis takes the earlier suggestion, robs his master and runs away, he will find a place for himself, the play implies, as one of the 'revolted tapsters' in Falstaff's company, men as good as dead long before they march to their deaths as upholders of the crown. Better that he should follow the drift of Hal's deliberately mystifying words and continue to clink pewter. As for the prince, his interest in the brief exchange, beyond what we have already sketched, is suggested by his boast to Poins moments before Francis enters: 'I have sounded the very base-string of humility. Sirrah, I am sworn brother to a leash of drawers and can call them all by their christen names, as Tom, Dick, and Francis' (II, iv, 5–8). The prince must sound the base-string of humility if he is to know how to play all of the chords and hence to be the master of the instrument, and his ability to conceal his motives and render opaque his language offers assurance that he himself will not be played on by another.

I have spoken of such scenes in *I Henry IV* as resembling what in Harriot's text I have called *recording*, a mode that culminates for Harriot in a glossary, the beginnings of an Algonkian-English dictionary, designed to facilitate further acts of recording and hence to consolidate English power in Virginia. The resemblance may be seen most clearly perhaps in Hal's own glossary of tavern slang: 'They call drinking deep, dyeing scarlet: and when you breathe in your watering, they cry 'hem!' and bid you play it off. To conclude, I am so good a proficient in one quarter of an hour that I can drink with any tinker in his own language during my life' (II, iv, 15–20). The potential value of these lessons, the functional interest to power of recording the speech of an 'under-skinker' and his mates, may be glimpsed in the expressions of loyalty that Hal laughingly recalls: 'They take it already upon their salvation that ... when I am King of England I shall command all the good lads in Eastcheap' (II, iv, 9–15).

There is, it may be objected, something slightly absurd in likening such moments to aspects of Harriot's text; *I Henry IV* is a play, not a tract for potential investors in a colonial scheme, and the only values we may be sure that Shakespeare had in mind, the argument would go, were theatrical values. But theatrical values do not exist in a realm of privileged literariness, of textual or even institutional self-referentiality. Shakespeare's theatre was not isolated by its wooden walls, nor was it merely the passive reflector of social and ideological forces that lay entirely outside of it: rather the Elizabethan and Jacobean theatre was itself a *social event*. Drama, and artistic expression in general, is never perfectly self-contained and abstract, nor can it be derived satisfactorily from the subjective consciousness of an isolated creator. Collective actions, ritual gestures, paradigms of relationship, and shared images of authority penetrate the work of art, while conversely the socially overdetermined work of art, along with a multitude of other institutions and utterances, contributes to the formation, realignment, and transmission of social practices.

Works of art are, to be sure, marked off in our culture from ordinary utterances, but this demarcation is itself a communal event and signals not the effacement of the social but rather its successful absorption into the work by implication or articulation. This absorption – the presence within the work of its social being – makes it possible, as Bakhtin has argued, for art to survive the disappearance of its enabling social conditions, where ordinary utterance, more dependent upon the extraverbal pragmatic situation, drifts rapidly toward insignificance or incomprehensibility (Bakhtin 1976, pp. 93–116). Hence art's genius for survival, its delighted reception by audiences for whom it was never intended, does not signal its freedom from all other domains of life, nor does its inward articulation of the social confer upon it a formal coherence independent of the world outside its boundaries. On the contrary, artistic form itself is the expression of social evaluations and practices.

One might add that *I Henry IV* itself insists that it is quite impossible to keep the interests of the theatre hermetically sealed off from the interests of power. Hal's characteristic activity is playing or, more precisely, theatrical improvisation – his parts include his father, Hotspur, Hotspur's wife, a thief in buckram, himself as prodigal and himself as penitent – and he fully understands his own behaviour through most of the play as a role that he is performing. We might expect that this role-playing gives way at the end to his true identity – 'I shall hereafter', Hal has promised his father, 'be more myself' (III, ii, 92–3) – but with the killing of Hotspur, Hal clearly does not reject all theatrical masks but rather replaces one with another. 'The time will come', Hal declares midway through the play, 'That I shall make this northern youth exchange/His glorious deeds for my indignities' (III, ii, 144–6); when that time *has* come, at the play's close, Hal hides with his 'favours' (that is, a scarf or other emblem, but the word also has in the sixteenth century the sense of 'face') the dead Hotspur's 'mangled face' (V, iv, 96), as if to mark the completion of the exchange.

Theatricality then is not set over against power but is one of power's essential modes. In lines that anticipate Hal's promise, the angry Henry IV tells Worcester, 'I will from henceforth rather be myself,/Mighty and to be fear'd, than my condition' (I, iii, 5–6). 'To be oneself' here means to perform one's part in the scheme of power as opposed to one's natural disposition, or what we would normally designate as the very core of the self. Indeed it is by no means clear that such a thing as a natural disposition exists in the play as anything more than a theatrical fiction; we recall that in Falstaff's hands 'instinct' itself becomes a piece of histrionic rhetoric, an improvised excuse when he is confronted with the shame of his flight from the masked prince: 'Beware instinct – the lion will not touch the true prince. Instinct is a great matter; I was now a coward on instinct. I shall think the better of myself, and thee, during my life; I for a valiant lion, and thou for a true prince' (II, iv, 271–5). Both claims – Falstaff's to natural valour, Hal's to legitimate royalty – are, the lines darkly imply, of equal merit.

Again and again in *1 Henry IV* we are tantalised by the possibility of an escape from theatricality and hence from the constant pressure of improvisational power, but we are, after all, in the theatre, and our pleasure depends upon the fact that there is no escape, and our applause ratifies the triumph of our confinement. The play then operates in the manner of its central character, charming us with its visions of breadth and solidarity, 'redeeming' itself in the end by betraying our hopes, and earning with this betrayal our slightly anxious admiration. Hence the odd balance in this play of spaciousness – the constant multiplication of separate, vividly realised realms – and claustrophobia – the absorption of all of these realms by a power at once vital and impoverished. The balance is almost eerily perfect, as if Shakespeare had somehow reached through in *1 Henry IV* to the very centre of the system of opposed and interlocking forces that held Tudor society together.

When we turn, however, to the plays that continue the chronicle of Hal's career, *2 Henry IV* and *Henry V*, not only do we find that the forces balanced in the earlier play have pulled apart – the claustrophobia triumphant in *2 Henry IV*, the spaciousness triumphant in *Henry V* – but that from this new perspective the familiar view of *1 Henry IV* as a perfectly poised play must be revised. What appeared as 'balance' may on closer inspection seem like radical instability tricked out as moral or aesthetic order; what appeared as clarity may seem now like a conjurer's trick concealing confusion in order to buy time and stave off the collapse of an illusion. Not waving but drowning.

2 Henry IV makes the characteristic operations of power less equivocal than they had been in the preceding play: there is no longer even the lingering illusion of distinct realms, each with its own system of values, its soaring visions of plenitude, and its bad dreams. There is manifestly a single system now, one based on predation and betrayal. Hotspur's intoxicating dreams of honour are dead, replaced entirely by the cold rebellion of cunning but impotent schemers. The warm, roistering sounds overheard in the tavern – sounds that seemed to signal a subversive alternative to rebellion – turn out to be the noise of a whore and bully beating a customer to death. And Falstaff, whose earlier larcenies were gilded by fantasies of innate grace, now talks of turning diseases to commodity (I, ii, 234–5).

Only Prince Hal seems, in comparison to the earlier play, less meanly calculating, subject now to fits of weariness and confusion, though this change serves less, I think, to humanise him (as Auerbach argued in a famous essay) than to make it clear that the betrayals are systematic. They happen to him and for him. He needn't any longer soliloquise his intention to 'Falsify men's hopes' by selling his wastrel friends: the sale will be brought about by the structure of things, a structure grasped in this play under the twinned names of time and necessity. So too there is no longer any need for heroic combat with a dangerous, glittering enemy like Hotspur (the only reminder of whose voice in this play is Pistol's parody of Marlovian swaggering); the rebels are deftly if ingloriously dispatched by the false promises of Hal's younger brother, the primly virtuous John of Lancaster. To seal his lies, Lancaster swears fittingly 'by the honour of my blood' – the cold blood, as Falstaff observes of Hal, that he inherited from his father.

The 'recording' of alien voices – the voices of those who have no power to leave literate traces of their existence – continues in this play, but without even the theatrical illusion of princely complicity. The king is still convinced that his son is a prodigal and that the kingdom will fall to ruin after his death – there is a certain peculiar consolation in the thought – but it is no longer Hal alone who declares (against all appearances) his secret commitment to disciplinary authority. Warwick assures the king that the prince's interests in the good lads of Eastcheap are entirely what they should be:

The Prince but studies his companions
Like a strange tongue, wherein, to gain the language,
'Tis needful that the most immodest word
Be look'd upon and learnt, which once attain'd,

> Your Highness knows, comes to no further use
> But to be known and hated. So, like gross terms,
> The Prince will in the perfectness of time
> Cast off his followers, and their memory
> Shall as a pattern or a measure live,
> By which his Grace must mete the lives of other,
> Turning past evils to advantages.

(IV, iv, 68–78)

At first the language analogy likens the prince's low-life excursions to the search for proficiency: perfect linguistic competence, the 'mastery' of a language, requires the fullest possible vocabulary. But the darkness of Warwick's words – 'to be known and hated' – immediately pushes the goal of Hal's linguistic researches beyond proficiency. When in *1 Henry IV* Hal boasts of his mastery of tavern slang, we are allowed for a moment at least to imagine that we are witnessing a social bond, the human fellowship of the extremest top and bottom of society in a homely ritual act of drinking together. The play may make it clear, as I have argued, that there are well-defined political interests involved, but these interests may be bracketed, if only briefly, for the pleasure of imagining what Victor Turner calls 'communitas' – a union based on the momentary breaking of the hierarchical order that normally governs a community (Turner 1974). And even when we pull back from this spacious sense of union, we are permitted for much of the play to take pleasure at the least in Hal's surprising skill, the proficiency he rightly celebrates in himself.

To learn another language is to acknowledge the existence of another people and to acquire the ability to function, however crudely, within its social world. Hal's remark about drinking with any tinker in his own language suggests, if only jocularly, that for him the lower classes are virtually another people, an alien tribe – immensely more populous than his own – within the kingdom. That this perception extended beyond the confines of Shakespeare's play is suggested by the evidence that middle- and upper-class English settlers in the New World regarded the American Indians less as another race than as a version of their own lower classes; one man's tinker is another man's Indian.

If Hal's glossary initially seems to resemble Harriot's, Warwick's account of Hal's practice quickly drives it past the functionalism of the word-list in the *Brief and True Report*, with its Algonkian equivalents for fire, food, shelter, and toward a different kind of glossary, one more specifically linked to the attempt to understand and control the lower classes. I refer to the sinister glossaries appended to sixteenth-century accounts of criminals and vagabonds. 'Here I set before the good reader the lewd, lousy language of these loitering lusks and lazy lorels', announces Thomas Harman, as he introduces (with a comical flourish designed to display his own rhetorical gifts) what he claims is an authentic list, compiled at great personal cost. His pamphlet, A *Caveat for Common Cursitors,* is the fruit, he declares, of personal research, difficult because his informants are 'marvellous subtle and crafty'. But 'with fair flattering words, money, and good cheer', he has learned much about their ways, 'not without faithful promise made unto them never to discover their names or anything they showed me'. Harman cheerfully goes on to publish what they showed him, and he ends his work not only with a glossary of 'peddlar's French' but with an alphabetical list of names, so that the laws made for 'the extreme punishment' of these wicked idlers may be enforced.

It is not at all clear that Harman's subjects – upright men, doxies, Abraham men, and the like – bear any relation to social reality, any more than it is clear in the case of Doll Tearsheet or Mistress Quickly. Much of the *Caveat,* like the other cony–catching pamphlets of the period, has the air of a jest book: time–honoured tales of tricksters and rogues, dished out cunningly as realistic observation. (It is not encouraging that the rogues' term for the stocks in which they were punished, according to Harman, is 'the harmans'.) But Harman is quite concerned to convey at least the impression of accurate observation and recording – clearly, this was among the book's selling points – and one of the principal rhetorical devices he uses to do so is the spice of betrayal: he repeatedly calls attention to his solemn promises never to reveal anything that he has been told, for his breaking of his word serves as an assurance of the accuracy and importance of what he reveals.

A middle-class Prince Hal, Harman claims that through dissembling he has gained access to a world normally hidden from his kind, and he will turn that access to the advantage of the kingdom by helping his readers to identify and eradicate the dissemblers in their midst. Harman's own personal interventions – the acts of detection and apprehension he proudly reports (or invents) – are not enough: only his book can fully expose the cunning sleights of the rogues and thereby induce the justices and shrieves to be more vigilant and punitive. Just as theatricality is thematised in the *Henry IV* plays as one of the crucial agents of royal power, so in the *Caveat for Common Cursitors* (and in much of the cony-catching literature of the period in England and France) printing is represented in the text itself as a force for social order and the detection of criminal fraud. The printed book can be widely disseminated and easily revised, so that the vagabonds' names and tricks may be known before they themselves arrive at an honest citizen's door; as if this mobility weren't quite tangible enough, Harman claims that when his pamphlet was only half-way printed, his printer helped him apprehend a particularly cunning 'counterfeit crank' – a pretended epileptic. In Harman's account the printer turns detective, first running down the street to apprehend the dissembler, then on a subsequent occasion luring him 'with fair allusions' and a show of charity into the hands of the constable. With such lurid tales Harman literalises the power of the book to hunt down vagabonds and bring them to justice.

The danger of such accounts, of course, is that the ethical charge will reverse itself: the forces of order – the people, as it were, of the book – will be revealed as themselves dependent on dissembling and betrayal, and the vagabonds either as less fortunate and well-protected imitators of their betters or, alternatively, as primitive rebels against the hypocrisy of a cruel society. Exactly such a reversal seems to occur again and again in the rogue literature of the period, from the doxies and morts who answer Harman's rebukes with unfailing if spare dignity to the more articulate defenders of vice elsewhere who insist that their lives are at worst imitations of the lives of the great:

> Though your experience in the world be not so great as mine [says a cunning cheater at dice], yet am I sure ye see that no man is able to live an honest man unless he have some privy way to help himself withal, more than the world is witness of. Think you the noblemen could do as they do, if in this hard world they should maintain so great a port only upon their rent? Think you the lawyers could be such purchasers if their pleas were short, and all their judgements, justice and conscience? Suppose ye that offices would be so dearly bought, and the buyers so soon enriched, if they counted not pillage an honest point of purchase? Could merchants, without lies, false making their wares, and selling them by a crooked light, to deceive the chapman in the thread or colour, grow so soon rich and to a baron's possessions, and make all their posterity gentlemen?

Yet though these reversals are at the very heart of the rogue literature, it would be as much of a mistake to regard their final effect as subversion as it would be to regard in a similar light the comparable passages – most often articulated by Falstaff – in Shakespeare's histories. The subversive voices are produced by the affirmations of order, and they are powerfully registered, but they do not undermine that order. Indeed as the example of Harman – so much cruder than Shakespeare – suggests, the order is neither possible nor fully convincing without both the presence and perception of betrayal.

This dependence on betrayal does not prevent Harman from levelling charges of hypocrisy and deep dissembling at the rogues and from urging his readers to despise and prosecute them. On the contrary, Harman's moral indignation seems paradoxically heightened by his own implication in the deceitfulness that he condemns, as if the rhetorical violence of the condemnation cleansed him of any guilt. His broken promises are acts of civility, necessary strategies for securing social well-being. The 'rowsy, ragged rabblement of rakehells' has put itself outside the bounds of civil conversation; justice consists precisely in taking whatever measures are necessary to eradicate them. Harman's false oaths are the means of identifying and ridding the community of the purveyors of false oaths. The pestilent few will 'fret, fume, swear, and stare at this my book' in which their practices, disclosed after they had received fair promises of confidentiality, are laid open, but the majority will band together in righteous reproach: 'the honourable will abhor them, the worshipful will reject them, the yeomen will sharply taunt them, the husbandmen utterly defy them, the labouring men bluntly chide them, the women with clapping hands cry out at them'. To like reading about vagabonds is to hate them and to approve of their ruthless betrayal.

'The right people of the play', a gifted critic of *2 Henry IV* observes, 'merge into a larger order; the wrong people resist or misuse that larger order' (Holland 1965, p. xxxvi). True enough, but like Harman's happy community of vagabond-haters, the 'larger order' of the Lancastrian State seems, in this play, to batten on the breaking of oaths. Shakespeare does not shrink from any of the felt nastiness implicit in this sorting out of the right people and the wrong people; he takes the discursive mode that he could have found in Harman and a hundred other texts and intensifies it, so that the founding of the modern State, like the founding of the modern prince, is shown to be based upon acts of calculation, intimidation, and deceit. And the demonstration of these acts is rendered an entertainment for which an audience, subject to just this State, will pay money and applaud.

There is, throughout *2 Henry IV* a sense of constriction that the obsessive enumeration of details – 'Thou didst swear to me upon a parcel-gilt goblet, sitting in my Dolphin chamber, at the round table by a sea-coal fire, upon Wednesday in Wheeson week. ...' – only intensifies. We may find, in Justice Shallow's garden, a few twilight moments of release from this oppressive circumstantial and strategic constriction, but Falstaff mercilessly deflates them – and the puncturing is so wonderfully adroit, so amusing, that we welcome it: 'I do remember him at Clement's Inn, like a man made after supper of a cheese-paring. When 'a was naked, he was for all the world like a forked radish, with a head fantastically carv'd upon it with a knife' (III, ii, 308–12).

What is left is the law of nature: the strong eat the weak. Yet this is not quite what Shakespeare invites the audience to affirm through its applause. Like Harman, Shakespeare refuses to endorse so baldly cynical a conception of the social order; instead actions that should have the effect of radically undermining authority turn out to be the props of that authority. In this play, even more cruelly than in *1 Henry IV*, moral values – justice, order, civility – are secured paradoxically through the apparent generation of their subversive contraries. Out of the squalid betrayals that preserve the State emerges the 'formal majesty' into which Hal at the close, through a final, definitive betrayal – the rejection of Falstaff – merges himself.

There are moments in *Richard II* in which the collapse of kingship seems to be confirmed in the discovery of the physical body of the ruler, the pathos of his creatural existence:

> ... throw away respect,
> Tradition, form, and ceremonious duty,
> For you have but mistook me all this while.
> I live with bread like you, feel want,
> Taste grief, need friends: subjected thus,
> How can you say to me I am a king?

(III, ii, 172–7)

By the close of *2 Henry IV* such physical limitations have been absorbed into the ideological structure, and hence justification, of kingship. It is precisely because Prince Hal lives with bread that we can understand the sacrifice that he and, for that matter, his father, have made. Unlike Richard II, Henry IV's articulation of this sacrifice is rendered by Shakespeare not as a piece of histrionic rhetoric but as a private meditation, the innermost thoughts of a troubled, weary man:

> Why rather, sleep, liest thou in smoky cribs,
> Upon uneasy pallets stretching thee,
> And hush'd with buzzing night-flies to thy slumber,
> Than in the perfum'd chambers of the great,
> Under the canopies of costly state,
> And lull'd with sounds of sweetest melody?

(III, i, 9–14)

Who knows? Perhaps it is even true; perhaps in a society in which the overwhelming majority of men and women had next to nothing, the few who were rich and powerful did lie awake at night. But we should understand that this sleeplessness was not a well-kept secret: the sufferings of the great are one of the familiar themes in the literature of the governing classes in the sixteenth century. Henry IV speaks in soliloquy, but as is so often the case in Shakespeare his isolation only intensifies the sense that he is addressing a large audience: the audience of the theatre. We are invited to take measure of his suffering, to understand – here and elsewhere in the play – the costs of power. And we are invited to understand these costs in order to ratify the power, to accept the grotesque and cruelly unequal distribution of possessions: everything to the few, nothing to the many. The rulers earn, or at least pay for, their exalted position through suffering, and this suffering ennobles, if it does not exactly cleanse, the lies and betrayals upon which this position depends.

As so often Falstaff parodies this ideology, or rather – and more significantly – presents it as humbug *before* it makes its appearance as official truth. Called away from the tavern to the court, Falstaff turns to Doll and Mistress Quickly and proclaims sententiously: 'You see, my good wenches, how men of merit are sought after. The undeserver may sleep when the man of action is called on' (II, iv, 374–7). Seconds later this rhetoric – marked out as something with which to impress whores and innkeepers to whom one owes money one does not intend to pay – recurs in the speech, and by convention of the soliloquy, the innermost thoughts of the king.

At such moments *2 Henry IV* seems to be testing and confirming an extremely dark and disturbing hypothesis about the nature of monarchical power in England: that its moral authority rests upon a hypocrisy so deep that the hypocrites themselves believe it. 'Then (happy) low, lie down! / Uneasy lies the head that wears a crown' (III, i, 30–1): so the old pike tells the young dace. But the old pike actually seems to believe in his own speeches, just as he may believe that he never really sought the crown, 'But that necessity so bow'd the state / That I and greatness were compell'd to kiss' (III, i, 72–3). We who have privileged knowledge of the network of State betrayals and privileged access to Falstaff's cynical wisdom can make this opaque hypocrisy transparent. And yet even in *2 Henry IV*, where the lies and the self-serving sentiments are utterly inescapable, where the illegitimacy of legitimate authority is repeatedly demonstrated, where the whole state seems – to adapt More's phrase – a conspiracy of the great to enrich and protect their interests under the name of commonwealth, even here the audience does not leave the theatre in a rebellious mood. Once again, though in a still more iron-age spirit than at the close of *1 Henry IV*, the play appears to ratify the established order, with the new-crowned Henry V merging his body into 'the great body of our state', with Falstaff despised and rejected, and with Lancaster – the cold-hearted betrayer of the rebels – left to admire his still more cold-hearted brother: 'I like this fair proceeding of the King's' (V, v, 97).

The mood at the close remains, to be sure, an unpleasant one – the rejection of Falstaff has been one of the nagging 'problems' of Shakespearean criticism – but the discomfort only serves to verify Hal's claim that he has turned away his former self. If there is frustration at the harshness of the play's end, the frustration is confirmation of a carefully plotted official strategy whereby subversive perceptions are at once produced and contained:

My father is gone wild into his grave;
For in his tomb lie my affections,
And with his spirits sadly I survive,
To mock the expectation of the world,
To frustrate prophecies, and to rase out
Rotten opinion. ...

(V, ii, 123–8)

105

The first part of *Henry IV* enables us to feel at moments that we are like Harriot, surveying a complex new world, testing upon it dark thoughts without damaging the order that those thoughts would seem to threaten. The second part of *Henry IV* suggests that we are still more like the Indians, compelled to pay homage to a system of beliefs whose fraudulence somehow only confirms their power, authenticity, and truth. The concluding play in the series, *Henry V*, insists that we have all along been both coloniser and colonised, king and subject. The play deftly registers every nuance of royal hypocrisy, ruthlessness, and bad faith, but it does so in the context of a celebration, a collective panegyric to 'This star of England', the charismatic leader who purges the commonwealth of its incorrigibles and forges the martial national state.

By yoking together diverse peoples – represented in the play by the Welshman Fluellen, the Irishman Macmorris, and the Scotsman Jamy, who fight at Agincourt alongside the loyal Englishmen – Hal symbolically tames the last wild areas in the British Isles, areas that in the sixteenth century represented, far more powerfully than any New World people, the doomed outposts of a vanishing tribalism. He does so, obviously, by launching a war of conquest against the French, but his military campaign is itself depicted as carefully founded upon acts of what I have called 'explaining'. The play opens with a notoriously elaborate account of the king's genealogical claim to the French throne, and, as we found in the comparable instances in Harriot, this ideological justification of English policy is an unsettling mixture of 'impeccable' reasoning (once its initial premises are accepted) and gross self-interest. The longer the Archbishop of Canterbury continues to spin out the public justifications for an invasion he has privately said would relieve financial pressure on the Church, the more the audience is driven toward scepticism. None of the subsequent attempts at explanation and justification offers much relief: Hal continually warns his victims that they are bringing pillage and rape upon themselves by resisting him, but from the head of an invading army these arguments lack a certain moral force. Similarly, Hal's meditation on the sufferings of the great – 'What infinite heart's ease / Must kings neglect that private men enjoy!' – suffers a bit from the fact that he is almost single-handedly responsible for a war that by his own account and that of the enemy is causing immense civilian misery. And after watching a scene in which anxious, frightened troops sleeplessly await the dawn, it is difficult to be fully persuaded by Hal's climactic vision of the 'slave' and 'peasant' sleeping comfortably, little knowing 'What watch the King keeps to maintain the peace' (IV, i, 283).

This apparent subversion of the glorification of the monarch has led some recent critics to view the panegyric as bitterly ironic or to argue, more plausibly, that Shakespeare's depiction of Henry V is radically ambiguous. But in the light of Harriot's *Brief and True Report*, we may suggest that the subversive doubts the play continually awakens serve paradoxically to intensify the power of the king and his war, even while they cast shadows upon this power. The shadows are real enough, but they are deferred – deferred until after Essex's campaign in Ireland, after Elizabeth's reign, after the monarchy itself as a significant political institution. Deferred indeed even today, for in the wake of full-scale ironic readings and at a time in which it no longer seems to matter very much, it is not at all clear that *Henry V* can be successfully performed as subversive. For the play's enhancement of royal power is not only a matter of the deferral of doubt: the very doubts that Shakespeare raises serve not to rob the king of his charisma but to heighten it, precisely as they heighten the theatrical interest of the play; the doubt-less celebrations of royal power with which the period abounds have no theatrical force and have long since fallen into oblivion.

The audience's tension then enhances its attention; prodded by constant reminders of a gap between real and ideal, facts and values, the spectators are induced to make up the difference, to invest in the illusion of magnificence, to be dazzled by their own imaginary identification with the conqueror. The ideal king must be in large part the invention of the audience, the product of a will to conquer which is revealed to be identical to a need to submit. *Henry V* is remarkably self-conscious about this dependence upon the audience's powers of invention. The prologue's opening lines invoke a form of theatre radically unlike the one that is about to unfold: 'A kingdom for a stage, princes to act, / And monarchs to behold the swelling scene!' (3–4). In such a theatre-State there would be no social distinction between the king and the spectator, the performer and the audience; all would be royal, and the role of the performance would be to transform not an actor into a king but a king into a god: 'Then should the warlike Harry, like himself, / Assume the port of Mars' (5–6). This is in effect the fantasy acted out in royal masques, but Shakespeare is intensely aware that his theatre is not a courtly entertainment, that his actors are 'flat unraised spirits,' and that his spectators are hardly monarchs – 'gentles all', he calls them, with fine flattery. 'Let us', the prologue begs the audience, 'On your imaginary forces work ... For 'tis your thoughts that now must deck our kings' (18, 28). This 'must' is cast in the form of an appeal and an apology – the consequence of the miserable limitations of 'this unworthy scaffold' – but the necessity extends, I suggest, beyond the stage: all kings are 'decked' out by the imaginary forces of the spectators, and a sense of the limitations of king or theatre only excites a more compelling exercise of those forces.

To understand Shakespeare's whole conception of Hal, from rakehell to monarch, we need in effect a poetics of Elizabethan power, and this in turn will prove inseparable, in crucial respects, from a poetics of the theatre. Testing, recording, and explaining are elements in this poetics that is inseparably bound up with the figure of Queen Elizabeth, a ruler without a standing army, without a highly developed bureaucracy, without an extensive police force, a ruler whose power is constituted in theatrical celebrations of royal glory and theatrical violence visited upon the enemies of that glory. Power that relies upon a massive police apparatus, a strong, middle-class nuclear family, an elaborate school system, power that dreams of a panopticon in which the most intimate secrets are open to the view of an invisible authority, such power will have as its appropriate aesthetic form the realist novel; Elizabethan power, by contrast, depends upon its privileged visibility. As in a theatre, the audience must be powerfully engaged by this visible presence while at the same time held at a certain respectful distance from it. 'We princes', Elizabeth told a deputation of Lords and Common in 1586, 'are set on stages in the sight and view of all the world.'

Royal power is manifested to its subjects as in a theatre, and the subjects are at once absorbed by the instructive, delightful, or terrible spectacles, and forbidden intervention or deep intimacy. The play of authority depends upon spectators – 'For 'tis your thoughts that now must deck our kings' – but the performance is made to seem entirely beyond the control of those whose 'imaginary forces' actually confer upon it its significance and force. These matters, Thomas More imagines the common people saying of one such spectacle, 'be king's games, as it were stage plays, and for the more part played upon scaffolds. In which poor men be but the lookers-on. And they that wise be will meddle no farther'. Within this theatrical setting, there is a remarkable insistence upon the paradoxes, ambiguities, and tensions of authority, but this apparent production of subversion is, as we have already seen, the very condition of power. I should add that this condition is not a theoretical necessity of theatrical power in general but an historical phenomenon, the particular mode of this particular culture. 'In sixteenth-century England', writes Clifford Geertz, comparing Elizabethan and Majapahit royal progresses, 'the political centre of society was the point at which the tension between the passions that power excited and the ideals it was supposed to serve was screwed to its highest pitch... In fourteenth century Java, the centre was the point at which such tension disappeared in a blaze of cosmic symmetry (Geertz 1977, p. 160).

It is precisely because of the English form of absolutist theatricality that Shakespeare's drama, written for a theatre subject to State censorship, can be so relentlessly subversive: the form itself, as a primary expression of Renaissance power, contains the radical doubts it continually provokes. There are moments in Shakespeare's career – *King Lear* is the greatest example – in which the process of containment is strained to the breaking point, but the histories consistently pull back from such extreme pressure. And we are free to locate and pay homage to the plays' doubts only because they no longer threaten us. There is subversion, no end of subversion, only not for us.

6 *A Midsummer Night's Dream* and the Shaping Fantasies of Elizabethan Culture: Gender, Power, Form*

Louis Montrose

If the human **subject** is historically produced, as contemporary theory proposes, the crucial question for New Historicism is the part played by cultural forms in this production. Louis Montrose's essay on *A Midsummer Night's Dream* addresses this question through a reading of a play which appears to disclaim any such importance, when Puck calls it 'a weak and idle theme, /No more yielding but a dream' (V, i, 414–15). Beginning with an interpretation of an actual Elizabethan dream, Montrose argues that the fantasies condensed in Shakespeare's comedy are a solution to the sexual contradictions of the English court, where a patriarchy was governed by a woman. But the Dream does not merely reflect Elizabethan psychology: **representations** are 'shaping fantasies' that create the desires they describe. So, this play's dream-work is to organise English family politics for future generations. Such a psychoanalytic approach is unusual for New Historicism which generally concurs with Foucault's dismissal of Freud. Montrose avoids any anachronistic Freudian generalisation, but his equation of culture with dream gives it the privileged status of the unconscious, demoting **agency** and reducing history itself to a cultural 'creation'.

1

I would like to recount an Elizabethan dream – not Shakespeare's *Midsummer Night's Dream*, but one dreamt by Simon Forman on 23 January 1597. Forman – a professional astrologer and physician, amateur alchemist, and avid playgoer – recorded in his diary the following account:

---

*Reprinted from *Representations*, 2 (1983), pp. 65–87.

I dreamt that I was with the Queen, and that she was a little elderly woman in a coarse white petticoat all unready; and she and I walked up and down through lanes and closes, talking and reasoning of many matters. At last we came over a great close where were many people, and there were two men at hard words. One of them was a weaver, a tall man with a reddish beard, distract of his wits. She talked to him and he spoke very merrily unto her, and at last did take her and kiss her. So I took her by the arm and put her away; and told her the fellow was frantic. And so we went from him and I led her by the arm still, and then we went through a dirty lane. She had a long, white smock, very clean and fair, and it trailed in the dirt and her coat behind. I took her coat and did carry it up a good way, and then it hung too low before. I told her she should do me a favour to let me wait on her, and she said I should. Then said I, 'I mean to wait *upon* you and not under you, that I might make this belly a little bigger to carry up this smock and coats out of the dirt.' And so we talked merrily and then she began to lean upon me, when we were past the dirt and to be very familiar with me, and methought she began to love me. And when we were alone, out of sight, methought she would have kissed me.

(A. L. Rowse, *The Case–Books of Simon Forman*. (London 1974), p. 31).

It was then that Forman awoke.

Within the dreamer's unconscious, the 'little elderly woman' who was his political mother may have been identified with the mother who had borne him. In an autobiographical fragment, Forman repeatedly characterizes himself as unloved and rejected by his mother during his childhood and youth; at the date of his dream, she was still alive, a very old woman. When he has taken the old woman of his dream away from the 'tall man with a reddish beard' who has kissed her, the dreamer begins to make his own erotic advances to her, anticipating that when they are alone, she will kiss *him*. The Oedipal triangle latent in this scenario is at once a psychological and social phenomenon: mother, mistress, and monarch merge in the dream figure of 'the Queen'. C. L. Barber has suggested that 'the very central and problematical role of women in Shakespeare – and in Elizabethan drama generally – reflects the fact that Protestantism did away with the cult of the Virgin Mary. It meant the loss of ritual resource for dealing with the internal residues in all of us of the once all-powerful and all-inclusive mother' (Barber 1980, p.196). What Barber fails to note is that a woman also had 'a very central and problematical role' in the Elizabethan state and that a concerted effort was made to appropriate the symbolism and affective power of the suppressed Marian cult in order to foster an Elizabethan cult. Both the internal residues and the religious rituals were potential resources for dealing with the political problems of the Elizabethan regime. Perhaps, at the same time, the royal cult may also have provided Forman and other Elizabethans with a resource for dealing with the internal residues of their relationships to the primary maternal figures of infancy. My concern is not to psychoanalyze Forman but rather to emphasize the historical specificity of psychological processes, the politics of the unconscious. Whatever the place of this dream in the dreamer's interior life, the text in which he represents it to himself allows us to glimpse the cultural contours of a psyche that is both distinctively male and distinctively Elizabethan.

The virginal sex-object of Forman's dream, the 'little elderly woman' scantily clad in white, corresponds with startling accuracy to descriptions of Elizabeth's actual appearance in 1597. In the year that Forman dreamt his dream, the ambassador extraordinary of the French king Henri IV described the English queen in his journal. At his first audience,

> She was strangely attired in a dress of silver cloth, white and crimson.... She kept the front of her dress open, and one could see the whole of her bosom, and passing low, and often she would open the front of this robe with her hands as if she was too hot.... Her bosom is somewhat wrinkled... but lower down her flesh is exceeding white and delicate, so far as one could see.

At the ambassador's second audience, the queen

> was clad in a dress of black taffeta, bound with gold lace .... She had a petticoat of white damask, girdled, and open in front, as was also her chemise, in such a manner that she often opened this dress and one could see all her belly, and even to her navel .... When she raises her head, she has a trick of putting both hands on her gown and opening it insomuch that all her belly can be seen.

In the following year, another foreign visitor who saw the queen noted that 'her bosom was uncovered, as all the English ladies have it till they marry'. Elizabeth's display of her bosom signified her status as a maiden. But, like the popular emblem of the life-rendering pelican (which Elizabeth wore as a pendant upon her bosom in one of her portraits), her breasts were also those of a selfless and bountiful mother. The image of the queen as a wet nurse seems to have had some currency. Of the earl of Essex's insatiable thirst for royal offices and honors, Naunton wrote that 'my Lord ... drew in too fast, like a childe sucking on an over-uberous Nurse'. The queen was the source of her subjects' social sustenance, the fount of all preferments; she was represented as a virgin-mother – part Madonna, part Ephesian Diana. Like her bosom, Elizabeth's belly must have figured her political motherhood. But, as the French ambassador insinuates, these conspicuous self-displays were also a kind of erotic provocation. The official portraits and courtly blazons that represent the splendor of the queen's immutable body politic are nicely complemented by the ambassador's sketches of the queen's sixty-five-year-old body natural. His perceptions of the vanity and melancholy of this personage in no way negate his numerous observations of her grace, vitality, and political cunning. Indeed, in the very process of describing the queen's preoccupation with the impact of her appearance upon her beholders, the ambassador demonstrates its impact upon him.

So, too, the aged queen's body exerts a power upon the mind of Dr Forman; and, in his dream, he exerts a reciprocal power upon the body of the queen. The virginal, erotic, and maternal aspects of the Elizabethan feminine that the royal cult appropriates from the domestic domain are themselves appropriated by one of the queen's subjects and made the material for his dreamwork. At the core of Forman's dream is his joke with the queen: 'I told her she should do me a favour to let me wait on her, and she said I should. Then said I, 'I mean to wait *upon* you and not under you, that I might make this belly a little bigger to carry up this smock and coats out of the dirt.' The joke – and, in a sense, the whole dream – is generated from Forman's verbal quibble: to *wait* upon / to *weight* upon. Within this subversive pun is concentrated the reciprocal relationship between dependency and domination. With one vital exception, all forms of public and domestic authority in Elizabethan England were vested in men: in fathers, husbands, masters, teachers, preachers, magistrates, lords. It was inevitable that the rule of a woman who was unmastered by any man would generate peculiar tensions within such a 'patriarchal' society. Sir John Harington, a courtier and godson of the queen recalled in a letter that when the Earl of Essex returned to court from Ireland in defiance of his royal commission, Elizabeth 'chaffed muche, walkede fastly to and fro, looked with discomposure in her visage; and, I remember, she catched my girdle when I kneelede to hir, and swore, "By God's Son I am no Queen; that *man* is above me; – Who gave him commande to come here so soon? I did sende hym on other busynesse."' Likewise, Forman's dream epitomizes the indissolubly political and sexual character of the cultural forms in which such tensions might be represented and addressed. In Forman's wordplay, the subject's desire for employment (to *wait* upon) coexists with his desire for mastery (to *weight* upon); and the pun is manifested physically in his desire to inseminate his sovereign, which is at once to serve her and to possess her. And because the figures in the dream are not only subject and prince but also man and woman, what the *subject* desires to perform, the *man* has the capacity to perform: for Forman to raise the queen's belly is to make her female body to bear the sign of his own potency. In the context of the cross-cutting relationships between subject and prince, man and woman, the dreamer insinuates into a gesture of homage, a will to power.

I find it a strange and admirable coincidence that the dreamer's rival for the queen should be a weaver – as if Nick Bottom had wandered out of Shakespeare's *Dream* and into Forman's. Forman's dream does indeed have affinities with the 'most rare vision' (*A Midsummer Night's Dream*, ed. H. Brooks, 1979, IV, i, 203)) that Shakespeare grants to Bottom. Bottom's dream, like Forman's, is an experience of fleeting intimacy with a powerful female who is at once lover, mother, and queen. The liaison between the fairy queen and the assified artisan is an outrageous theatrical realization of a personal fantasy that was obviously not Forman's alone. Titania treats Bottom as if he were both her child and her lover. And she herself is ambivalently nurturing and threatening, imperious and enthralled. She dotes upon Bottom and indulges in him all those desires to be fed, scratched, and coddled that make Bottom's dream into a parodic fantasy of infantile narcissism and dependency. The sinister side of Titania's possessiveness is manifested in her binding up of Bottom's tongue and in her intimidating command, 'Out of this wood do not desire to go: / Thou shalt remain here, whether thou wilt or no' (III, i, 145–6). But if Titania manipulates Bottom, the amateur actor, she herself is manipulated by Oberon, the play's internal dramatist. A fantasy of male dependency upon woman is expressed and contained within a fantasy of male control over woman; the social reality of the player's dependency upon a queen is inscribed within the imaginative reality of the dramatist's control over a queen. Both Forman's private dream-text and Shakespeare's public play-text embody a culture specific dialectic between personal and public images of gender and power; both are characteristically *Elizabethan* cultural forms.

It has long been recognized that *A Midsummer Night's Dream* has affinities with Elizabethan courtly entertainments. In his recent edition of the play, Harold Brooks cautiously endorses the familiar notion that it was 'designed to grace a wedding in a noble household'. He adds that 'it seems likely that Queen Elizabeth was present when the *Dream* was first acted… She delighted in homage paid to her as the Virgin Queen, and receives it in the myth-making about the Imperial votaress' (*Arden* ed, pp. liii, lv). Although attractive and plausible, such topical connections must remain wholly conjectural. The perspective of my own analysis of the play's court connection is dialectical rather than causal, ideological rather than occasional. For, whether or not Queen Elizabeth was physically present at the first performance of *A Midsummer Night's Dream*, her pervasive *cultural presence* was a condition of the play's imaginative possibility. This is not to imply that *A Midsummer Night's Dream* is merely an inert product of Elizabethan culture. The play is rather a new *production* of Elizabethan culture, enlarging the dimensions of the cultural field and altering the lines of force within it. Thus, in the sense that the royal presence was itself represented within the play, it may be said that the play henceforth conditioned the imaginative possibility of the queen.

When Shakespeare's Duke Theseus proclaims that 'The lunatic, the lover, and the poet / Are of imagination all compact', that 'Lovers and madmen have such seething brains, / Such shaping fantasies, that apprehend / More than cool reason ever comprehends', he fails to apprehend that he himself and the fictional society over which he rules have been shaped by the imagination of a poet. My intertextual study of Shakespeare's *Midsummer Night's Dream* and symbolic forms shaped by other Elizabethan lunatics, lovers, and poets construes the play as calling attention to itself, not only as an end but also as a source of cultural production. Thus, in writing of 'shaping fantasies', I mean to suggest the dialectical character of cultural representations: the fantasies by which the text of *A Midsummer Night's Dream* has been shaped are also those to which it gives shape. I explore this dialectic within a specifically *Elizabethan* context of cultural production: the interplay between representations of gender and power in a stratified society in which authority is everywhere invested in men – everywhere, that is, except at the top.

2

Harold Brooks summarizes the consensus of modern criticism when he writes that 'love and marriage is the [play's] central theme: love aspiring to and consummated in marriage, or to a harmonious partnership within it' (*Arden* ed, p. cxxx). As Paul Olson suggested some years ago, the harmonious marital unions of *A Midsummer Night's Dream* are also in harmony with doctrines of Tudor apologists for the patriarchal family: marital union implies a domestic hierarchy; marital harmony is predicated upon the wife's obedience to her husband (Olson 1957). The opposed emphases of Brooks and Olson – the former, romantic; the latter, authoritarian – abstract and idealize what are in fact complementary features of the dramatic process whereby *A Midsummer Night's Dream* figures the social relationship of the sexes in courtship, marriage, and parenthood. The play imaginatively embodies what Gayle Rubin has called a 'sex/gender system': a sociohistorical construction of sexual identity, difference, and relationship; an appropriation of human anatomical and physiological features by an ideological discourse; a culture-specific fantasia upon Nature's universal theme (Rubin 1975). My concern is with how *A Midsummer Night's Dream* and other Elizabethan texts figure the Elizabethan sex/gender system and the queen's place within it.

The beginning of *A Midsummer Night's Dream* coincides with the end of a struggle in which Theseus has been victorious over the Amazon warrior:

Hippolyta, I woo'd thee with my sword,
And won thy love doing thee injuries;
But I will wed thee in another key,
With pomp, with triumph, and with revelling.

(I, i, 16–19)

Representations of the Amazons are ubiquitous in Elizabethan texts. All of the essential features are present in popular form in William Painter's 'Novel of the Amazones', which opens the second book of *The Palace of Pleasure*. Here we read that the Amazons 'were most excellent warriors': that 'they murdred certaine of their husbands' at the beginning of their gynecocracy; that, 'if they brought forth daughters, they norished and trayned them up in armes, and other manlik exercise.... If they were delivered of males, they sent them to their fathers, and if by chaunce they kept any backe, they murdred them, or else brake their armes and legs in sutch wise as they had no power to beare weapons, and served for nothynge but to spin, twist, and doe other feminine labour.' The Amazons' penchant for male infanticide is complemented by their obvious delight in subjecting powerful heroes to their will. In Spenser's *Faerie Queene*, for example, Arthegall, hero of the Legend of Justice, becomes enslaved to Radigund, 'A Princesse of great powre, and greater pride, / And Queene of Amazons, in armes well tride' (E. Spenser, *Poetical Works* ed. J. C. Faith [Oxford 1912], *Faerie Queene* V, iv, 33). Defeated by Radigund in personal combat, Arthegall must undergo degradation and effeminization of the kind endured by Hercules and by the Amazons' maimed sons.

Sixteenth-century travel narratives often recreate the ancient Amazons of Scythia in South America or in Africa. Invariably, the Amazons are relocated just within the receding boundary of *terra incognita*. Thus, in Sierra Leone in 1582, the chaplain of an English expedition to the Spice Islands recorded the report of a Portuguese trader that 'near the mountains of the moon there is a queen, empress of all these Amazons, a witch and a cannibal who daily feeds on the flesh of boys. She ever remains unmarried, but she has intercourse with a great number of men by whom she begets offspring. The kingdom, however, remains hereditary to the daughters, not to the sons.' This cultural fantasy assimilates Amazonian myth, witchcraft, and cannibalism into an anti-culture that precisely inverts European norms of political authority, sexual license, marriage practices, and inheritance rules. The attitude toward the Amazons expressed in such Renaissance texts is a mixture of fascination and horror. Amazonian mythology seems symbolically to embody and to control a collective anxiety about the power of the female not only to dominate or reject the male but to create and destroy him. It is an ironic acknowledgment by an androcentric culture of the degree to

which men are in fact dependent upon women: upon mothers and
nurses, for their birth and nurture; upon mistresses and wives, for the
validation of their manhood.

Shakespeare engages his wedding play in a dialectic with this
mythological formation. The Amazons have been defeated before the
play begins; and nuptial rites are to be celebrated when it ends. *A
Midsummer Night's Dream* focuses upon different crucial transitions in the
male and female life cycles: the fairy plot, upon taking 'a little changeling
boy' from childhood into youth, from the world of the mother into the
world of the father; the Athenian plot, upon taking a maiden from youth
into maturity, from the world of the father into the world of the husband.
The pairing of the four Athenian lovers is made possible by the magical
powers of Oberon and made lawful by the political authority of Theseus.
Each of these rulers is preoccupied with the fulfillment of his own desires
in the possession or repossession of a wife. Only after Hippolyta has been
mastered by Theseus may marriage seal them 'in everlasting bond of
fellowship' (I, i, 85). And only after 'proud Titania' has been degraded by
'jealous Oberon' (II, i, 60, 61), has 'in mild terms begg'd' (IV, i, 57) his
patience, and has readily yielded the changeling boy to him, may they be
'new in amity' (IV, i, 86).

The diachronic structure of *A Midsummer Night's Dream* eventually
restores the inverted Amazonian system of gender and nurture to a
patriarchal norm. But the initial plans for Theseus's triumph are
immediately interrupted by news of yet another unruly female. Egeus
wishes to confront his daughter Hermia with two alternatives: absolute
obedience to the paternal will or death. Theseus intervenes with a third
alternative: if she refuses to marry whom her father chooses, Hermia must
submit 'Either to die the death or to abjure / Forever the society of men' (I,
i, 65–6). If Theseus finally overbears Egeus' will (IV, i, 178), it is because the
father's obstinate claim to 'the ancient privilege of Athens' (I, i, 41)
threatens to obstruct the very process by which Athenian privilege and
Athens itself are reproduced. Hermia and Helena are granted their desires
– but those desires have themselves been shaped and directed by a social
imperative. Thus, neither for Oberon nor for Theseus is there any
contradiction between mastering the desires of a wife and patronizing the
desires of a maiden.

Theseus has characteristically Protestant notions about the virtue of
virginity: maidenhood is a phase in the life cycle of a woman who is
destined for married chastity and motherhood. As a permanent state,
'single blessedness' (I, i, 78) is mere sterility. Theseus expands Hermia's
options only in order to clarify her constraints. In the process of
tempering the father's domestic tyranny, the duke affirms his own
interests and authority. He represents the life of a vestal as a *punishment*,
and it is one that fits the nature of Hermia's crime. Each of the men who

surround the maid – father, lovers, lord – claims a kind of property in her. Yet Hermia dares to suggest that she has a claim to property in herself: she refuses to 'yield [her] virgin patent up / Unto his lordship whose unwished yoke / [Her] soul consents not to give sovereignty' (I, i, 80–2). She wishes the limited privilege of giving herself. Theseus appropriates the source of Hermia's fragile power: her ability to deny men access to her body. He usurps the power of virginity by imposing upon Hermia his own power to deny her the use of her body. If she will not submit to its use by her father and by Demetrius, she must 'live a barren sister all [her] life' (I, i, 72). The female body is a supreme form of property and a locus for the contestation of authority. The self-possession of single blessedness is a form of power against which are opposed the marriage doctrines of Shakespeare's culture and the very form of his comedy.

In the opening scene, Egeus claims that he may do with Hermia as he chooses because she is his property: 'As she is mine, I may dispose of her' (I, i, 42). This claim is based upon a stunningly simple thesis: she is his because he has *made* her. Theseus explains to Hermia the ontogenetic principle underlying her father's vehemence:

> To you your father should be as a god:
> One that compos'd your beauties, yea, and one
> To whom you are but as a form in wax
> By him imprinted, and within his power
> To leave the figure or disfigure it.

> (I, i, 47–51)

Theseus represents paternity as a cultural act, an art: the father is a demiurge or *homo faber*, who composes, in-forms, imprints himself upon, what is merely inchoate matter. Conspicuously excluded from Theseus' account and from the whole play is the relationship between mother and daughter – the kinship bond through which Amazonian society reproduces itself. The central female characters of Shakespeare's comedies are not mothers but mother-to-be, maidens who are passing from fathers to husbands in a world made and governed by men. Hermia and Helena have no mothers; they have only fathers. And Theseus's lecture on the shaping of a *daughter* is, in effect, a fantasy of male parthenogenesis.

Titania's votaress is the only biological mother in *A Midsummer Night's Dream*. But she is an absent presence who must be evoked from Titania's memory because she has died in giving birth to a *son*. Assuming that they do not maim their sons, the Amazons are only too glad to give them away to their fathers. In Shakespeare's play, however, Oberon's paternal power must be directed against Titania's maternal possessiveness:

> For Oberon is passing fell and wrath,
> Because that she as her attendant hath
> A lovely boy, stol'n from an Indian king –
> She never had so sweet a changeling;
> And jealous Oberon would have the child
> Knight of his train to trace the forest wild;
> But she perforce withholds the loved boy,
> Crowns him with flowers, and makes him all her joy.
>
> (II, i, 20–7).

A boy's transition from the female-centered world of his early childhood to the male-centered world of his youth is given a kind of phylogenetic sanction by myths recounting a cultural transition from matriarchy to patriarchy. Such a myth is represented at the very threshhold of *A Midsummer Night's Dream*: Theseus's defeat of the Amazonian matriarchate sanctions Oberon's attempt to take the boy from an infantilizing mother and to make a man of him. Yet 'jealous' Oberon is not only Titania's rival for the child but also the child's rival for Titania: making the boy 'all her joy', 'proud' Titania withholds herself from her husband; she has 'forsworn his bed and company' (II, i, 62–3). Oberon's preoccupation is to gain possession not only of the boy but of the woman's desire and obedience; he must master his own dependency upon his wife.

Titania has her own explanation for her fixation upon the changeling:

> His mother was a votress of my order
> And in the spiced Indian air, by night,
> Full often hath she gossip'd by my side;
> And sat with me on Neptune's yellow sands,
> Marking th'embarked traders on the flood:
> When we have laugh'd to see the sails conceive
> And grow big-bellied with the wanton wind;
> Which she, with pretty and with swimming gait
> Following (her womb then rich with my young squire),
> Would imitate, and sail upon the land
> To fetch me trifles, and return again
> As from a voyage rich with merchandise.
> But she, being mortal, of that boy did die;
> And for her sake do I rear up her boy;
> And for her sake I will not part with him.
>
> (II, i, 123–37)

Titania's attachment to the changeling boy embodies her attachment to the memory of his mother. What Oberon accomplishes by substituting Bottom for the boy is to break Titania's solemn vow. As in the case of the Amazons, or that of Hermia and Helena, the play again enacts a male disruption of an intimate bond between women: first by the boy, and then by the man. It is as if, in order to be freed and enfranchised from the prison of the womb, the male child must *kill* his mother: 'She, being mortal, of that boy did die.' One can read the line as suggesting that mother and son are potentially mortal to each other: the matricidal infant complements the infanticidal Amazon. As later with Bottom, Titania both dotes upon and dominates the child, prolonging his imprisonment to the womb: 'And for her sake I will not part with him.' Thus, within the changeling plot are embedded transformations of the male fantasies of motherhood that are figured in Amazonian myth.

Titania represents her bond to her votaress as one that is rooted in an experience of female fecundity, an experience for which men must seek merely mercantile compensations. The women 'have laugh'd to see the sails conceive / And grow big-bellied with the wanton wind'; and the votaress has parodied such false pregnancies by sailing to fetch trifles while she herself bears riches within her womb. The notion of maternity implied in Titania's speech counterpoints the notion of paternity formulated by Theseus in the opening scene. In Theseus's description, neither biological nor social mother – neither *genetrix* nor *mater* – plays a role in the making of a daughter; in Titania's description, neither *genitor* nor *pater* plays a role in the making of a son. The father's daughter is shaped from without; the mother's son comes from within her body: Titania dwells upon the physical bond between mother and child, as manifested in pregnancy and parturition. Like an infant of the Elizabethan upper classes, however, the changeling is nurtured not by his natural mother but by a surrogate. By emphasizing her own role as a foster mother to her gossip's offspring, Titania links the biological and social aspects of parenthood together within a wholly maternal world, a world in which the relationship between women has displaced the relationship between wife and husband. Nevertheless, despite the exclusion of a paternal role from Titania's speech, Shakespeare's embryological notions here remain distinctly Aristotelian, distinctly phallocentric: the mother is represented as a *vessel*, as a container for her son; she is not his *maker*. In contrast , the implication of Theseus's description of paternity is that the male is the only begetter; a daughter is merely a token of her father's potency. Thus these two speeches may be said to formulate, in poetic discourse, a proposition about the genesis of gender and power: men make women, and they make themselves through the medium of women. Such a proposition reverses the Amazonian practice, in which women use men merely for their own reproduction. But much more importantly, it seems an overcompensation for the *natural* fact that men do indeed come from women; an overcompensation for the *cultural* facts that consanguineal and affinal ties between men are established through mothers, wives, and daughters.

We may recall here that what we tend to think of as the facts of life have been established as *facts* relatively recently in human history, with the development of microbiology that began in Europe in the later seventeenth century. That seminal and menstrual fluids are in some way related to generation and that people have both a father and a mother are, of course, hardly novel notions. My point is that, in Shakespeare's age, they still remained *merely* notions. Although biological maternity was readily apparent, biological paternity, was a cultural construct for which ocular proof was unattainable. More specifically, the evidence for *unique* biological paternity, for the generative link between a particular man and child, has always been exiguous. As Launcelot Gobbo puts it, 'It is a wise father that knows his own child' (*The Merchant of Venice*, II, ii, 76–7). In Shakespearean drama, this uncertainty is frequently the focus of anxious concern, whether that concern is to validate paternity or to call it into question. Thus, Lear tells Regan that if she were *not* glad to see him, 'I would divorce me from thy mother's tomb, / Sepulchring an adult'ress' (*King Lear*, II, iv, 131–2). And Leontes exclaims, upon first meeting Florizel, 'Your mother was most true to wedlock, Prince / For she did print your royal father off, / Conceiving you' (*The Winter's Tale*, V, i 124–6). In the former speech, a vulnerable father invokes his previously unacknowledged wife precisely when he wishes to repudiate his daughter; in the latter, a vulnerable husband celebrates female virtue as the instrument of male self-reproduction. A thematic complex that pervades the Shakespearean canon is dramatized in *A Midsummer Night's Dream*: a set of claims for a spiritual kinship among men that is unmediated by women, for the procreative powers of men, and for the autogeny of men.

The festive conclusion of *A Midsummer Night's Dream*, its celebration of romantic and generative heterosexual union, depends upon the success of a process whereby the female pride and power manifested in misanthropic warriors, possessive mothers, unruly wives, and wilful daughters are brought under the control of husbands and lords. But while the dramatic structure articulates a patriarchal ideology, it also intermittently undermines its own comic propositions. The naturalization of the social doctrine of domestic hierarchy in the marriage of 'jealous' Oberon and 'proud' Titania calls attention to itself as an equivocal strategy of legitimation, one that authorizes not only the authority of husbands but also the unruliness of wives. The all-too-human struggle between the fairy king and queen – the play's already married couple – provides an ironic prognosis for the new marriages. The play ends upon the threshold of another generational cycle, in which the procreation of new children will also produce new mothers and new fathers. Within this ending is a potential for renewing the forms of strife exhibited at the opening of the play. Regardless of authorial intention, Oberon's blessing of the marriage bed of Theseus and Hippolyta evokes precisely what it seeks to suppress: the cycle of sexual and familial violence, fear, and betrayal begins again at the very engendering of Hippolytus. Shakespeare's romantic comedy is in fact contaminated throughout by a kind of intertextual irony. As Harold Brooks's edition has conclusively demonstrated, the text of Shakespeare's play is permeated by echoes not only of Plutarch's 'Life of Theseus' but also of Seneca's *Hippolitus* and his *Medea* – by an archaeological record of the texts that shaped the poet's fantasy as he was shaping his play. Thus, sedimented within the verbal texture of *A Midsummer Night's Dream* are traces of those recurrent acts of bestiality and incest, of parricide, uxoricide, filicide, and suicide, that the ethos of romantic comedy would evade. Shakespeare's sources weave the chronicle of Theseus's rapes and disastrous marriages, his habitual victimization of women, into the lurid history of female depravity that includes Pasiphae, Medea, and Phaedra. And Shakespeare's text discloses – perhaps, in a sense, despite itself – that patriarchal norms are compensatory for the vulnerability of men to the powers of women.

3

Such textual disclosures also illuminate the interplay between sexual politics in the Elizabethan family and sexual politics in the Elizabethan monarchy, for the woman to whom *all* Elizabethan men were vulnerable was Queen Elizabeth herself. Within legal and fiscal limits, she held the power of life and death over every Englishman, the power to advance or frustrate the worldly desires of all her subjects. Her personality and personal symbolism helped to mold English culture and the consciousness of Englishmen for several generations.

Although the Amazonian metaphor might seem suited to strategies for praising a woman ruler, it was never popular among Elizabethan encomiasts. Its associations must have been too sinister to suit the personal tastes and political interests of the queen. However, Sir Walter Ralegh did boldly compare Elizabeth to the Amazons in his *Discovery of Guiana*. In his digression on the Amazons, who are reported to dwell 'not far from Guiana', Ralegh repeats the familiar details of their sexual and parental practices and notes that they 'are said to be very cruel and bloodthirsty, especially to such as offer to invade their territories'. At the end of his narrative, Ralegh exhorts Elizabeth to undertake a conquest of Guiana:

Her Majesty heereby shall confirme and strengthen the opinions of al nations, as touching her great and princely action. And where the south border of *Guiana* reacheth to the Dominion and Empire of the *Amazones*, those women shall heereby heare the name of a virgin, which is not onely able to defend her owne territories and her neighbors, but also to invade and conquere so great Empyres and so farre removed.

Ralegh's strategy for persuading the queen to advance his colonial enterprise is to insinuate that she is both like and unlike an Amazon, that Elizabethan imperialism threatens not only the empire of Guiana but the empire of the Amazons, and that Elizabeth can definitively cleanse herself from contamination by the Amazons if she sanctions their subjugation. The Amazonomachy that Ralegh projects into the imaginative space of the New World is analogous to that narrated by Spenser within the imaginative space of Faeryland. Radigund, the Amazon queen, can be defeated only by Britomart, the martial maiden who is Artegall's betrothed and the fictional ancestress of Elizabeth. Radigund is Britomart's double, split off from her as an allegorical personification of everything in Artegall's beloved that threatens him. Having destroyed Radigund and liberated Artegall from his effeminate 'thraldome', Britomart reforms what is left of Amazon society: she

> The liberty of women did repeale,
> Which they had long usurpt; and them restoring
> To mens subjection, did true Justice deale:
> That all they as a Goddesse her adoring,
> Her wisedome did admire, and hearkned to her loring.
>
> (*FQ*, V, vii, 42)

Unlike some of the popular sixteenth-century forms of misrule well discussed by Natalie Davis, this instance of sexual inversion would seem to be intended as an exemplum 'of order and stability in a hierarchical society', which 'can clarify the structure by the process of reversing it' (Davis 1975, p. 130). For Ralegh's Elizabeth, as for Spenser's Britomart, the woman who has the prerogative of a goddess, who is authorized to be out of place, can best justify her authority by putting other women in their places.

A few paragraphs before Ralegh exhorts Elizabeth to undertake an Amazonomachy, he exhorts his gentlemen-readers to commit a cultural rape:

> Guiana is a Countrey that hath yet her Maydenhead, never sackt, turned, nor wrought, the face of the earth hath not beene torne, nor the vertue and salt of the soyle spent by manurance, the graves have not beene opened for gold, the mines not broken with sledges, nor their Images puld down out of their temples. It hath never been entred by any armie of strength and never conquered and possessed by any Christian Prince.

Ralegh's enthusiasm is, at one and the same time, for the unspoiled quality of this world and for the prospect of despoiling it. Guiana, like the Amazons, is fit to be wooed with the sword and won with injuries. Such metaphors have a peculiar resonance in the context of an address to Elizabeth. Certainly, it is difficult to imagine Ralegh using them to represent the plantation of Virginia, which had been named by and for the Virgin Queen. When, in the poem to the second book of *The Faerie Queene*, Spenser conjoins 'the Amazons huge river' and 'fruitfullest Virginia' (*FQ*, 2, Proem, 2), he is invoking not only two regions of the New World but two archetypes of Elizabethan culture: the engulfing Amazon and the nurturing Virgin. Later in the same book, they are conjoined again in Belphoebe, the virgin huntress who figures Queen Elizabeth in her body natural. Belphoebe is introduced into the poem with an extended blazon that concludes in an ominous epic simile comparing her both with the goddess Diana and with Penthesilea ' that famous Queene / Of *Amazons*, whom *Pyrrhus* did destroy ' (*FQ*, II, iii, 31). The female body – and, in particular, the symbolic body of the queen – provides a cognitive map for Elizabethan culture, a matrix for the Elizabethan forms of desire, and a field upon which the relations of Elizabethan power are played out.

The queen herself was too politic, and too ladylike, to wish to pursue the Amazonian image very far. Instead, she transformed it to suit her purposes, representing herself as an androgynous martial maiden, like Spenser's Britomart. Such was her appearance at Tilbury in 1588, where she had come to review the troops mustered in preparation for a Spanish invasion. On that momentous occasion, she rode a white horse and dressed in white velvet; she wore a silver cuirass on her breast and carried a silver truncheon in her hand. The theme of her speech was by then already very familiar to her listeners: she dwelt upon the womanly frailty of her body natural and the masculine strength of her body politic – a strength deriving from the love of her people, the virtue of her lineage, and the will of her God: 'I have always so behaved myself that, under God, I have placed my chiefest strength and safeguard in the loyal hearts and good will of my subjects….I know I have the body of a weak and feeble woman, but I have the heart and stomach of a king, and of a king of England too.' As the female ruler of what was, at least in theory, a patriarchal society, Elizabeth incarnated a contradiction at the very center of the Elizabethan sex/gender system. After the death of their royal mistress, Cecil wrote to Harington that she had been 'more than a man, and, in troth, sometime less than a woman'. Queen Elizabeth was a cultural anomaly; and this anomalousness made her powerful and dangerous. By the skillful deployment of images that were at once awesome and familiar, this perplexing creature tried to mollify her male subjects while enhancing her authority over them.

At the beginning of her reign, Elizabeth formulated the strategy by which she turned the political liability of her gender to advantage for the next half century. She told her first parliaments that she was content to have as her epitaph 'that a Queen, having reigned such a time, lived and died a virgin'; that her coronation ring betokened her marriage to her subjects; and that, although after her death her people might have many stepdames, yet they should never have 'a more natural mother than [she] meant to be unto [them] all'. When she told the earl of Leicester, 'I will have here but one Mistress, and no Master', she epitomized her policy on gender and power. As Bacon observed in his memorial of Elizabeth, 'the reigns of women are commonly obscured by marriage; their praises and actions passing to the credit of their husbands; whereas those that continue unmarried have their glory entire and proper to themselves ... . And even those whom she herself raised to honour she so kept in hand and mingled one with the other, that while she infused into each the greatest solicitude to please her, she was herself ever her own mistress.' Elizabeth's self-mastery and mastery of others were enhanced by the promotion of her maidenhood into a cult of virginity; the displacement of her wifely duties from a household to a nation; and the modulation of her temporal and ecclesiastical supremacy into a nurturing maternity. She appropriated not only the suppressed cult of the Blessed Virgin but also the Tudor notion of the Ages of Woman. By fashioning herself into a singular combination of Maiden, Matron, and Mother, the queen transformed the normal domestic life cycle of an Elizabethan female into what was at once a social paradox and religious mystery. Her emblem was the phoenix; her motto, *semper eadem, semper una*. Because she was always uniquely herself, Elizabeth's rule was not intended to undermine the male hegemony of her culture. Indeed, the emphasis upon her *difference* from all other women may have helped to reinforce it. As she herself wrote in response to Parliament in 1563, 'though I can think [marriage] best for a private woman, yet I do strive with myself to think it not meet for a prince'. The royal exception could prove the patriarchal rule in society at large.

Nevertheless, from the very beginning of her reign, Elizabeth's parliaments and counselors urged her to marry and produce an heir. There was a deeply felt and loudly voiced need to insure a legitimate succession, upon which the welfare of the whole people depended. But there seems to have been another, more obscure motivation behind these requests: the political nation, which was wholly a nation of men, could sometimes find it frustrating or degrading to serve a prince who was, after all, merely a woman. Late in Elizabeth's reign, the French ambassador observed that 'her government is fairly pleasing to the people, who show that they love her, but it is little pleasing to the great men and nobles; and if by chance she should die, it is certain that the English would never again submit to the rule of a woman'. In the 1560s and 1570s, Elizabeth witnessed allegorical entertainments boldly criticizing her attachment to a life of 'single blessedness'. For example, in the famous Kenilworth entertainments sponsored by the Earl of Leicester in 1575, Diana praised the state of fancy-free maiden meditation and condemned the 'wedded state, which is to thraldome bent'. But Juno had the last word in the pageant: 'O Queene, o worthy queene / Yet never wight felt perfect blis / But such as wedded beene.' By the 1580s, the queen was past childbearing; Diana and her virginal nymph, Eliza, now carried the day in such courtly entertainments as Peele's *Araygnment of Paris*. Although 'as fayre and lovely as the queene of Love', Peele's Elizabeth was also 'as chast as Dian in her chast desires'. By the early 1590s, the cult of the unaging royal virgin had entered its last and most extravagant phase. In the 1590 Accession Day pageant, there appeared ' a Pavilion.... like unto the sacred Temple of the Virgins Vestal'. Upon the altar there were presents for the queen – offerings from her votaries. At Elvetham, during the royal progress of 1591, none other than 'the Fairy Queene' gave to Elizabeth a chaplet that she herself had received from 'Auberon, the Fairy King'. From early in the reign, Elizabeth had been directly engaged by such entertainments: debates were referred to her arbitration; the magic of her presence civilized savage men, restored the blind to sight, released errant knights from enchantment, and rescued virgins from defilement. These social dramas of celebration and coercion played out the delicately balanced relationship between the monarch and her greatest subjects. And because texts and descriptions of most of them were in print within a year of their performance, these occasional and ephemeral productions could achieve a considerable cultural impact.

A Midsummer Night's Dream is permeated by images and devices that suggest these characteristic forms of Elizabethan court culture. Whether or not its provenance was in an aristocratic wedding entertainment, however, Shakespeare's play is neither focused upon the queen nor structurally dependent upon her presence or her intervention in the action. On the contrary, it might be said to depend upon her absence, her exclusion. In the third scene of the play, after Titania has remembered her Indian votaress, Oberon remembers his 'imperial votaress'. He has once beheld,

> Flying between the cold moon and the earth,
> Cupid all arm'd; a certain aim he took
> At a fair vestal, throned by the West,
> And loos'd his love-shaft smartly from his bow
> As it should pierce a hundred thousand hearts.
> But I might see young Cupid's fiery shaft
> Quench'd in the chaste beams of the watery moon;
> And the imperial votress passed on,

> In maiden meditation, fancy-free.
> Yet mark'd I where the bolt of Cupid fell:
> It fell upon a little western flower,
> Before milk-white, now purple with love's wound:
> And maidens call it 'love-in-idleness'.

(II, i, 156–68)

The resonant monologues of Titania and Oberon are carefully matched and contrasted: the fairy queen speaks of a mortal mother from the east; the fairy king speaks of an invulnerable virgin from the west. Their memories express two myths of origin: Titania's provides a genealogy for the changeling and an explanation of why she will not part with him; Oberon's provides an aetiology of the metamorphosed flower that he will use to make her part with him. The floral symbolism of female sexuality begun in this passage is completed when Oberon names 'Dian's bud' (IV, i, 72) as the antidote to 'love-in-idleness'. With Cupid's flower, Oberon can make the fairy queen 'full of hateful fantasies' (II, i, 258); and with Dian's bud, he can win her back to his will. The vestal's invulnerability to fancy is instrumental to Oberon in his reaffirmation of romantic, marital, and parental norms that have been inverted during the course of the play. Thus, Shakespeare's royal compliment re-mythologizes the cult of the Virgin Queen in such a way as to sanction a relationship of gender and power that is personally and politically inimical to Elizabeth.

Shakespeare's comic heroines are in transition between the statuses of maiden and wife, daughter and mother. These transitions are mediated by the wedding rite and the act of defloration, which are brought together at the end of *A Midsummer Night's Dream*. When the newlyweds have retired, Oberon and Titania enter the court in order to bless the 'bride-bed' where the marriages are about to be consummated. By the act of defloration, the husband takes physical and symbolic possession of his bride. The sexual act in which the man draws blood from the woman is evoked at the beginning of the play, in Theseus's vaunt: 'Hippolyta, I woo'd thee with my sword, / And won thy love doing thee injuries.' And it is immanent in the image that Oberon uses to describe the very origin of desire: 'the bolt of Cupid fell / ... Upon a little western flower, / Before milk-white, now purple with love's wound.' Cupid's shaft violates the flower when it has been deflected from the vestal: Oberon's purple passion flower is procreated in a displaced and literalized defloration.

Unlike the female *dramatis personae*, Oberon's vestal virgin is *not* subject to Cupid's shaft, to the frailties of the flesh and the fancy. Nor is she subject to the mastery of men. And it is precisely her bodily and mental impermeability that make possible Oberon's pharmacopoeia. Thus, ironically, the vestal's very freedom from fancy guarantees the subjection of others. She is necessarily excluded from the erotic world of which her own chastity is the efficient cause. Within *A Midsummer Night's Dream*, the public and domestic domains of Elizabethan culture intersect in the figure of the imperial votaress. When a female ruler is ostensibly the virgin mother of her subjects, then the themes of male procreative power, autogeny, and mastery of women acquire a seditious resonance. In royal pageantry, the queen is always the cynosure; her virginity is the source of magical potency. In *A Midsummer Night's Dream*, however, such magical powers are invested in the king. Perhaps three or four years before the first production of *A Midsummer Night's Dream*, in a pastoral entertainment enacted at Sudeley during the royal progress of 1592, the queen's presence was sufficient to undo the metamorphosis of Daphne, to release her from her arboreal imprisonment, and to protect her from the lustful advances of Apollo. According to Shakespeare's Oberon, Helena's pursuit of Demetrius necessitates a metamorphosis of Ovid's text: 'The story shall be chang'd: / Apollo flies, and Daphne holds the chase' (II, i, 230–1). The response of the fairy king is neither to extinguish desire nor to make it mutual but rather to restore the normal pattern of pursuit: 'Fare thee well, nymph; ere he do leave this grove / Thou shalt fly him and he shall seek thy love' (II, i, 245–6). Unlike Elizabeth, Oberon uses his mastery over Nature to subdue others to their passions. Spenser and other courtly writers often fragment the royal image, reflecting aspects of the queen 'in mirrours more then one' (*FQ*, 3, Proem, 5). Similarly, Shakespeare splits the triune Elizabethan cult image between the fair vestal, an unattainable *virgin*; and the fairy queen, an intractable *wife* and a dominating *mother*. Oberon uses one against the other in order to reassert male prerogatives. Thus, in the logic of its structure, Shakespeare's comedy symbolically neutralizes the royal power to which it ostensibly pays homage.

Shortly before her death, Sir John Harington wrote of Elizabeth as 'oure deare Queene, my royale godmother, and this state's natural mother'. Shortly after her death, he reflected slyly on how she had manipulated the filial feelings of her subjects: 'Few knew how to aim their shaft against her cunninge. We did all love hir, for she saide she loved us, and muche wysdome she shewed in thys matter'. In Harington's image of the court, a metaphor from archery resonates as a metaphor of masculine genital aggression. But, like Oberon's Cupid, these children/courtiers are frustrated in their desire to master the sovereign mother/mistress with whom they are engaged in a subtle but ceaseless contest of wills. Bacon provides what is perhaps the most astute contemporary analysis of the queen's erotic strategies:

> As for those lighter points of character, – as that she allowed herself to be wooed and courted, and even to have love made to her; and liked it; and continued it beyond the natural age for such vanities; – if any of the sadder sort of persons be disposed to make a great matter of this, it may be observed that there is something to admire in these very things, which

ever way you take them. For if viewed indulgently, they are much like the accounts we find in romances, of the Queen in the blessed island, and her court and institutions, who allows of amorous admiration but prohibits desire. But if you take them seriously, they challenge admiration of another kind and of a very high order; for certain it is that these dalliances detracted but little from her fame and nothing from her majesty, and neither weakened her power nor sensibly hindered her business.

As Bacon suggests, the queen's personal vanity and political craft are mutually reinforcing. He appreciates the generic affinities of the royal cult, its appropriation and enactment of the conventions of romance. And he also appreciates that, like contemporaneous romantic fictions, the queen's romance could function as a political allegory. However, symbolic forms may do more than *represent* power: they may actually help to *generate* the power that they represent. Thus – although Bacon does not quite manage to say so – the queen's dalliances did not weaken her power but strengthened it, did not hinder her business but furthered it.

By the same token, the queen's subjects might put the discourse of royal power to their own uses. Consider the extravagant royal entertainment of 1581, in which Philip Sidney and Fulke Greville performed as 'Foster Children of Desire'. 'Nourished up with [the] infective milke' of Desire – 'though full oft that dry nurse Dispaier indevered to wainne them from it' – the Foster Children boldly claimed and sought to possess The Fortress of Perfect Beauty, an allegorical structure simultaneously identified with the queen's body and with her state. Elizabeth beheld the 'desirous assault' against her, in which 'two canons were shot off, the one with sweet powder, and the other with sweet water', and 'floures and such fansies' were thrown 'against the wals'. During two days of florid speeches, spectacular self-displays, and mock combats, these young, ambitious, and thwarted courtiers acted out a fantasy of political demand, rebellion, and submission in metaphors of resentment and aggression that were alternately filial and erotic. They seized upon the forms in which their culture had articulated the relationship between sovereign and subjects: they demanded sustenance from their royal mother, favors from their royal mistress. The Foster Children were finally forced to acknowledge the paradox of Desire: 'No sooner hath Desire what he desireth, but that he dieth presentlie: so that when Beautie yeeldeth once to Desire, then can she never want to be desired againe. Wherefore of force this principle must stand, it is convenient for Desire ever to wish, and necessarie that he alwaies want'. The nobility, gentlemen, and hangers-on of the court generated a variety of pressures that constantly threatened the fragile stability of the Elizabethan regime. At home, personal rivalries and political dissent might be sublimated into the agonistic play forms of courtly culture; abroad, they might be expressed in warfare and colonial enterprise – displaced into the conquest of lands that had yet their maidenheads.

The queen dallied, not only with the hearts of courtiers but also with the hearts of commoners. For example, in 1600, a deranged sailor named Abraham Edwardes sent 'a passionate ... letter unto her Majesty', who was then sixty-eight years old. Edwardes was later committed to prison 'for drawing his dagger in the [royal] presence chamber'. The clerk of the privy council wrote to Cecil that 'the fellow is greatly distracted, and seems rather to be transported with a humour of love, than any purpose to attempt anything against her Majesty'. He recommended that this poor lunatic and lover 'be removed to Bedlam'. By her own practice of sexual politics, the queen may very well have encouraged the sailor's passion – in the same sense that her cult helped to fashion the courtly performances and colonial enterprises of courtiers like Sidney or Ralegh, the dream-life of Doctor Forman, the dream-play of Master Shakespeare. This being said, it must be added that the queen was as much the creature of her image as she was its creator – the creature of images fashioned by Sidney and Ralegh, Forman and Shakespeare – and that her power to shape her own strategies was itself shaped by her society and constrained within the horizon of its cultural assumptions. It would be an oversimplification to imply that the spiritual, maternal, and erotic transformations of Elizabethan power were merely instances of Machiavellian policy – were intentional mystifications and nothing more. Relationships of dependency and autonomy, desire and fear, characterize both the public and domestic domains of Elizabethan experience. If sexual and family experience were invariably politicized, economic and political experience were invariably eroticized. The social and psychological force of Elizabethan symbolic forms depended upon a play between the distinction and conflation of these domains.

The much-noted 'metadrama' of *A Midsummer Night's Dream* – its calling of attention to its own artifice, its own artistry – analogizes the powers of parents, princes, and playwrights, the fashioning of children, subjects, and plays. Shakespeare's text is not only a cultural production but a representation of cultural production; a representation of fantasies about the shaping of the family, the polity, and the theatre. When Oberon blesses the bride-beds of 'the couples three' (V, i, 393), he metaphorizes the engendering of their offspring as an act of *writing*: 'And the blots of Nature's hand / Shall not in their issue stand' (V, i, 395–6). And when Theseus wryly describes the poet's 'fine frenzy' (V, i, 12), the text of *A Midsummer Night's Dream* obliquely represents the parthenogenetic process of its own creation:

And as imagination bodies forth
The forms of things unknown, the poet's pen

> Turns them to shapes, and gives to airy nothing
> A local habitation and a name.

(V, i, 14–17)

In its preoccupation with the transformation of the personal into the public, the metamorphosis of dream and fantasy into poetic drama, *A Midsummer Night's Dream* does more than *analogize* the powers of prince and playwright: It dramatizes – or, rather, *meta*-dramatizes – the relations of power *between* prince and playwright. The play bodies forth the theatre poet's contest, not only with the generativity of Elizabethan mothers but with the generativity of the royal virgin; it contests the princely claim to cultural authorship and social authority. To the extent that the cult of Elizabeth informs the play, it is itself transformed within the play. *A Midsummer Night's Dream* is, then, in a double sense, a *creation* of Elizabethan culture: for it also creates the culture by which it is created, shapes the fantasies by which it is shaped, begets that by which it is begotten.

7 Alice Arden's Crime*

CATHERINE BELSEY

Cultural Materialism which developed in Britain while New Historicism emerged in America, is distinguished by an insistence that, if reality is constructed in language, it is in constant contest. Renaissance drama is important, therefore, not only for what it tells us about the **difference** of the past, but because that **difference** reminds us that the meanings we assign are not unchanging. In *The Subject of Tragedy* Catherine Belsey examines the generation of a concept of the autonomous, unified individual, whose supposed freedom is the basis of liberal **humanism**. She dates this to the seventeenth century, demonstrating that a sense of human autonomy is absent from medieval plays like *Everyman*. But the fact that is was unresolved in Renaissance culture makes it the 'subject' of Elizabethan tragedy, where a free **subject** is defined as male, by virtue of woman's passivity and silence. But even in a patriarchy, Belsey shows in the extract, the dominant **discourse** fails to define women entirely, and a story like that of the murderess Alice Arden reveals 'unruly women' slipping free of the prison of humanist language. Here feminism allies with **Cultural Materialism** in a critique more polemical than that of New Historicism, which is often viewed as a male preserve.

Defining the crime

On Sunday 15 February 1551 Alice Arden of Faversham in Kent procured and witnessed the murder of her husband. She and most of her accomplices were arrested, tried and executed. The goods of the murderers, worth a total of £184.10s.4$\frac{1}{2}$d , and certain jewels, were forfeit to the Faversham treasury. The city of Canterbury was paid 44 shillings for executing George Bradshaw, who was also present at the murder, and for

* Reprinted from *The Subject of Tragedy: Identity and Difference in Renaissance Drama* (London, Methuen, 1985), pp. 129–48.

burning Alice Arden alive. At a time when all the evidence suggests that crimes of violence were by no means uncommon, Alice Arden's crime was cited, presented and re-presented, problematized and reproblematized, during a period of at least eighty years after it was committed. Holinshed, pausing in his account of the events which constitute the main material of the *Chronicles of England, Scotland and Ireland* to give a detailed analysis of the murder, explains that the case transgresses the normal boundaries between public and private, and so, 'for the horribleness thereof, although otherwise it may seeme to be but a private matter, and therefore as it were impertinent to this historie, I have thought good to set it foorth somewhat at large' (*Arden of Faversham*, ed. M.L. Wine (London, 1973), p. 148).

This 'horribleness', which identifies Alice Arden's domestic crime as belonging to the public arena of history is not, it could be argued, a matter of the physical details of the murder, nor even of the degree of premeditation involved. On the contrary, the scandal lies in Alice Arden's challenge to the institution of marriage, itself publicly in crisis in the period. Marriage becomes in the sixteenth and seventeenth centuries the site of a paradoxical struggle to create a private realm and to take control of it in the interests of the public good. The crime coincides with the beginning of this contest. *Arden of Faversham*, which can probably be dated about 1590, is contemporary with a major intensification of the debate about marriage, and permits its audience glimpses of what is at stake in the struggle.

There are a great many extant allusions to Alice Arden's crime. It was recorded in the *Breviat Chronicle* for 1551, in the diary of Henry Machyn, a London merchant-tailor, and in Stow's *Annals of England* (1592, 1631), as well as in Holinshed's *Chronicles* (1577, 1587). Thomas Heywood gives it two lines in his seventeen-canto poem on the history of the world, *Troia Britannica* (1609), and John Taylor in *The Unnaturall Father* (1621, 1630) invokes it as an instance of God's vengeance on murderers. In addition to the play, which ran to four editions between 1592 and 1633, '[The] complaint and lamentation of Mistresse Arden' was printed in ballad form, probably in 1633.

The official record of the murder was given in the Wardmote Book of Faversham, reprinted in Wine's Revels edition of the play, together with Holinshed's account and the ballad. According to the Wardmote Book, Arden was 'heynously' and 'shamefully' murdered, and the motive was Alice's intention to marry Mosby, a tailor whom she carnally kept in her own house and fed with delicate meats, with the full knowledge of her husband. The value-judgment established here is constant in all the accounts, and the word 'shameful' defines the crime in the *Breviat Chronicle* (*Arden of Faversham*, p. xxxvii), in Holinshed, on the title page of the first edition of the play and again in the ballad. What is contested in these representations is not, on the whole, the morality of the murder, but its explanation, its meaning. Specific areas of the story are foregrounded or reduced, with the effect of modifying the crime's significance. The low social status of Mosby, and Arden's complaisance, for instance, both intensify the disruption of matrimonial conventions, and these elements are variously either accounted for or played down. Arden's role in the story differs considerably from one narrative to another.

What are the implications of the constant efforts at redefinition? In Holinshed's analysis Arden was a gentleman, a tall and comely person, and Mosby 'a blacke swart man'. According to the marginal gloss in the second edition of the *Chronicles,* Alice's irrational preference is an instance of the radical difference between love and lust, and her flagrant defiance of the marriage bond accountable in terms of human villainy: 'Thus this wicked woman, with hir complices, most shamefullie murdered hir owne husband, who most entirelie loved hir all his life time' (*Arden of Faversham,* pp. 148, 155). But running through Holinshed's narrative is another account of the murder, not wholly consistent with this view of Arden as innocent victim, which emphasizes God's vengeance on his greed for property. In this account Arden's avarice, repeatedly referred to in the story, is finally his undoing. His complaisance is a consequence of his covetousness: 'bicause he would not offend hir, and so loose the benefit which he hoped to gaine at some of hir freends hands in bearing with hir lewdnesse, which he might have lost if he should have fallen out with hir: he was contented to winke at her filthie disorder' (ibid., p. 149). After Arden's death, the field where the conspirators had placed his corpse miraculously showed the imprint of his body for two years afterwards. This field was Arden's property, and in 1551 he had insisted that the St Valentine's fair be held there, 'so reaping all the gaines to himselfe, and bereaving the towne of that portion which was woont to come to the inhabitants'. For this he was bitterly cursed by the people of Faversham (ibid., p.157). The field itself had been 'cruellie' and illegally wrested from the wife of Richard Read, a sailor, and she too had cursed him, 'wishing manie a vengeance to light upon him, and that all the world might woonder on him. Which was thought then to come to passe, when he was thus murdered, and laie in that field from midnight till the morning' on the day of the fair. Again the marginal gloss spells out the moral implications: 'God heareth the teares of the oppressed and taketh vengeance: note an example in Arden' (ibid., p.159). The murder is thus part of the providential scheme.

These two versions of Arden – as a loving husband and as a rapacious landlord – coexist equally uneasily in the play. Here the element of complaisance is much reduced: Arden has grounds for suspicion but not certainty. Mosby's baseness is a constant theme, and underlines Alice's irrationality. But what is new in the play is the parallel between Arden's dubious business deals and Alice's. A good part of the plot is taken up with Alice's negotiations with possible murderers . Michael is to carry out the crime in exchange for Susan Mosby. Clarke is to provide a poison, and subsequently a poisoned picture, in exchange for Susan Mosby. Greene gets £10 and a promise of £20 more, with land to follow, for his 'plain dealing' in carrying out the murder (I, 517). Greene subcontracts the work to Black Will and Shakebag for £10. Finally, in desperation, Alice increases her offer to this team to £20, and £40 more when Arden is dead. They leave triumphantly with their gold when the work is completed. Mosby, too, is part of this world of economic individualism, and there are indications that his motive is not of love of Alice so much as desire to come by Arden's money (e.g. VIII, 11–44). He quarrels with Alice in terms of 'credit', 'advantages', 'fortune' and 'wealth' (VIII, 80–92). If the play has any explanation to offer of Alice Arden's crime it is social and economic rather than providential. The event is primarily an instance of the breakdown of order – the rape of women and property – which follows when the exchange of contracts in a market economy supplants old loyalties, old obligations, old hierarchies.

But there are elements of the play which this reading leaves out of account. Some of the dialogue between Alice and Mosby invites a response which contradicts the play's explicit project, defined on the title page, of showing 'the great malice and dissimulation of a wicked woman, [and] the unsatiable desire of filthy lust'. In these speeches it is marriage which is identified as an impediment to true love, and images familiar from the poetry of the period seem to offer the audience a position of some sympathy with Alice's repudiation of the marriage bond:

Alice Why should he thrust his sickle in our corn,
        Or what hath he to do with thee, my love,
        Or govern me that am to rule myself?
        Forsooth, for credit sake, I must leave thee!
        Nay, he must leave to live that we may love,
        May live, may love; for what is life but love?
        And love shall last as long as life remains,
        And life shall end before my love depart.
Mosby Why, what's love, without true constancy?
        Like to a pillar built of many stones,
        Yet neither with good mortar well compact
        Nor cement to fasten it in the joints
        But that it shakes with every blast of wind
        And, being touched, straight falls unto the earth
        And buries all his haughty pride in dust.
        No, let our love be rocks of adamant,
        Which time nor place nor tempest can asunder.

                                     (X, 83–99)

The natural and elemental images and the Biblical echoes momentarily
ennoble Alice's defiance of patriarchy. Early in the play Clarke makes
explicit this other face of the crime:

> Let it suffice I know you love him well
> And fain would have your husband made away,
> Wherein, trust me, you show a noble mind,
> That rather than you'll live with him you hate
> You'll venture life and die with him you love.

(I, 267–71)

In these instances the play presents Alice Arden's challenge to the
institution of marriage as an act of heroism. Alice rejects the metaphysics of
presence which guarantees the social enforcement of permanent
monogamy, in favour of a free sexuality, unauthorized within the play as a
whole, but glimpsed at isolated moments:

> Sweet Mosby is the man that hath my heart;
> And he [Arden] usurps it, having nought but this,
> That I am tied to him by marriage.
> Love is a god, and marriage is but words;
> And therefore Mosby's title is the best.
> Tush! Whether it be or no, he shall be mine
> In spite of him, of Hymen, and of rites.

(I, 98–104)

The ballad, almost certainly derived from the play, redefines the problem
yet again. For the first time the woman is the unequivocal subject of the
narrative, in contrast to the play, where the title indicates that it is Arden's
tragedy rather than Alice's. The ballad reduces the story to two main
elements – Alice's love and the series of contracts for the murder. These
negotiations are recounted in all their detail within a text of only 192 lines.
Arden's rapacity is ignored, and Holinshed's 'blacke swart' Mosby
becomes a man of 'sugred tongue, good shape, and lovely looke' (11). The
ballad is a record of contracts made and broken for love. There is no
explicit doubt of Alice's wickedness: her 'secret dealings' come to light and
are duly punished by her death (167). At the same time a curious
formulation, perhaps a slip of the pen, picks up something of the element
of ambivalence in the play: 'And then by justice we were straight
condemn'd,/Each of us came unto a shamelesse end' (11, 165–6). 'Shamelesse'
here is unexpected – appropriate to their (impudent) behaviour, perhaps,
but not to their (disgraceful) execution. On a reading of the word obsolete
since the fifteenth century, 'shameless' could mean 'free from disgrace'

(*OED*, 3). Perhaps a parapraxis betrays the unconscious of the text, a world well lost for love, and Alice Arden heroic on the scaffold, exposing herself to death through death.

However that may be, these repeated reinterpretations of the events, reproblematizations of the murder, may be read as so many attempts to elicit a definitive meaning for Alice Arden's crime. In each case this definitive meaning remains elusive, in the sense that each text contains elements not accounted for in its overall project. What is at stake in these contests for the meaning of the murder is marriage itself

Murderous women

The existing historical evidence gives no reason to believe that there was a major outbreak of women murdering their husbands in the sixteenth century. What it does suggest, however, is a widespread belief that they were likely to do so. The Essex county records for the Elizabethan period, for instance, reveal no convictions for this crime, but they list several cases of frightened husbands seeking the protection of the courts. In 1574 a Barnston man complained that his wife, 'forgetting her duty and obedience as a wife, had sundry times maliciously attempted to bereave her husband of his life, so that he stand in great fear' both of her and of two men from Dunmow, her 'adherents', who haunted his house at night. In 1590 a man called Philpott complained that John Chandler, then living with Philpott's wife, had given his consent to Philpott's death, and Rowland Gryffyth deposed that he had been hired to carry out the murder. The records of the ecclesiastical courts in the same county include two cases, both in 1597, of men who refused to live with their wives for fear that they would be murdered by them.

When the crime was actually committed, it seems that notoriety instantly followed. In 1573 Anne Sanders (or Saunders) consented to the murder of her husband, a London merchant, by her lover, George Browne. The case rapidly became as widely known as the Arden murder. It was recorded by Arthur Golding in a pamphlet published in the same year and again in 1577; it was probably the subject of an anonymous pamphlet called 'A Cruell Murder Donne in Kent' published in 1577; the story was told by Holinshed and Stow again; and it was recounted by Antony Munday in *A View of Sundry Examples* (1580). Like the Arden case, the Sanders murder elicited a play, *A Warning for Fair Women* (*c.* 1590), and a ballad, 'The wofull lamentacon of Mrs Anne Saunders, which she wrote with her own hand, being prisoner in Newgate, justly condemned to death'. In the ballad Anne Sanders begs all women to be warned by her example; the play, unable to account in any other terms for so scandalous a crime, shows Anne, in an allegorical dumb show instigated by the furies, suddenly torn between chastity and lust, then pledging herself to Browne in a ceremony which evokes the 'sacrament prophane in mistery of wine' between Paridell and the adulterous Hellenore in *The Faerie Queene* (III, ix, 30).

In 1591 Mistress Page of Plymouth was executed with her lover and two other men for the murder of her husband. A ballad by Thomas Deloney appeared at once, recording 'The lamentation of Mr Pages wife of Plimouth, who, being forc'd to wed him, consented to his murder, for the love of G. Strangwidge'. Here the ambivalences implicit in the Arden narratives are foregrounded to produce a radical contradiction between sympathy and condemnation. The ballad gives a graphic account of the miseries of enforced marriage:

My closen eies could not his sight abide;
My tender youth did lothe his aged side;
Scant could I taste the meate whereon he fed;
My legges did lothe to lodge within his bed.

At the same time,

Methinkes the heavens crie vengeance for my fact,
Methinkes the world condemns my monstrous act,
Methinkes within my conscience tells me true,
That for that deede hell fier is my due.

In the circumstances it is particularly regrettable that *Page of Plymouth* by Jonson and Dekker, performed by the Admiral's Men in 1599, is now lost, as is *The History of Friar Francis*, produced, according to Henslowe's diary, in 1593/4, though not necessarily for the first time. According to Heywood in 1612, when *The History of Friar Francis* was performed at King's Lynn it had the gratifying effect of inducing an apparently respectable woman in the audience to confess that seven years earlier she had poisoned her husband for love of a gentleman in precisely the same way as the protagonist of the play. Heywood is here writing in defence of the moral efficacy of stage plays, and it is worth noting that of the three instances he cites of the providential operation of the drama, two concern women murdering their husbands. In the second case it was the method of murder shown on the stage which caused 'a woman of great gravity' to shriek loudly, and after several days of torment to confess that she had driven a nail into the temples of her husband twelve years before. She was duly tried, condemned and burned.

The control of marriage

According to John Taylor, writing in 1621, 'Arden of Feversham, and Page of Plimmouth, both their murders are fresh in memory, and the fearfull ends of their wives and their ayders in those bloudy actions will never be forgotten'. This was seventy years after Alice Arden's crime. The prominence allotted to these cases, the suspicion which seems to have been prevalent in Essex in the period, and Heywood's instances of the salutory effects of stage plays in bringing such crimes to light, all point to a preoccupation with the possibility of women murdering their husbands which is not accounted for in any of the individual texts. In *Arden of Faversham* Alice Arden defines her problem specifically in terms of the institutional regulation of sexuality by marriage:

> nothing could enforce me to the deed
> But Mosby's love. Might I without control
> Enjoy thee still, then Arden should not die;
> But, seeing I cannot, therefore let him die.

(I, 273–6)

It is a contest for the control of sexuality in the period which throws marriage into crisis and precipitates the instability of the institution that is evident in crimes like Alice Arden's.

The history of marriage in the Middle Ages is a history of an effort to regulate sexuality by confining it within a framework of permanent monogamy. From the twelfth century onwards the Church gradually extended its control over marriage, making efforts to contain instances of divorce and bigamy by urging with increasing insistence the public solemnization of matrimony after due reading of the banns on consecutive Sundays. Since at the same time private marriage in the presence of witnesses was held to be valid and binding, it was easy enough to produce just cause or impediment after the event. The banns were no guarantee against bigamy, since they were easily evaded by those who had anything to fear. In consequence, the process of taking control was slow and laborious, so that in 1540 it was still the case that bigamy was widespread, and that 'no mariage coulde be so surely knytt and bounden but it shulde lye in either of the parties power and arbitre ... to prove a precontracte a kynnerede an alliance or a carnall knowledge to defeate the same'. Many of the cases which came before the ecclesiastical courts depended on such ingenuities, but Michael M. Sheehan finds, after investigating the late fourteenth-century register of the consistory court of the Bishop of Ely, that there at least 'the court was primarily a body for the proof and defence of marriage rather than an instrument of easy annulment'. The commitment of the court to the stability of marriage above all other considerations may be illustrated by one of the cases Sheehan cites. The marriage between John Poynant and Joan Swan was annulled on the grounds of the husband's impotence. Joan married again, and John took up with Isabel Pybbel. When Isabel became pregnant John prepared to marry her, but the court investigated the matter and found that, since John was apparently not impotent after all, his marriage to Joan Swan should be restored. John protested, claiming affinity within the forbidden degrees between Joan and Isabel, but the court was not impressed, and the original marriage was eventually reinstated.

The Anglican church took over on behalf of the sovereign this effort to control the institution of marriage through the ecclesiastical courts, but not without a struggle which generated a high degree of uncertainty about the nature and permanence of marriage. The introduction of registers of births, marriages and deaths in 1539 was a move towards central control of the population, but at the same time the Reformation introduced a liberalization of marriage which found a focus in a debate about divorce that remained legally unresolved, apart from a brief interlude during the commonwealth, until the nineteenth century.

The Catholic church had permitted separation *a mensa et thoro* (from bed and board) for adultery, cruelty, apostasy or heresy, and divorce *a vinculo matrimonii* on the basis of impotence or of a prior impediment to valid marriage on grounds of consanguinity, affinity or precontract. The act of 1540 attempted to abolish precontract as grounds for divorce, but had no practical effect. Meanwhile, most of the newly Protestant states had introduced divorce with remarriage for the innocent party in cases of adultery and desertion. Similar legislation was urged in England, and was incorporated in the *Reformatio Legum Ecclesiasticarum* of 1552. This was defeated in the House of Commons, but the divorce provision had been sanctioned independently, when a commission under Cranmer had approved the remarriage of the divorced Northampton in 1548, and this was confirmed by parliament in 1552. In practice, however, the ecclesiastical courts largely refused to put the law into operation, and in consequence the position of marriage remained extremely confused and controversial for the rest of the century. The divorce debate reached a high point in the 1590s, with the result that in the Canons of 1597 convocation declared all remarriage after divorce illegal. These were not sanctioned by Elizabeth, but the principle was reiterated in the Canons of 1604 which were approved by James I, though without silencing the controversy.

The divorce debate polarized already conflicting definitions of marriage. Broadly, the Anglican and absolutist position was that marriage was indissoluble, that couples were joined by God for the avoidance of fornication and the procreation of children, and there was no remedy but patience for marital disharmony and discontent. The liberal position of the Puritans is familiar from Milton's divorce tracts, which carry the radical

Protestant arguments to their logical climax. Equally broadly, the Puritans
defined marriage as a civil covenant, a thing indifferent to salvation. It
depended on consent, and where this was lacking the couple could not be
said to be joined by God, and could therefore justly be put asunder. The
Reformers varied in the causes of divorce they were prepared to admit.
Only Milton gave real prominence to discord as a cause, while Henry Smith,
at the other extreme though still within the pro-divorce lobby, recognized
divorce for adultery but vigorously repudiated incompatibility as grounds:

> If they might bee separated for discorde, some would make a commoditie
> of strife; but now they are not best to be contentious, for this lawe will
> hold their noses together, till wearines make them leave struggling, like
> two spaniels which are coupled in a chaine, at last they learne to goe
> together, because they may not goe asunder.

Not all the Reformers were so optimistic about the couple learning to go
together. According to Martin Bucer, whose *De Regno Christi* was addressed
to Edward VI when the author was Professor of Divinity at Cambridge, the
Church's refusal to permit divorce compelled it to tolerate 'whordoms and
adulteries, and worse things then these', 'throwing men headlong into
these evils'. 'Neither', he argued, 'can God approve that to the violation of
this holy league (which is violated as soon as true affection ceases and is
lost,) should be added murder'. John Rainolds, writing in 1597, insists that
if divorce is forbidden, crimes like Alice Arden's are bound to follow: a
husband may be forced to live in permanent suspicion, or worse : 'And
how can he choose but live still in feare and anguish of minde, least shee add
drunckennesse to thirst, and murder to adultery: I meane least she serve him
as Clytemnestra did Agamemnon, as Livia did Drusus, as Mrs Arden did
her husband?'

There is some evidence for the bitterness of the struggle. John Dove, who
preached a sermon against divorce in 1601, records that many people found
his view offensive, 'as unseasonable for the time, and unpleasing to the
auditory'. Rainolds wrote his plea for divorce in 1597, but explains in a letter
to Pye published in 1606 that the Archbishop of Canterbury at that time
'thought it not meete to be printed: as containing dangerous doctrine'. He
urges Pye to cut out any references to him (Rainolds) in his own argument if
he wants to get into print, especially since the Canons of 1604 have hardened
the orthodox line. Rainolds's own *Defence of the Judgment of the Reformed
Churches* was published in 1609. The Archbishop's censorship seems to have
been even-handed, since at about the same time he also discouraged
Edmund Bunny from publishing his case against divorce – in order to avoid
controversy, on the grounds that he had already 'staied' one of the contrary
persuasion. Bunny's book appeared in 1610. Later William Whately argued
for divorce on grounds of desertion as well as adultery in books published in

1617 and 1624. Whately was brought before the Court of High Commission, and promptly reverted to the Anglican doctrine of the indissolubility of marriage. Even between the liberals there was considerable sectarianism on this issue. Milton, of course, encountered a good deal of controversy, and was denounced by his fellow-Puritans for his divorce pamphlets. And at the very beginning of the debate an interesting piece of sleight of hand shows how delicate the whole issue must have been. In 1541 Miles Coverdale's translation of Bullinger's treatise on marriage was published as *The Christen State of Matrimonye*. Primarily a plea for marriage as a union of minds, and a corresponding repudiation of the Catholic doctrine of celibacy as a way of perfection, this included a chapter recommending divorce not only for adultery but also for 'lyke and greater occasions'. *The Christen State of Matrimonye* was remarkably popular. Three new editions appeared within five years, and two more before the end of the century. Meanwhile, in 1542 there appeared *The Golden Boke of Christen Matrimonye* 'newly set forth in English by Theodore Basille'. 'Theodore Basille' was Thomas Becon, and *The Golden Boke* was actually Coverdale's translation of Bullinger again with four chapters silently erased, including the one on divorce.

The contest for the meaning of marriage cannot be isolated from the political struggles which characterize the century between the Reformation and the Revolution. Both sides make explicit the parallel between the family and the state, marriage and the monarchy. 'A householde is as it were a little commonwealth'. 'A familie, is a naturall and simple society of certaine persons, having mutuall relation one to another, under the private government of one'. At one extreme Milton argues for liberty within marriage as directly analogous to liberty in the commonwealth:

> He who marries, intends as little to conspire his own ruine, as he that swears allegiance: and as a whole people is in proportion to an ill government, so is one man to an ill mariage. If they against any authority, covnant, or statute, may by the soveraign edict of charity, save not only their lives, but honest liberties from unworthy bondage, as well may he against any private covnant, which hee never enter'd to his mischief, redeem himself from unsupportable disturbances to honest peace, and just contentment.

And if this position was not made explicit in the radical treatises before 1642, nonetheless it was identified by Anglican orthodoxy as implicit in the Puritan arguments. According to Bunny, divorce can lead only to 'disorder'. Marriage cannot be dissolved at will any more than can the bond between master and servant, parent and child, 'the prince and the subject'. And for this reason, 'the more heed should bee taken, that no such gap should be opened to any, as wherby the looser sort, when they should get their desire in this, should cast about to obtaine the like in other things also of greater consequence'. Dove, whose name entirely belies his political position, argues strenuously that, 'As when a servant runneth from his master the chaine of bondage doth pursue him, and bring him backe againe to his maister, so when a woman leaveth her husband, the lawe of matrimony is as a chaine to draw her back againe to her husband'. The libertines who believe in divorce pervert the scriptures for their own licentious ends, 'Even as others will proove rebellion and high treason out of the scriptures, that the people are above their King'. The parallel between domestic patriarchy and absolute monarchy is a commonplace of the seventeenth century, and reaches its most notorious formulation, of course, in Robert Filmer's *Patriarcha*.

Alice Arden, held in the chain of bondage which is marriage, in a period when liberty is glimpsed but not authorized, is caught up in a struggle larger than her chroniclers recognize. But it may be the political significance of Arden's assassination which causes Holinshed to identify Alice Arden's crime as marking the border between private and public, pamphlet and history.

The new family

There is an indication in *Arden of Faversham* that in opting for Mosby in place of Arden, a freely chosen sexuality based on concord in place of the constraints of the institution of permanent marriage, Alice Arden may be committing herself to a form of power more deadly still, and less visible. Mosby's individualism is precisely that:

> Yet Mistress Arden lives; but she's myself,
> And holy church rites makes us two but one.
> But what for that I may not trust you, Alice?
> You have supplanted Arden for my sake
> And will extirpen me to plant another.
> 'Tis fearful sleeping in a serpent's bed,
> And I will cleanly rid my hands of her.
> But here she comes, and I must flatter her ...

(VIII, 37–44)

The episode could be read as an allegory of the transition to the liberal-humanist family, itself a mechanism of regulation more far-reaching but less visible than the repressive ecclesiastical courts. Arden's absolute rights over Alice are clear, and his threats are directed not against his wife but against the man who means to rob him of her, for which he

Shall on the bed which he thinks to defile
See his dissevered joints and sinews torn
Whilst on the planchers pants his weary body,
Smeared in the channels of his lustful blood.

(I, 40 – 3)

This overt power and violence give way in Mosby's version of marriage to distrust and surveillance veiled by flattery; in an individualist society of 'equals' absolutist modes of control are replaced by reciprocal fear between partners within the social body. Further, flattery and death are the metaphorical destiny of the wife in the new family. Her standing improves (though always in subjection to her husband) but at the cost of new and more insidious forms of control.

Liberal marriage, founded on consent, is 'appointed by God himselfe, to be the fountaine and seminary of all sorts and kinds of life, in the commonwealth and in the church'. To this end the family becomes quite explicitly an ideological apparatus, 'a schoole wherein the first principles and grounds of government and subjection are learned: whereby men are fitted to greater matters in church or commonwealth'. In Puritan definitions of marriage and the family as 'the fountain and seminary of good subjects', it is made very clear that 'the holy and righteous government thereof, is a direct meane for the good ordering both of church and commonwealth; yea that the lawes thereof beeing rightly informed, and religiously observed, are availeable to prepare and dispose men to the keeping of order in other governments'. To ensure that the family becomes an adequate model and source of good government, the treatises recommend family prayers, grace before meals, keeping the sabbath, the education of the children and the servants, and the inculcation of the fundamental principles of law and order. The family, separated from the public realm of politics, none the less becomes a microcosm of it and, by practice and by precept, a training ground for the ready acceptance of the power relations established in the social body:

For this first societie is as it were the schoole, wherein are taught and learned the principles of authoritie and subjection. And looke as the superiour that faileth in his charge, will proove uncapable of publike imployment, so the inferiour, who is not framed to a course of oeconomicall subjection, wil hardly undergoe the yoake of civill obedience.

The liberalism of the Reformers implies a constant scrutiny of marriage for fitness of mind and disposition, since harmony and concord are the precondition of a realm of hearth and home regulated from within. Vigilantly protected from sedition, and isolated from public and political affairs, the family is held in place in the social body as a model of the proper distribution of authority and submission, and thus the fountain and seminary of good subjects.

Read as an event which troubled the politics of the state, Alice Arden's crime was a defiance of absolutism and, in common with the constant reproblematization of such crimes in the period, as well as the great numbers of divorces established in the sixteenth century without recourse to the civil or ecclesiastical authorities, it constitutes evidence of the instability of central control at the time. It is this which accounts for the repeated attempts to define and redefine the crime, and which explains why it was so important and so impossible to furnish it with a final meaning. The assassination of Arden is never justified, but it is variously identified as a part of God's providential plan, as a tragedy, as the effect of social and economic change, or as an act of unauthorized heroism, a noble transgression of an absolute law. The representations of the crime are (sometimes contradictory, never neutral) contributions to a discursive struggle for the meaning of resistance to absolutism.

Read as an episode which troubled the politics of gender, Alice Arden's crime throws into relief a corresponding instability in the meaning of the family. The divorce debate, reaching a crisis in the 1590s, the decade which also produced three plays about women murdering their husbands, is the site of a discursive contest between distinct meanings of marriage. Offering a promise of freedom from the 'chain' (recurring metaphor for absolutism) of marriage, the liberal position on divorce leads in reality to a new mode of control, no longer centralized and overt, but internalized and invisible. The new family of the seventeenth century, still under 'the government of one', remains a place in which power is exercised privately in the interests of public order. Alice Arden's bid for freedom, as the play implies, would have led, had it succeeded, to a new form of subjection, both for the woman within the family and for the family within the state. No text of the 1590s could formulate this point in these terms. Indeed, the explicit identification of the family as a mechanism of social control probably has its tentative beginnings in the nineteenth century. None the less, Mosby's threat that he will subject Alice to surveillance, flattery and death indicates a glimpse in this text of an issue which is more complex than the simple opposition between authority and freedom, control and consent.

Women are defined by their difference from men, and the central place of this difference has been the reproductive process. Alice Arden's crime drew attention to the problem of Alice Arden's sexuality, and of the institution which had failed to hold it in place. For this reason too it was both important and impossible to furnish it with a final explanation. To defy the meaning of marriage is to reopen the question of the implications of sexual difference and thus the meaning of what it is to be a woman. Perhaps ultimately this above all was Alice Arden's crime.

8 Shakespeare's Roman Carnival*

RICHARD WILSON

If New Historicism followed Foucault in seeing power as monolithic, **Cultural Materialism** responded that the dominant do not control the whole of culture, or even their own cultural forms. This is clear in the case of English Renaissance drama, which dates from a period when art was beginning to separate from popular culture, but when the playhouse still depended on the **carnival** tradition for its licensing. Shakespeare's theatre was a scene of scrimmage between conflicting **discourses,** and Richard Wilson's essay examines this instability in the instance of *Julius Caesar,* perhaps the first production of the Globe. Out of its own determinants, as an institution on the **margin** of the city, like the prison or hospital, the playhouse produced a blueprint for the control of English culture in a time of revolution. The play shows that access to the places where **discourses** are made is all-important; but it cannot then efface the violence which went into its own making, any more than the Globe could expel the London apprentices. This is a reading of Shakespearean **carnival** which differs from that of American New Historicists, in insisting that if the rules of the cultural game do shape struggle, they are made to be broken by social **agency**, like those of Shrovetide football.

Julius Caesar was the first Shakespearean play we know to have been acted at the Globe and was perhaps performed for the opening of the new Bankside playhouse in 1599. The Swiss tourist Thomas Platter saw it on 21st September, and his impressions locate the work within the different cultural practices that went to make the playhouse. To our minds, accustomed to a decorous image of both Shakespeare and ancient Rome, it is just this collision of codes and voices which makes the traveller's report seem so jarring and bizarre:

*Reprinted from *ELH* (*English Literary History*), 54, 1 (Spring 1987), pp. 31–44.

> After lunch, at about two o'clock, I and my party crossed the river, and there in the house with the thatched roof we saw an excellent performance of the tragedy of the first emperor, Julius Caesar, with about fifteen characters; and after the play, according to their custom, they did a most elegant and curious dance, two dressed in men's clothes and two in women's.

Along with the chimney-pots, feather hats and chiming clocks in the play itself, we can absorb the shock of 'the house with the thatched roof', but the elegant jig of Caesar and the boy dressed as Caesar's wife is too alienating a mixture for us of the 'merry and tragical'. Even the Swiss visitor thought it a curious local custom, and he was lucky to see it, because by 1612 'all Jigs, Rhymes and Dances after Plays' had been 'utterly abolished', to prevent the 'tumults and outrages whereby His Majesty's peace is often broke', alleged to be caused by the 'cut-purses and other lewd and ill-disposed persons' who were attracted by them into the auditorium in droves at the close of each performance. Platter was an observer of a theatre already expelling gatecrashers and purging itself of the popular customs that had legitimized their unwelcome intrusion. He was witnessing what Francis Barker admits were 'the seeds of an incipient naturalism growing up' inside the Elizabethan theatre, and the inauguration of a new kind of drama in England, where clowns would learn to 'speak no more than is set down for them', and laughter – as Hamlet prescribes – would be conditional on the 'necessary question of the play' (Barker 1984, p.18). Authority in this theatre would come to be concentrated in 'the speech' written in what Hamlet proprietorially tells the players are 'my lines' (*Hamlet* ed. H.Jenkins [London 1982], III, ii 1–45), and the mastery of the author as producer would be founded on the suppression of just those practices which Platter thought so picturesque: the unwritten scenario of the mummers' dance, transvestite mockery, Dick Tarlton's 'villainous' comic improvisation, and the raucous collective gesture of disrespect for 'His Majesty's peace'. Elite and popular traditions coexist in embarrassed tension in Platter's travel diary, where the excellence of the classical tragedy consorts so oddly with the curiosity of the antic hay. The diarist did not realize, of course, that the sequence he recorded represented the scission between two cultures and for one of them the literal final fling, nor that 'the house with the thatched roof' was the scene, even as he applauded the performance, of bitter social separation.

The opening words of *Julius Caesar* seem to know themselves, nevertheless, as a declaration of company policy towards the theatre audience. They are addressed by the Roman Tribune Flavius to 'certain Commoners' who have entered 'over the stage', and they are a rebuke to their temerity: 'Hence! home, you idle creatures, get you home/Is this a holiday?' Dressed in their festive best apparel these 'mechanical' men have mistaken the occasion for a' holiday', and to the rhetorical question 'Is this a holiday?' they are now given the firm answer that for them, at least, it is an ordinary 'labouring day' (I,i, 1–60). This is an encounter, then, that situates what follows explicitly within the contemporary debate about the value or 'idleness ' of popular culture, a debate in which, as Christopher Hill has written, 'two modes of life, with their different needs and standards, are in conflict as England moves out of the agricultural Middle Ages into the modern industrial world' (Hill 1986, p.163). And as Flavius and his colleague Marullus order the plebeians back to work, it is a confrontation that confirms Hill's thesis that the Puritan attack on popular festivity was a strategy to control the emerging manufacturing workforce. The Tribunes oppose 'holiday' because it blurs distinctions between the 'industrious' and the 'idle', just as their counterparts the London Aldermen complained the theatres lured 'the prentices and servants of the City from their works'. In fact, the Tribunes' speeches echo *The Anatomy of Abuses* (1583) by the merchants' censor Philip Stubbes, and in so doing the actors of the Globe were disarming one of the most powerful, because pragmatic, objections to their trade. As Thomas Nashe protested when the first playhouse was opened on the South Bank in 1592, professional players were not to be confused with 'squirting bawdy comedians'; they were distinct from 'the pantaloon, whore and zany' of street theatre. Their patrons were 'Gentlemen of the Court, and the Inns of Court, and captains and soldiers' (a clientele corroborated by the 1602 police raid on the playhouses), and the citizens could rest assured that 'they heartily wish they might be troubled with none of their youth nor their prentices'. So theatre- owners such as Philip Henslowe were careful to obey the ban on 'interludes and plays on the Sabbath', closing their doors on city workers (as James I complained) on the only afternoon when they were regularly free. If working men were present to hear the beginning of *Julius Caesar* and stayed despite it, the implication is clear that they had no business to be there. Theatre, we infer, is now itself a legitimate business with no room for the 'idle'.

The first scene acted at the Globe can be interpreted, then, as a manoeuvre in the campaign to legitimize the Shakespearean stage and dissociate it from the subversiveness of artisanal culture. As historians such as Peter Burke have demonstrated, revelry and rebellion were entangled in Renaissance popular entertainments, and it was no coincidence that insurrections such as the Peasants' Revolts of 1381 and 1450, the Evil May Day riot of 1517, or Kett's Rebellion of 1549 should have been sparked off at seasonal plays or have had vivid carnivalesque features. The juridical function of folk drama had been to cement the ties and obligations of an agrarian community, and when these were threatened in the transition to capitalist social relations, it was through the 'rough music' of folk customs

– mummings, wakes and charivaris – that the new masters were called to ritual account. The world of carnival, with its travesty and inversion, was a standing pretext for protest; but if, as happened increasingly in the early modern period, rulers chose to ignore the 'wild justice' of festivity, there could be what Burke calls 'a 'switching' of codes, from the language of ritual to the language of rebellion', when 'the wine barrel blew its top' (Burke 1978, p. 203). This is what happened spectacularly in the bloody Carnival at Romans in 1580, and it was what happened less explosively in London during the crisis years of the 1590s, when hunger and unemployment drove 'disordered people of the common sort' (in the Aldermanic phrase) 'to assemble themselves and make matches for their lewd ungodly practices' at Shrovetide, May Day or Midsummer: festivals when, like the workers in *Julius Caesar,* they could still 'cull out a holiday' from the industrial week. Associating all revels with rebellion, the authorities were instinctively sure that riotous 'apprentices and servants drew their infection' from the playhouses where people also caught the plague; but, as Nashe insisted, this analogy was a kind of category mistake, which miscalculated the new theatres' social role. If the playhouse was, as coroners reported, the site of 'frays and bloodshed', it was as the target of violence, not the origin, as when apprentices rampaged traditionally on Shrove Tuesday to 'put play houses to the sack and bawdy houses to the spoil' (in 1617 wrecking the Cockpit Theatre with the loss of several lives). The rough music of charivari was hollered in anger from outside the playhouse walls.

'The disorders of the 1590s were the most serious to menace the metropolis in the decades up to the Civil War', writes the urban historian Peter Clark in a recent essay, and what concerns him is how this unprecedented metropolitan crisis was contained (Clark 1985, p. 54). The answer must lie at least partly in the success with which the language of carnival as a discourse of legitimation was commandeered by the commercial players and then tamed. For as scenes like the opening of *Julius Caesar* remind us, and as history, in Foucault's words, 'constantly teaches us, discourse is not simply that which translates struggles or systems of domination, but is the thing for which struggle takes place' (Foucault 1981, p. 52). It was no mere evasion of authority, therefore, which led to the theatre being situated on the criminalized southern bank of the Thames, where Platter and his party rowed to unbrace and recreate themselves after lunch. In the complex zoning of the metropolis that dates precisely from this time, Southwark was to occupy the position of the policed and segregated annexe to the business and residential districts on the river's northern side. Within its licensed liberties, the Bankside was to have the status of a permanent but strictly circumscribed carnival in the city's economy of repression and indulgence, a disposal-valve in its regulation of productivity and waste. Suspect and sinistral, until the final suppression of Hogarth's Southwark Fair in 1762, the South Bank was to function as the unconscious of the capital of trade. Nor, in this geography of desire, was it accidental that the Globe was built beside those very institutions that, in Foucault's analysis, shaped the discourses of modern subjectivity. Ringed by reconstructed prisons such as The Marshalsea and The Clink, and flanked by the newly refounded St Thomas's Hospital, the playhouse meshed with a chain of buildings charged with those dividing practices whereby the productive subject was defined by isolation from its negative in the sick, the mad, the aged, the criminal, the bankrupt, and the unemployed: separated, as Flavius urges and the 1569 Charter of St Thomas's decreed, from 'all Idle, Begging people'. The wooden operating theatre of St Thomas's survives as the celebrated arena where the body was cut into diseased and healthy parts. The 'Wooden O' of the Globe next door, which must have resembled it in design so much, operated in analogous ways on the body politic to divide and control the visceral language of carnival, separating out productive revelry (or art) from the idleness and infection of rebellion.

If Thomas Platter was a naive theatre critic, as a sociologist he was shrewder. 'England', he observed, 'is the servants' prison, because their masters and mistresses are so severe.' The foreign visitor could see what has been confirmed in detail by Lee Beier in his study of masterless men and the vagrancy problem in Shakespearean England, that the public order system which Foucault dated from the founding of the Paris General Hospital in 1656 was already being established in London by 1599 (Beier 1985, p.164). It was a system based, however, less on crude severity than on the strategy of self-regimentation and surveillance which Brutus proposes in *Julius Caesar* when he argues for a controlled and strictly rational rebellion:

> And let our hearts, as subtle masters do,
> Stir up their servants to an act of rage,
> And after seem to chide 'em. This shall make
> Our purpose necessary, and not envious.

(II,i, 175–8)

The Shakespearean text belongs to a historical moment when a revolutionary bourgeois politics has not naturalized its own productive processes, and Brutus's *realpolitik* is a complete statement of the technique of the modern state whereby subversion is produced in both consciousness and society to legitimize the order that subjects it. Unruly passions and apprentices are both checked in this regime, as Hal also demonstrates in his career as *agent provocateur* in Eastcheap, by being known and hated: incited to be rejected. This is a system of discipline whose subtlety, as Brutus recognizes, depends not on how it obstructs but on how it manipulates desire, so that sexuality, for example, will no longer be so much forbidden as the very ground through which power controls the community and the individual. And it is just this 'subtle, calculated technology of subjection', as analysed by Foucault, operating in the new factory, hospital or school of Elizabethan London, which surely explains why Bakhtin says so little in his work on the subversiveness of carnival about either Shakespeare or England (Foucault 1977, p.221). His ideas were recently applied to Elizabethan drama by Michael Bristol, who argues for what he terms the 'carnivalization' of Shakespearean literature. The argument is not convincing because, as Umberto Eco has remarked, what Bakhtinians crucially forget in their idealization of carnival is precisely the revenge of Lent: that is to say, the confinement of desire within a dialectic of transgression and containment. If carnival were always so emancipatory, Eco adds, 'it would be impossible to explain why power uses circuses' (Eco 1984, p.3).

The conditions of modern subjectivity are inscribed within the Shakespearean text. Thus, when Portia tries to persuade her husband to share 'the secrets of [his] heart' by divulging the plot she calls the 'sick offence within your mind', she challenges him: 'Dwell I but in the suburbs/Of your good pleasure? If it be no more,/Portia is Brutus' harlot' (II,i, 268–306). Body, language and thought are all held in ideological subjection in the bourgeois order Brutus represents, but when he succumbs to Portia's emotional blackmail he destroys himself by failing to quarantine desire in the suburbs of his self, where it should have been confined like the brothels of the Bankside. In *Julius Caesar* carnival – the language of desire and the flesh – is a discourse that is always mastered by the dominant. Thus, the opening scenes take place on the Roman 'feast of Lupercal': 14th February, St Valentine's Day and the approximate date of *Mardi Gras*. So Shakespeare's revelling artisans connect with those 'bands of prentices, 3,000 or 4,000 strong, who on Shrove Tuesday do outrages in all directions, especially in the suburbs', in contemporary accounts, and whose Kingdoms and Abbeys of Misrule have been researched, in their European manifestations, by Natalie Zemon Davis (Davis 1975). In the play their carnival ceremonies have been appropriated by Caesar to legitimize his intended coronation. Antony therefore runs in the 'holy chase' to 'touch' Calpurnia for fertility (I,ii, 7–8), while Caesar himself performs in the Shroving game by pretending to give 'the rabblement' the freedom that they shout for. This would be the tactic of King James's *Book of Sports* (1618), of royalist propagandists such as Herrick, and ultimately of the Restoration, when (contrary to Bakhtin's thesis) the rituals 'of May-poles, Hock-carts, Wassails, Wakes' could be harnessed to the legitimation of a programme of social conservatism. It belongs to the world of what Hill calls 'synthetic monarchy', of Elizabeth's Accession Day anniversary and the Stuart revival of 'touching' (Hill 1975, p.353). And by this appropriation of the discourse of festival Caesar turns politics into theatre as 'the tag-rag people clap and hiss him, according as he pleas'd and displeas'd them, as they do the players' (I,ii, 255). He is the Carnival King, a Lord of Misrule who governs by exploiting his subjects' desires with his 'foolery' (I,ii, 232), manipulating 'fat,/Sleek-headed men' (I,ii, 190), as he indulges Antony in plays and music when he 'revels long a'nights' (II,i, 116). Provoking them 'to sports, to wildness, and much company' (II,i, 189), Caesar is the master of revels who knows that 'danger' belongs to the 'lean and hungry' who can discipline the body to their purposes. So his Roman carnival becomes a model of authoritarian populism, the true regimen of bread and circuses.

According to Anne Barton the theatre image in *Julius Caesar* is uniquely positive and 'the actors are no longer shadowy figures: they are the creators of history' (Barton 1967, p.141). This may be true, but it over simplifies the process that the play rehearses whereby discourses, which are the means of struggle, are themselves shaped by that struggle as it unfolds. It unfolds in the Shakespearean text like carnival itself, as a masquerade in which successive ideologies which had seemed to be authoritative are 'discovered' and discarded as power is displaced. On *Mardi Gras* the aim is to see without being seen behind the carnival mask; and here the eye of power strips the mask of discourse from its antagonist, revealing – as Cassius demonstrates with his satirical broadsheets 'wherein Caesar's ambition shall be glanced at' – the naked drives discursive practices hide (I,ii, 315). Thus the plebeians who are masterless in their holiday guise are exposed by the Tribune's Puritan analysis as Caesar's 'idle creatures'; but Puritan discourse is itself 'put to silence' when it tries to 'pull the scarfs' from Caesar's images (I,ii, 282). That demystification belongs to the knives of the aristocratic fraction, whose mask of constitutionalism – with its common law reverence for ancient custom and contempt for the absolutist yoke – is worn 'like Roman actors do' (II,i, 226), until Antony seizes the pulpit/stage in turn and reveals the carnivorous butchery their Lenten rhetoric conceals. This is the radical potentiality of Renaissance tragedy that Jonathan Dollimore (Dollimore 1984) and others would mobilize as a critical weapon: the revelry with which one discourse decodes the authority of another, as Antony deconstructs the discursivity of the 'honourable men' (III,ii, 120–230). With 'their hats pluck'd about their ears,/And half their faces buried in their cloaks' (II,i, 73–4) or masked by handkerchiefs (II,i, 315), the plotters who meet in Pompey's theatre assume the anonymity of carnival and arrogate its dispensation to kill a scapegoat in their coup against Caesar, just as the real rebels of the Dutch Revolt had started their uprising against the Spanish governor at Carnival in 1563 dressed in motley and jester's cap and bells. In the Renaissance, as Stephen Greenblatt contends, 'theatricality is one of power's essential modes' (Greenblatt 1985, p.33); so when their 'antic disposition' is ripped from these revellers, it is fittingly by the consummate theatricality and power of speech of a champion gamesman and seasoned masker. 'A masque is treason's licence' in Jacobean drama, but the incremental logic of this revelry will be to strip all power, including that of rebels, of its legitimacy, exposing the face of bare ambition beneath the 'veil'd look' (I,ii, 36) of rites and ceremonies (III,i, 241).

The Carnival at Romans in 1580 described by Emmanuel Le Roy Ladurie provides a paradigm of Renaissance festival as a 'psychological drama or ballet' whose players danced or acted out class struggle through the 'symbolic grammar' of processions and masquerades. There the poor had celebrated a mock funeral of the rich whose flesh they pretended to eat on *Mardi Gras*, until the law and order party had organized a massacre in retaliation, arraying themselves for the ambush in carnival costume and carrying carnival torches (Ladurie 1981, pp. 192–215). The Roman carnival in *Julius Caesar* follows a similar timetable and pattern through the cannibalistic feast of Caesar's assassination and the mock-trial of the conspirators at the funeral, to the counter revolution of a revanchist repression. In Shakespearean Rome, as in actual Romans, the symbolic discourse of public festival is a system whose social significance will be dictated by the strongest. Likewise, poems, plays, letters, music, names, dreams, prophecies, clouds, storms, stars, entrails and flights of birds are all discredited as 'idle ceremonies' (II,i, 197) in *Julius Caesar*, the random signifiers on which praxis enforces meaning. This is a deconstructive carnival that leads ineluctably to the burlesque textuality of Caesar's bloodstained 'vesture' as interpreted by Antony in the Forum through its gaps and 'wounded' tears, and finally, when the corpse is divested of even that last tattered shred of discursivity, to the exposure of Caesar's naked 'will': the 'bleeding piece of earth' which is metonymic of all desire and power (III,ii, 130–60). Twenty-seven times in thirty lines the favourite Shakespearean phallic pun is repeated through all its libidinous connotations as it is taken up by Antony and passed around the crowd, to substantiate in a riot of polysemy that at the point where text and body fuse, discourse and power are one. Caesar had offered his murderers wine on the Ides of March. Now his carved meat becomes with cannibalistic literalism the carnival sacrament of a festive fraternity of blood.

Power constructs its own discursivity in Shakespearean tragedy by appropriating the radical subversiveness of carnival, and a text such as *Julius Caesar* seems knowingly to meditate upon its participation in this process of sublimation and control. Thus, Caesar's will, which is his butchered flesh, is also by etymological extension his testament – his will power disseminated through his signed and written text – where the potency denied him in his sterile marriage and abortive reign is regenerated from his posthumous stimulation of the desires of the crowd he makes his heir. Where there's a will, in the modern state, there is also a way for power to make its own, and Caesarism works here through a system of licence and surveillance that exactly parallels the real dividing practices of Shakespearean London. Sequestered in the suburb of the city, desire can henceforth be partitioned and canalized in the interest of the governing group:

Antony	Moreover, he hath left you all his walks,
	His private arbours, and new-planted orchards,
	On this side Tiber: he hath left them you,
	And to your heirs for ever: common pleasures,
	To walk abroad and recreate yourselves.
	Here was a Caesar! When comes such another?
Plebeian	Never, never! Come away, away!
	We'll burn his body in the holy place,
	And with the brands fire the traitors' houses,
	Take up the body.

(III,ii, 249–58).

So the incendiary brands of carnival are transformed into instruments of counter-revolution (as in London the Corpus Christi and Midsummer cressets became the flambeaux for the Lord Mayor's Show and the stolen fire of Halloween illuminated the thanks-giving for Stuart deliverance from the Gunpowder Plot). Caesar's authoritarian paternalism deflects the *vox populi* towards the institution of the monarchy by the invigilation of the people's private desires. Likewise, the sexual licence of the Bankside funfair would prove the conduit through which power would recreate itself by the regulation of the public's common pleasures in the impending bourgeois age. The corpse exhibited by Antony stands in something of the same relation to the organization of modern subjectivity, therefore, as the exemplary cadaver in Rembrandt's picture of *The Anatomy Lesson of Dr Tulp* discussed by Francis Barker. It is the material ground, the 'earth' (III,i, 254), on which bourgeois ideology will proceed to write its own interpretation of society and human life, inscribing a discourse of reason and morality on a scene of lust and blood that 'else were a savage spectacle' (III,i, 223). This is quite literally how Antony uses the body for demonstration, when he effaces his own discursive practice in the interpellation of the members of the crowd as obedient subjects of the revived monarchic state:

For I have neither wit, nor words, nor worth,
Action, nor utterance, nor the power of speech
To stir men's blood; I only speak right on.
I tell you that which you yourselves do know,
Show you sweet Caesar's wounds, poor poor dumb mouths,
And bid them speak for me.

(III,ii, 223–8)

Like Tulp's dissection, Antony's anatomy lesson – to be repeated with the body of Brutus – reproduces the spectacular corporeality of the carnivalesque in the service of the new power of the disciplinary society, forcing the corpse to signify 'that which you yourselves do know' about what it is to say 'This was a man!' (V,v, 75). And as Antony turns desire in the mob to authoritarian ends, this is also the manouevre of the Shakespearean text, which reworks the ceremonies of an older kind of ritual – 'to execute, to dismember, to eat' – not simply to erase them but, as Barker notes of Rembrandt's painting, 'to take them over, to appropriate the ancient vengeful motifs and to rearticulate them for its own new purposes'. Text and picture belong to a moment, that is to say, when the bourgeoisie still has need of the energies of 'the earlier pageant of sacramental violence', and when its 'image fashions an aesthetic which is rationalistic, classical, realistic, but one to which the iconography of a previous mode of representation is not completely alien'. As Barker goes on to explain, 'if it continues to evoke the signs of a punitive corporeality', bourgeois representation 'also aims to draw off and reorganise the charge of these potent residues, and to invest them, transformed', in the name of the rational spirit of capitalism, 'which will soon free itself entirely from the old body, even if it trades at first on the mystique and the terror of that abandoned materiality' (Barker 1984, p.76). So Antony must yoke 'mischief' to his politics and 'let it work' for the restoration of the social status quo (III,ii, 262). By syphoning the subversiveness of popular festivity in the representation of a deflected and contained rebellion, the Shakespearean text anticipates the counter-revolution of the Cromwellian Commonwealth and faithfully enacts the coercive strategy of those subtle London masters who 'stir up servants to an act of rage' (II,i, 176) the better to control them. Located on the threshold of revolutionary upheaval, *Julius Caesar* is the image of bourgeois ascendency as 'necessary, and not envious' (II,i, 178), separated from popular or sectarian movements, and the natural issue of 'a general honest thought' – as Antony claims over the body of Brutus – 'and common good to all' (V,v, 71– 2).

Julius Caesar is the representation of a world turned upside-down to be restored, where citizens' houses are set alight by the mob in order that property values should be upheld. The question that it seems to address in this paradoxical operation is the one which would become, according to Christopher Hill, the critical dilemma of the Commonwealth, posed eventually by a pamphleteer of 1660: 'Can you at once suppress the sectaries and keep out the King?' (Hill 1975, p.347). Because it arises from a historical juncture when the English bourgeoisie was engaged in a reorganization of the absolutist state to effect this end, it is a text that discloses the materiality of power with self-important openness. In particular, this early Globe play reflects candidly on the process whereby hegemony is obtained through the control of discourse, a process in which the inauguration of the playhouse was itself a major intervention. Victory in *Julius Caesar* goes to those who administer and distribute the access to discourse, and the conspirators lose possession of the initiative in the action the moment that they concede Antony permission to 'speak in the order of [the] funeral' (III,i, 230–50). Inserting his own demagogic rhetoric into Brutus's idealistic scenario, Antony disrupts that order of discourse, rearranges the 'true rites and lawful ceremonies' (III,i, 241) of the republic to facilitate his counter-coup, and imposes his domination through the populist device of Caesar's will. Censorship, Barker insists, was 'a constitutive experience' in the seventeenth-century construction of both the bourgeois subject and the modern state, and one which predicated the very possibility of bourgeois enunciation. This text proclaims that fact when Antony revises the clauses of the will to finance his army, cuts off Cicero's Greek irony with the orator's 'silver hairs' (II,i, 1–10), and 'damns' his enemies 'with a spot' when 'their names are prick'd out' on his proscription list (IV,i, 1–10). The murder by the mob of the poet Cinna for his 'bad verses' (III,iii, 30) and mistaken name merely confirms what Cassius and Brutus learn to their cost, that power goes with those who command the materiality of signs (III,iii, 30–5). Tzvetan Todorov proposes that the Incas and Aztecs fell victim to the Spanish *conquistadors* because of their inferior system of signification, defeated, he believes, by Cortez's capacity to decipher their semiotic conduct whilst baffling them with his own (Todorov 1984). Likewise, the republicans fail in *Julius Caesar* when they lose control of signs. Quarrelling over the meaning of their correspondence and at cross- purposes in their reading of the 'signs of battle' (V,i, 14–24), Brutus and Cassius become deaf even to Homer's textual warning when they hear *The Iliad* read (IV,iii, 129–37), while the words of Caesar that the Romans record when they 'mark him and write his speeches in their books' (I,ii, 125) come back to haunt the assassins at the end in the form of the Ghost, which appears the instant Brutus finds 'the leaf turn'd down' in his book and opens it to read, presumably, the avenging text *'Veni, vidi, vici'* (IV,iii, 251–75). 'Words before blows' (V,i, 27) is the battle-order in this play, which rehearses the English Revolution by enacting the Gramscian doctrine that the iron fist is preceded by the velvet glove, and that power is first enthroned in pulpits, poetry and plays.

Carnival, *Julius Caesar* reminds us, was never a single, unitary discourse in the Renaissance, but a symbolic system over which continuous struggle to wrest its meaning was waged by competing ideologies. It is the pretence of the Shakespearean text, however, that the masquerade of false appearances comes to its end in bourgeois realism, as Antony closes the action and announces his domination when he discounts all 'objects, art and imitations' as 'out of use and stal'd by other men' (IV,i, 37–8), learning to separate the idleness of drama from the business of politics. Thus the rupture forced by holiday in history would be sealed during the course of the seventeenth century as the English bourgeoisie elided its own revolutionary past. To make this representation of tragic acquiescence possible, nonetheless, the playhouse had been made the bloody site of contestation between social groups. 'The Triumph of Lent' is what Peter Burke calls the seventeenth-century suppression of the carnivalesque 'World Turned Upside Down'. It was a triumph achieved only after many eruptions into the Shakespearean space of festive rout, and to grasp the operation of the new theatre as an institution of division it is only necessary to recall those intrusions from outside the enclosure of the 'Wooden O': interruptions like the episode at Shrewsbury in 1627 when the actors of the Globe were driven out of town in the middle of a performance by fairground revellers with flaming brands, or the one that recurred on Shrove Tuesday in the capital itself, according to reports, when players half-way through an 'excellent tragedy' were 'forc'd to undress and put off their tragic habits' by the holiday crowd, and made to

> conclude the day with *The Merry Milkmaids*. And unless this were done, and the popular humour satisfied (as sometimes it so fortun'd that the players were refractory), the benches, the tiles, the laths, the stones, oranges, apples, nuts, flew about most liberally; and as there were mechanics of all professions there upon these festivals, every one fell to his trade and dissolved the house in an instant, and that made the ruin of a stately fabric.

The floor of the new playhouse was not yet quite an arena which the dominant ideology could call its own, and excluded or enclosed the festive melee still found the means on occasion to deconstruct – or transvalue – the sign system of the imposing 'house with the thatched roof'.

9 Hamlet's Unfulfilled Interiority*

FRANCIS BARKER

New Historicism has tended, like Foucault, to spurn a psychoanalytic approach to Renaissance texts, because Freud's theory of the unconscious is held to be inappropriate to a culture in which modern **subjectivity** was inchoate. Francis Barker's book *The Tremulous Private Body* was an attempt to historicise the sense of an inner self by applying Jacques Lacan's updated Freudian psychoanalysis to texts such as *Hamlet*. In the extract Barker develops Lacan's bad French pun that Hamlet is an *hommelette*, rather than a fully-rounded *homme*, whose identity is a vacuum waiting to be filled with modern interiority. Although the external role to be acted out in a Renaissance court is a sham, the Prince of Denmark is not provided with the autonomy and unity which will constitute the inner life of a bourgeois **subject**. That will emerge after the English Revolution, in the coded and guilt-stricken secret diary of a Pepys. Shakespeare's tragedy therefore straddles a world dying, where status was signified through the **body**, and one yet powerless to be born, where the **body** will be repressed to sanctify the soul. This is a reading that locates Elizabethan drama in a cultural continuum of which we are products, and it has been influential for the **Cultural Materialist** reading of the Renaissance as the 'history of the present'.

That Hamlet's first argument with his stepfather takes place in the crowded council chamber marks off this spectacular, corporeal sovereignty from the polity which is to succeed it. There is, however, no difficulty in recognizing, even from the present, the scene of the state. The language and the costume may not be that of our own day, but nor are we – on the surface – without sure points of reference here. Conducted under a

---

*Reprinted from *The Tremulous Private Body: Essays in Subjection* (London: Methuen, 1984), pp. 29–40.

different historical form, but clearly identifiable as such even from the contemporary standpoint of a very different experience of the political, central affairs of state are centrally enacted: the succession of rule, and the emergency of war. Claudius's opening disquisition on the haste with which his marriage to Gertrude has followed on the death of the former king her husband, by way of a nicely turned contrast between mourning and celebration, manages to sound at once sorrowing and festive. It is the accomplished palliative speech of an adept politician reassuring anxieties at home. He is convincing, genial, magnanimous, clearly adroit in managing councils of state. The next item of business touches foreign policy: Fortinbras has sharked up his list of lawless resolutes in the marches and now challenges for the control of disputed territory. Old rights are involved, not least the honour of the dead king, which Claudius does not fail to mention, skilfully linking the external threat to the internal problem, subtly buttressing his legitimacy by establishing himself as a defender of the memory of his predecessor against the foreign invader. War grows out of such things, and Denmark's armourers and shipwrights are already preparing for the conflict, but Claudius will pursue the options of diplomacy before unleashing the violence of this warlike state against the mercenaries. A certain political circumspection governs his instructions to the ambassadors who are fiercely ordered not to overstep the limits of their commission. In this, the primal scene of the play, the fully political concerns of the internal and external security of the realm itself are dramatized. Written at a moment in England's political history when both press heavily on the real kingdom, the scene delineates process of government with a clarity that is as economical as it is essential. The destiny of an entire society is gathered into these few lines and placed before audiences who will themselves participate at a drama of historical crisis. Denmark and England each stand on a threshold of change: by the end a certain greatness will have gone out of one; revolution will transform the other.

But there is an anachronistic temptation to read back from the present and identify, in the next business of the scene, as it shifts from the empowering of the ambassadors to the matter of Laertes's departure from court, with a *caesura* dividing off the political state from the more intimate textures of family life. Hardly high policy on a level with what has already been transacted in this busy hall, does this episode not serve to reformulate the scene, and to manage a transition from the public space to the personal and domestic argument with Hamlet that is to follow? To think so would be to commit a signal historical mistake. At most the items on this agenda are organized according to a descending order of importance, and even that is questionable in view of the subsequent unfolding of the action. The narrative of the drama (which should not, in any event, be confused with the form of the social situation it discloses) will foreground the particular trajectories of Hamlet substantially, and Laertes to an extent; but this must not be allowed to occlude its location of these destinies within the menace of the wider crisis, and more profoundly, within a density and order of being that defers the modern division.

In sharp contrast to the separations which the Pepysian text describes, in this polity, Laertes's departure is fully *in place* in the business of state. The king's permission – sued for in full council – doubles, complements, sanctions and completes the reluctant permission of the biological father. The scene inscribes within itself not a separation of spheres but that relation of subordinate correspondence, theorized with varying degrees of mysticism at the time, between the father who is as a king in the family and the king who is as a father in the state. Nor should this similitude be thought as pallid analogy or distant likeness. It is stricter than homology, and constitutes an essential link in a chain of ideal connections that ground sociality itself in a theory of kingship and kinship which was practised in an array of political, juridical and cultural institutions, and which articulates a social body that is layered, figured, but one. Organized under the general form of hierarchy, sanctioned in practice by force and metaphysically by God the King and God the Father whose just order it reflects, the single realm describes a full place, tense with patterns of fealty, reciprocity, obligation and command. The figure of the king guarantees, as locus and source of power and as master-signifier, a network of subsidiary relations which constitute the real practice and intelligibility of the lives of subjects.

If the body of the Passion is the foundation of this world's signifying, at the same time the body of the king is its coherent temporal instance, the body that encompasses all mundane bodies within its build. But the subjection at work here is not that modern form for which the ambitiously inappropriate name of 'consciousness' is frequently used. Pre-bourgeois subjection does not properly involve subjectivity at all, but a condition of dependent membership in which place and articulation are defined not by an interiorized self-recognition – complete or partial, percipient or unknowing, efficient or rebellious – (of none the less socially constituted subject-positions), but by incorporation in the body politic which is the king's body in its social form. With a clarity now hard to recapture, the social plenum is the body of the king, and membership of this anatomy is the deep structural form of all being in the secular realm. Where post-Pepysian subjection will distance the external world in order to construct subjectivity as the (imaginary) property of inner selfhood, this sovereignty achieves its domination by other means, across an articulated but single ground. It establishes a constitution within which subjects are profoundly implicated not because they 'know their place' (as in the modern form when it is effective) but because alterity of placement is always-already encoded as unthinkable. Or at least no more conceivable than the absurd proposition that the arm could take the place of the spleen. This did not prevent rebellion, but the heavy price legitimacy extracts for such an act is the burden of dismembering the frame of place and sense itself.

In this scene, in *Hamlet*, the king and the biological father happen to be different people. But not far away in the *oeuvre*, in a significantly more conservative text, they are identical. When Lear sets his tragic action in motion by dividing the indivisible kingdom, there are a number of different registers to his error (one of the glories of the Renaissance is the pre-Rationalist *complexity* of its error). The historical register involves regression across a century of painful development. Under the Tudor dynasty England had emerged from internal wars to lay the groundwork of a nation state. The Crown, in breaking the authority of the feudal magnates and in rearticulating under its own sovereignty that of the Church, acquired the national monopoly of the means of both persuasion and violence. By skilful manipulation of class and factional alliances both with and over the heads of the lords ecclesiastical and temporal, it reorganized the power previously vested in them. The imposition of a professional central bureaucracy, and of local administrative and judicial government staffed increasingly by royal appointees, appeared to disseminate control at the same time as it effectively gathered it to the writ of the Crown. But Lear, in his *historical* folly, refragments the realm by dividing it among his daughters and re-establishing, under a nominal and ineffectual monarch, powerful and competitive baronial factions, whose gender only serves to underline their monstrous character.

If today an effort of retrospective imagination is needed in order to perceive the catastrophic enormity of this, to contemporaries its implications were plain and fearsome. And not simply because of the threat posed by this dismemberment of the integrity of the realm. For in another register, but at the identical moment and not as a consequential effect, Lear's action – which is already close to that madness that will soon bear down on him – also disarticulates the order of the family. If Hamlet's first argument with Claudius takes place in state, in the first scene of *Lear* the fusion (of what is in any case not yet separate) is also total. Even without that signal blindness which permeates the play as a terrible instance of debility in the spectacular kingdom and whose first act is to misrecognize Cordelia and cast her, rather than her sisters, in the role of rebellious daughter-subject, the king's original intention of a tripartite division of the realm and the family violates an essential coherence between them both. Its intention threatens to disassemble authority relations fundamental to this patriarchal sovereignty, and to the very code of being it describes. Lear cannot abdicate his position, in family or state, as if it were the public office of a later polity. In this settlement, soon to be unsettled and surrendered to lawlessness because the place of the king–father from which the law is uttered is soon to be emptied, subjects are located in places not by the *apparently* auxiliary contingency of the later constitution, but by an essential fit, by necessary bonds of nature articulating the political anatomy of the king's body. Although disorder in the family, in the state and in the faculties of the soul – and, indeed, in cosmic nature – can act as metaphors for each other, their substantial interrelation is more profound than poetic artifice: they are all grounded at once in the same inner correspondence whose transgression risks the disarticulation of reality itself. It is with the same gesture of division that Lear fissures his kingdom, his family and his reason, for on this scene the state, kinship and sense repeat and extend into each other without break.

Thus Laertes's suit for permission to travel and the fourth item on the agenda which is much more problematic from the standpoint of the present – Hamlet's melancholic excess of mourning and the Oedipal drama that begins to speak itself there – are heard in the crowded council chamber. What would appear under the new regime as private matters exist in an as yet undivided continuum with the succession and the gathering war. The public and the private as strong, mutually defining, mutually exclusive categories, each describing separate terrains with distinct contents, practices and discourses, are not yet extant. In *Hamlet* and in *Lear*, and in the wider sovereignty they disclose, the space of being, the society, the world – what you will – is ordered along different lines from those that fissure our own situation. This is not to insist that there is no aloneness there. Ophelia's lonely epithet for Hamlet himself – 'The glass of fashion and the mould of form,/The observ'd of all observers' (*Hamlet*, ed. H.Jenkins [London, 1982], IV,i,156–7) – certainly marks out around the prince, in significantly specular language, a penumbra of solitude. But this is not a private condition. The keynote is the very visibility with which the space is delineated: it is the pertinent metaphor, as concrete as any could be, for the indivisibility of the plenum. The sovereignty that governs this space – however insecure it is growing as it registers in the resort to the figure of the spy, or in Lear's and Gloucester's blindness, its progressive *failure to see* – is represented by the all-pervading access which the spectacle provides. This is why so many stand around, paying attention or not, near the action at the throne, in the centre of the kingdom and of the family. They and we are attentive or indifferent, but necessary spectators here, not because the action only acquires its meaning when it is apprehended by an audience for whom it is played out, but because no other conditions are extant. In the same way as what is seen does not take place in public, so what is not seen by all does not work itself out in private. What is secret in this world – the conspiracies of the night, two figures who stand together on an empty beach – does not correspond to that modern condition of privacy in which the Pepysian subject is incarcerated. Here even solitude, while it may be a form of torture, is a figure of the whole, contingent on the local and momentary situation, but not a rent in the social fabric as such.

And yet, to return to the great hall, which has been named with an aptness that is uncanny the *presence* chamber (for everything in this sovereignty is exactingly present, sanctioned by the real or in principle proximity of the body of the king), we must take the measure of the one great exception to the rule of this world: beside the throne, slightly apart from the others, his head bowed in thought, stands the Oedipal prince. In what are almost the first words we hear him speak, a claim is made for modern depth, for qualitative distinction from the corporeal order of the spectacle:

> Seems, madam! nay it is, I know not 'seems'.
> 'Tis not alone my inky cloak, good mother,
> Nor customary suits of solemn black,
> Nor windy suspiration of forced breath,
> No, nor the fruitful river in the eye,
> Nor the dejected haviour of the visage,
> Together with all forms, modes, shapes of grief,
> That can denote me truly. These indeed seem,
> For they are actions that a man might play,
> But I have that within that passes show,
> These but the trappings and the suits of woe.
>
> (I,ii, 75–86)

Hamlet asserts against the devices of the world an essential interiority. If the 'forms, modes, shapes' fail to denote him truly it is because in him a separation has already opened up between the inner reality of the subject, living itself, as 'that within that passes show', and an inauthentic exterior: and in that opening there begins to insist, however prematurely, the figure that is to dominate and organize bourgeois culture. Seen from the viewpoint of this speech, the narrative of *Hamlet* is nothing but the prince's evasion of a series of positionalities offered to him by the social setting. From the moment when the ghost of his father lays on him the burden of vengeance, his passage through the drama is the refusal of – or, at most, the parodic and uncommitted participation in – the roles of courtier, lover, son, politician, swordsman, and so on. Even the central task of revenge provides, in its deferral, no more than a major axis of the play's duration. But in dismissing these modes, or 'actions' as he calls them, Hamlet utters, against the substance of the spectacular plenum which is now reduced in his eyes to a factitious artificiality 'that a man might play', a first demand for the modern subject. In the name, now, not of the reign of the body but of the secular soul, an interior subjectivity begins to speak here – one which, if it encounters the world in anything more than a quizzical and contemplative manner, must alienate itself into an environment which inevitably traduces the richness of the subject by its mute and resistant externality. An early embarrassment for bourgeois ideology, and one of which Hamlet is in part an early victim, was that even as it had to legitimize the active appropriation of the world, it also had to encode its subject as an individual, privatized and largely passive 'consciousness' systematically detached from a world which is thus beyond its grasp: for all its insistence on the world as tractable raw object it none the less constructs a subjectivity whose form is that of the unique and intransitive soul, centred in meanings which are apparently its alone.

But this interiority remains, in *Hamlet*, gestural. 'The heart of my mystery' (III,ii, 368–9), as he describes it to Guildenstern in another place, is the real opacity of the text. Unlike those other obscurities of seeming which are *proper* to the spectacle, the truth and density of *this* mystery can never be apprehended. The deceptions of the plenum which surrounds Hamlet are always ultimately identifiable as such, and therefore only obscure for a few or within some tactical situation of the drama as it unfolds: they are never beyond the reach of its epistemology. But Hamlet's inner mystery is not of this order. Neither those who seek it out within the play, who try to discover whether he is mad in reality or 'in craft', nor the audience who overhear so many examples of the rhetorical form proper to this isolated subjectivity, the soliloquy, are ever placed by the text in a position from which it can be grasped. It perdures as a central obscurity which cannot be dramatized. The historical prematurity of this subjectivity places it outside the limits of the text-world in which it is as yet emergent only in a promissory form. The text continually offers to fulfil the claim of that first speech, but whenever it appears that the claimed core of that within which passes the show of the spectacle will be substantially articulated, Hamlet's riddling, antic language shifts its ground and the text slides away from essence into a further deferral of the mystery. But if the text cannot dramatize this subjectivity, it can at least display its impossibility, when Hamlet offers a metaphor of himself, of his self, to Guildenstern who is an instrument, purely, of the king, and signally lacking any form of interiority. Challenging Guildenstern to 'pluck out the heart' of his mystery – in language sufficiently corporeal to point the failure – Hamlet gives him the recorder which he cannot play, although he would, in Hamlet's conceit, 'sound' the 'compass' of the prince. The hollow pipe is the refutation of the metaphysic of soul which the play signals but cannot realize. For Hamlet, in a sense doubtless unknown to him, is truly this hollow reed which will 'discourse most eloquent music' but is none the less vacuous for that. At the centre of

Hamlet, in the interior of his mystery, there is, in short, nothing. The promised essence remains beyond the scope of the text's signification: or rather, signals the limit of the signification of this world by marking out the site of an absence it cannot fill. It gestures towards a place for subjectivity, but both are anachronistic and belong to a historical order whose outline has so far only been sketched out.

It is into this breach in Hamlet that successive generations of criticism – especially Romantic and post-Romantic variants – have stepped in order to fill the vacuum and, in explaining Hamlet, to explain him away. This effort to dissipate the challenge he represents is partly explained by the need to remake the Jacobean settlement in the eternal image of the bourgeois world, and partly by a more subversive potential in the prince. Accounts of his unresolved Oedipus complex, his paranoia – both clinical and vulgar – his melancholic nobility of soul in a world made petty by politics have all served the purposes of bourgeois criticism's self-recognition. In erasing the alterity of this other world it has sought to discover there the same preocccupations and structures as those which govern its own discourse. Politically liberal versions of this unconscious and ideologically loaded modernization of the pre-revolutionary sovereignty, articulating what is either a mild criticism or simply the inheritance of a soured Cartesianism, have even discovered in the prince – fully fledged – that alienated modern individual dejected in the market-place of inauthentic values. Each has found it necessary to discover in him one recension or another of the subjectivity which defines the modern soul. But in so doing they have necessarily overstated the fullness of the consciousness actually dramatized by the text. The lack of closure in its relentless scepticism, its relativizing, unstable discourse, have been blocked and frozen in order to provide the fixity necessary to recuperate it to a conception of essential subjectivity *fully realized*. In place of the text's pattern of offer and refusal of this interiority, strung out along the chain of Hamlet's rich but fleeting language, a single 'problem', or knot of problems, is diagnosed, and is then said to denote him truly. The startling effect has been to reproduce the text as the great tragedy of ... *bourgeois* culture.

But the point is not to supply this absence, to make whole what is lacking, but to aggravate its historical significance. *Hamlet* is a contradictory, transitional text, and one not yet fully assimilated into the discursive order which has claimed it: the promise of essential subjectivity remains unfulfilled. From its point of vantage on the threshold of the modern but not yet within it, the text scandalously reveals the emptiness at the heart of that bourgeois trope. Rather than the plenitude of an individual presence, the text dramatizes its impossibility. Not only is the myth by which the autonomous individual is made the undetermined unit of being, in contrast to an inert social world, alien to this dramatic regime, but even when, in a later settlement, the philosophical legislation and discursive underpinning necessary to support the device have been provided, it will achieve a success whose stability, as the example of Pepys shows, is at best fragile. When it does emerge in the discourse of Descartes or a Pepys, in a different kind of writing from that of the Jacobean spectacle as its substantial and founding mode, it will immediately begin to be naturalized as the figure under which the social conditions of another sovereignty will be lived. Itself socially constructed none the less, and not in any event identical with those, or any, social conditions themselves – for in dividing the subject from the outer world it enacts an imaginary desocialization of subjectivity – it will take up its place as the central figure in which bourgeois society will be experienced in interiority and subjection. Its dramatic impossibility in *Hamlet* is, therefore, the more critically valuable for those like ourselves who must still live it out. Rather than a gap to be filled, the vacuity in Hamlet is a 'failure' to be celebrated against the more systematically vacuous dominion of the order of subjectivity it both signals and resists.

But if Hamlet's promised but unfulfilled interiority in its sharpest form is unacceptable to bourgeois ideology because it is not sufficiently fixated, it is equally intolerable to the plenum which surrounds him because it has already moved too far in that direction. The text, too, effects its own closure of the fissure that the prince opens in its fabric, and averts the challenge to its order which the prince represents. This is why it mobilizes so many simulacra of him. Fortinbras, Laertes, even the semi-mythical Pyrrhus of the First Player's speech – whose sword also hesitates above the head of a king – are each interference repetitions of Hamlet by which the text disperses across its surface (in a distribution fitted to the spatial dimension of the spectacle) other, external versions of the prince, in order to fend off the insistence of his unique essentiality. And it is why, in order that the play may end, a second Hamlet must be introduced. For rather than the maturation or development of 'character' that we have been taught to look for in Shakespeare, there is a quasi-Brechtian discretion between the figure who is deported to England and the figure who returns having suffered a sea-change. The agnostic melancholic is replaced by the man of action who does battle with the pirates, and who devises an effective stratagem against the king's agents which he sardonically reports to Horatio: 'So Guildenstern and Rosencrantz go to't'. 'Why, man, they did make love to this employment'(V, ii, 56–7). The Hamlet who delays (and whose delaying is but the linear deployment of the 'vertical' absence within) is replaced by one who simply waits, for whom 'it will be short, the interim is mine' (V, ii, 74): and who is soon dead; by one whose first appearance, at Ophelia's graveside, is signalled by the fact that the riddling, sliding language of the first Hamlet has now migrated to the mouth of the gravedigger from whom, ironically, the second must now try to elicit simple answers to simple questions; and, finally, by one who goes to his death inserted into the traditional Christian values – the 'special providence in the fall of a sparrow' (V, ii, 217–18) and the 'divinity that shapes our ends,/Rough-hew them how we will' (V, ii, 10–11) – that were so profoundly questioned by the figure he supplants. By these devices, arbitrarily and theatrically secured, the challenge of Hamlet's incipient modernity is extinguished – for a time – and the prince recuperated to the order of the spectacle which his opacity had troubled.

10 *Macbeth:* History, Ideology and Intellectuals*

Alan Sinfield

Cultural Materialism contends that if culture is a determinant of events, then how it is *reproduced* (by teachers or actors in the case of Renaissance drama) is as vital as its production. Moreover, in recognition of the materiality of culture, critics have a strategic duty to declare their partisanship. Alan Sinfield's essay on *Macbeth* offered a model of how an oppositional analysis of a **canonical** text might read it 'across the grain' of the received opinion that such literature reinforces official order. Despite its reputation as royalist propaganda, Sinfield finds *Macbeth* to be riven with the contradictions of a **state** founded on the very violence it disavows. A product of the moment when the British monarchy secured a monopoly of violence, Shakespeare's play divulges the strategy by which a modern state **legitimates** bloodshed done in its name, and it thus challenges critics to take positions on state violence perpetrated today. Sinfield is reminded by IRA terrorism that the legitimacy of the state created by James I remains a 'live issue', so in pointing up the immediacy of *Macbeth* he is acting on the principle that the role of intellectuals is 'to expose, rather than promote, state **ideology**'. The influence here is the Marxism of Althusser, rather than the 'hands-off' anthropology which inclines American New Historicism to political neutrality.

It is often said that Macbeth is about 'evil', but we might draw a more careful distinction: between the violence which the state considers legitimate and that which it does not. Macbeth, we may agree, is a dreadful murderer when he kills Duncan. But when he kills Macdonwald – 'a rebel' (*Macbeth*, I,ii,10) – he has Duncan's approval:

> For brave Macbeth (well he deserves that name),
> Disdaining Fortune, with his brandish'd steel,

*Reprinted from *Critical Quarterly*, 28, 1/2 (Spring/Summer 1986), pp. 63–77.

> Which smok'd with bloody execution,
> Like Valour's minion, carv'd out his passage,
> Till he fac'd the slave;
> Which ne'er shook hands, nor bade farewell to him,
> Till he unseam'd him from the nave to th' chops,
> And fix'd his head upon our battlements.
> *Duncan* O valiant cousin! worthy gentleman!
>
> (*Macbeth*, ed. K.Muir, [London, 1962], I,ii,16–24)

Violence is good, in this view, when it is in the service of the prevailing dispositions of power; when it disrupts them it is evil. A claim to a monopoly of legitimate violence is fundamental in the development of the modern state; when that claim is successful, most citizens learn to regard state violence as qualitatively different from other violence and perhaps they don't think of state violence at all (consider the actions of police, army and judiciary as opposed to those of pickets, protesters, criminals and terrorists). *Macbeth* focuses major strategies by which the state asserted its claim at one conjuncture.

Generally in Europe in the sixteenth century the development was from Feudalism to the Absolutist State. (Anderson 1974; Poulantzas 1973, pp. 157–68). Under Feudalism, the king held authority among his peers, his equals, and his power was often little more than nominal; authority was distributed also among overlapping non-national institutions such as the church, estates, assemblies, regions and towns. In the Absolutist State, power became centralised in the figure of the monarch, the exclusive source of legitimacy. The movement from one to the other was of course contested, not only by the aristocracy and the peasantry, whose traditional rights were threatened, but also by the gentry and urban bourgeoisie, who found new space for power and influence within more elaborate economic and governmental structures. Because of these latter factors especially, the Absolutist State was never fully established in England. Probably the peak of the monarch's personal power was reached by Henry VIII; the attempt of Charles I to reassert that power led to the English Revolution. In between, Elizabeth and James I, and those who believed their interests to lie in the same direction, sought to sustain royal power and to suppress dissidents. The latter category was broad; it comprised aristocrats like the Earls of Northumberland and Westmorland who led the Northern Rising of 1569 and the Duke of Norfolk who plotted to replace Elizabeth with Mary Queen of Scots in 1571, clergy who refused the state religion, gentry who supported them and who tried to raise awkward matters in parliament, writers and printers who published criticism of state policy, the populace when it complained about food prices, enclosures, or anything.

The exercise of state violence against such dissidents depended upon the achievement of a degree of legitimation – upon the acceptance by many people that state power was, at least, the lesser of two evils. A principal means by which this was effected was the propagation of an ideology of Absolutism, which represented the English state as a pyramid, any disturbance of which would produce general disaster, and which insisted increasingly on the 'divine right' of the monarch. This system was said to be 'natural' and ordained by 'God'; it was 'good' and disruptions of it 'evil'. This is what some Shakespeareans have celebrated as a just and harmonious 'world picture'. Compare Perry Anderson's summary: 'Absolutism was essentially just this: *a redeployed and recharged apparatus of feudal domination*, designed to clamp the peasant masses back into their traditional social position' (Anderson 1974, p. 18).

The reason why the state needed violence and propaganda was that the system was subject to persistent structural difficulties. *Macbeth*, like very many plays of the period, handles anxieties about the violence exercised under the aegis of Absolutist ideology. Two main issues come into focus. The first is the threat of a split between legitimacy and actual power – when the monarch is not the strongest person in the state. Such a split was altogether likely during the transition from Feudalism to the Absolutist State; hence the infighting within the dominant group in most European countries. In England the matter was topical because of the Essex rebellion in 1601: it was easy for the charismatic earl, who had shown at Cadiz that Englishmen could defeat Spaniards, to suppose that he would make a better ruler than the aging and indecisive Elizabeth, for all her legitimacy. So Shakespeare's Richard II warns Northumberland, the kingmaker, that he is bound, structurally, to disturb the rule of Bolingbroke:

> thou shalt think,
> Though he [Bolingbroke] divide the realm and give thee half,
> It is too little, helping him to all
>
> (*Richard II*, ed. P. Ure [1956], V, i, 59–61)

Jonathan Dollimore and I have argued elsewhere that the potency of the myth of Henry V in Shakespeare's play, written at the time of Essex's ascendancy, derives from the striking combination in that monarch of legitimacy and actual power (Dollimore and Sinfield 1985b). At the start of *Macbeth* the manifest dependency of Duncan's state upon its best fighter sets up a dangerous instability (this is explicit in the sources). In the opening soliloquy of Act I, scene vii, Macbeth freely accords to Duncan entire legitimacy: he is Duncan's kinsman, subject and host, the king has been 'clear in his great office', and the idea of his deposition evokes religious imagery of angels, damnation and cherubins. But that is all the power the king has that does not depend upon Macbeth; against it is ranged 'Vaulting ambition', Macbeth's impetus to convert his actual power into full regal authority.

The split between legitimacy and actual power was always a potential malfunction in the developing Absolutist State. A second problem was less dramatic but more persistent. It was this: what is the difference between Absolutism and tyranny? – having in mind contemporary occurrences like the Massacre of St Bartholomew's in France in 1572, the arrest of more than a hundred witches and the torturing and killing of many of them in Scotland in 1590–91, and the suppression of the Irish by English armies. The immediate reference for questions of legitimate violence in relation to *Macbeth* is the Gunpowder Plot of 1605. This attempted violence against the state followed upon many years of state violence against Roman Catholics: the Absolutist State sought to draw religious institutions entirely within its control, and Catholics who actively refused were subjected to fines, imprisonment, torture and execution. Consider the sentence passed upon Jane Wiseman in 1598:

> The sentence is that the said Jane Wiseman shall be led to the prison of the Marshalsea of the Queen's Bench, and there naked, except for a linen cloth about the lower part of her body, be laid upon the ground, lying directly on her back: and a hollow shall be made under her head and her head placed in the same; and upon her body in every part let there be placed as much of stones and iron as she can bear and more; and as long as she shall live, she shall have of the worst bread and water of the prison next her; and on the day she eats, she shall not drink, and on the day she drinks she shall not eat, so living until she die.

This was for 'receiving, comforting, helping and maintaining priests', and refusing to reveal, under torture, who else was doing the same thing, and for refusing to plead. There is nothing abstract or theoretical about the state violence to which the present essay refers. Putting the issue succinctly in relation to Shakespeare's play, what is the difference between Macbeth's rule and that of contemporary European monarchs?

In *Basilikon Doron* (1599) King James tried to protect the Absolutist State from such pertinent questions by asserting an utter distinction between 'a lawfull good King' and 'an usurping Tyran':

> The one acknowledgeth himselfe ordained for his people, having received from God a burthen of government, whereof he must be countable: the other thinketh his people ordeined for him, a prey to his passions and inordinate appetites, as the fruites of his magnanimitie: And therefore, as their ends are directly contrarie, so are their whole actions, as meanes, whereby they preasse to attaine to their endes.

Evidently James means to deny that the Absolutist monarch has anything significant in common with someone like Macbeth. Three aspects of James's strategy in this passage are particularly revealing. First, he depends upon an utter polarisation between the two kinds of ruler. Such antitheses are characteristic of the ideology of Absolutism: they were called upon to tidy the uneven apparatus of Feudal power into a far neater structure of the monarch versus the rest, and protestantism tended to see 'spiritual' identities in similarly polarised terms. James himself explained the function of demons like this: 'since the Devill is the verie contrarie opposite to God, there can be no better way to know God, then by the contrarie'. So it is with the two kinds of rulers: the badness of one seems to guarantee the goodness of the other. Second, by defining the lawful good king against the usurping tyrant, James refuses to admit the possibility that a ruler who has *not* usurped will be tyrannical. Thus he seems to cope with potential splits between legitimacy and actual power by insisting on the unique status of the lawful good king, and to head off questions about the violence committed by such a ruler by suggesting that all his actions will be uniquely legitimate. Third, we may notice that the whole distinction, as James develops it, is in terms not of the *behaviour* of the lawful good king and the usurping tyrant, respectively, but in terms of their *motives*. This seems to render vain any assessment of the actual manner of rule of the Absolute monarch. On these arguments, any disturbance of the current structure of power relations is against God and the people, and consequently any violence in the interest of the status quo is acceptable. Hence the legitimate killing of Jane Wiseman. (In fact, the distinction between lawful and tyrannical rule eventually breaks down even in James's analysis, as his commitment to the state leads him to justify even tyrannical behaviour in established monarchs).

It is often assumed that *Macbeth* is engaged in the same project as King James: attempting to render coherent and persuasive the ideology of the Absolutist State. The grounds for a Jamesian reading are plain enough – to the point where it is often claimed that the play was designed specially for the king. At every opportunity Macbeth is disqualified ideologically and his opponents ratified. An entire antithetical apparatus of nature and supernature – the concepts through which a dominant ideology most commonly seeks to establish itself – is called upon to witness against him as usurping tyrant. 'Nature' protests against Macbeth (II,iv), Lady Macbeth welcomes 'Nature's mischief' (I,v, 50) and Macbeth will have 'Nature's germens tumble all together, /Even till destruction sicken' (IV, i, 59–60). Good and evil are personified absolutely by Edward the Confessor and the Witches, and the language of heaven and hell runs through the play; Lady Macbeth conjures up 'murth'ring minister' (I,v, 48) and Macbeth acknowledges 'The deep damnation of his [Duncan's] taking-off' (I, vii, 20). It all seems organised to validate James's contention, that there is all the difference in this world and the next between a usurping tyrant and a lawful good king. The whole strategy is epitomised in the account of

Edward's alleged curing of 'the Evil' – actually scrofula – 'A most miraculous work in this good King' (IV, iii, 146–7). James himself knew that this was a superstitious practice, and he refused to undertake it until his advisers persuaded him that it would strengthen his claim to the throne in the public eye. As Francis Bacon observed, notions of the supernatural help to keep people acquiescent (e.g. the man in pursuit of power will do well to attribute his success 'rather to divine Providence and felicity, than to his own virtue or policy'). *Macbeth* draws upon such notions more than any other play by Shakespeare. It all suggests that Macbeth is an extraordinary eruption in a good state – obscuring the thought that there might to any propensity to structural malfunctioning in the system. It suggests that Macbeth's violence is wholly bad, whereas state violence committed by legitimate monarchs is quite different.

Such manoeuvres are even more necessary to a Jamesian reading of the play in respect of the deposition and killing of Macbeth. Absolutist ideology declared that even tyrannical monarchs must not be resisted, yet Macbeth could hardly be allowed to triumph. Here the play offers two moves. First, the fall of Macbeth seems to result more from (super)natural than human agency: it seems like an effect of the opposition of good and evil ('Macbeth / Is ripe for shaking, and the Powers above / Put on their instruments' – IV, iii, 237–9). Most cunningly, although there are material explanations for the moving of Birnam Wood and the unusual birth of Macduff, the audience is allowed to believe, at the same time, that these are (super)natural effects (thus the play works upon us almost as the Witches work upon Macbeth). Second, in so far as Macbeth's fall is accomplished by human agency, the play is careful to suggest that he is hardly in office before he is overthrown. The years of successful rule specified in the chronicles are erased and neither Macduff nor Malcolm has tendered any allegiance to Macbeth. The action rushes along, he is swept away as if he had never truly been king. *Even so*, the contradiction can hardly vanish altogether. For the Jamesian reading it is necessary for Macbeth to be a complete usurping tyrant in order that he shall set off the lawful good king, and also, at the same time, for him not to be a ruler at all in order that he may properly be deposed and killed. Macbeth kills two people at the start of the play: a rebel and the king, and these are apparently utterly different acts of violence. That is the ideology of Absolutism. Macduff also, killing Macbeth, is killing both a rebel and a king, but now the two are apparently the same person. The ultimate intractability of this kind of contradiction disturbs the Jamesian reading of the play.

Criticism has often supposed, all too easily, that the Jamesian reading of *Macbeth* is necessary on historical grounds – that other views of state ideology were impossible for Shakespeare and his contemporaries. But this was far from being so: there was a well-developed theory allowing for resistance by the nobility, and the Gunpowder Plotters were manifestly unconvinced by the king's arguments. Even more pertinent is the theory of the Scotsman George Buchanan, as we may deduce from the fact that James tried to suppress Buchanan's writings in 1584 after his assumption of personal rule; in *Basilikon Doron* he advises his son to 'use the Law upon the keepers' of 'such infamous invectives'. With any case so strenuously overstated and manipulative as James's, we should ask what alternative position it is trying to put down. Arguments in favour of Absolutism constitute one part of *Macbeth*'s ideological field – the range of ideas and attitudes brought into play by the text; another main part may be represented by Buchanan's *De jure regni* (1579) and *History of Scotland* (1582). In Buchanan's view sovereignty derives from and remains with the people; the king who exercises power against their will is a tyrant and should be deposed. The problem in Scotland is not unruly subjects, but unruly monarchs: 'Rebellions there spring less from the people than from the rulers, when they try to reduce a kingdom which from earliest times had always been ruled by law to an absolute and lawless despotism'. Buchanan's theory is the virtual antithesis of James's; it was used eventually to justify the deposition of James's son.

Buchanan's *History of Scotland* is usually reckoned to be one of the sources of *Macbeth*. It was written to illustrate his theory of sovereignty and to justify the overthrow of Mary Queen of Scots in 1567. In it the dichotomy of true lawful king and usurping tyrant collapses, for Mary is the lawful ruler *and* the tyrant, and her deposers are usurpers and *yet* lawful also. To her are attributed many of the traits of Macbeth: she is said to hate integrity in others, to appeal to the predictions of witches, to use foreign mercenaries, to place spies in the households of opponents and to threaten the lives of the nobility; after her surrender she is humiliated in the streets of Edinburgh as Macbeth fears to be. It is alleged that she would not have shrunk from the murder of her son if she could have reached him. This account of Mary as arch-tyrant embarrassed James, and that is perhaps why just eight kings are shown to Macbeth by the Witches (IV, i, 119). Nevertheless, it was well established in protestant propaganda and in Spenser's *Faerie Queene*, and the Gunpowder Plot would tend to revivify it. Any recollection of the alleged tyranny of Mary, the lawful ruler, prompts awareness of the contradictions in Absolutist ideology, disturbing the customary interpretation of *Macbeth*. Once we are alert to this disturbance, the Jamesian reading of the play begins to leak at every joint.

One set of difficulties is associated with the theology of good, evil and divine ordination which purports to discriminate Macbeth's violence from that legitimately deployed by the state. I have written elsewhere of the distinctive attempt of Reformation Christianity to cope with the paradoxical conjunction in one deity of total power and goodness, and will here only indicate the scope of the problem. *Macbeth*, in the manner of

Absolutist ideology and Reformation Christianity, strongly polarises 'good' and 'evil', but, at the same time, also like the prevailing doctrine, it insists on complete divine control of all human events. This twin determination produces a deity that sponsors the 'evil' it condemns and punishes. Orthodox doctrine, which was Calvinist in general orientation, hardly flinched from this conclusion (for example, James said in his *Daemonologie* that fallen angels are 'Gods hang-men, to execute such turnes as he employes them in'). Nevertheless, fictional reworkings of it often seem to point up its awkwardness, suggesting an unresolvable anxiety. Traditional criticism registers this factor in *Macbeth* in its inconclusive debates about how far the Witches make Macbeth more or less excusable or in charge of his own destiny. The projection of political issues onto supposedly (super)-natural dimensions seems to ratify the Absolutist State but threatens also to open up another range of difficulties in contemporary ideology.

Macbeth also reveals a range of directly political problems to the reader rendered wary by Buchanan's analysis. They tend to break down the antithesis, upon which James relied, between the usurping tyrant and the legitimately violent ruler. Many of them have been noted by critics, though most commonly with the idea of getting them to fit into a single, coherent reading of the play. For a start, Duncan's status is in doubt: it is unclear how far his authority runs, he is imperceptive, and his state is in chaos well before Macbeth's violence against it. G. K. Hunter in the introduction to his Penguin edition (1967) registers unease at the 'violence and bloodthirstiness' of Macbeth's killing of Macdonwald (pp. 9–10). Nor is Malcolm's title altogether clear, since Duncan's declaration of him as 'Prince of Cumberland' (I, iv, 35–42) suggests what the chronicles indicate, namely that the succession was not necessarily hereditary; Macbeth seems to be elected by the thanes (II, iv, 29–32).

I have suggested that *Macbeth* may be read as working to justify the overthrow of the usurping tyrant. Nevertheless, the *awkwardness* of the issue is brought to the surface by the uncertain behaviour of Banquo. In the sources he collaborates with Macbeth, but to allow that in the play would taint King James's line and blur the idea of the one monstrous eruption. Shakespeare compromises and makes Banquo do nothing at all. He fears Macbeth played 'most foully for't' (III, i, 3) but does not even communicate his knowledge of the Witches' prophecies. Instead he wonders if they may 'set me up in hope' (III, i, 10). If it is right for Malcolm and Macduff, eventually, to overthrow Macbeth, then it would surely be right for Banquo to take a clearer line.

Furthermore, the final position of Macduff appears quite disconcerting, once we read it with Buchanan's more realistic, political analysis in mind: Macduff at the end stands in the same relation to Malcolm as Macbeth did to Duncan in the beginning. He is now the king-maker on whom the legitimate monarch depends, and the recurrence of the whole sequence may be anticipated (in production this might be suggested by a final meeting of Macduff and the Witches). For the Jamesian reading it is necessary to feel that Macbeth is a distinctively 'evil' eruption in a 'good' system; awareness of the role of Macduff in Malcolm's state alerts us to the fundamental instability of power relations during the transition to Absolutism, and consequently to the uncertain validity of the claim of the state to the legitimate use of violence. Certainly Macbeth is a murderer and an oppressive ruler, but he is one version of the Absolutist ruler, not the polar opposite.

Malcolm himself raises very relevant issues in the conversation in which he tests Macduff: specifically tyrannical qualities are invoked. At one point, according to Buchanan, the Scottish lords 'give the benefit of the doubt' to Mary and her husband, following the thought that 'more secret faults' may be tolerated 'so long as these do not involve a threat to the welfare of the state' (*Tyrannous Reign*, p. 88). Macduff is prepared to accept considerable threats to the welfare of Scotland:

> Boundless intemperance
> In nature is a tyranny; it hath been
> Th' untimely emptying of the happy throne,
> And fall of many kings. But fear not yet
> To take upon you what is yours: you may
> Convey your pleasures in a spacious plenty,
> And yet seem cold – the time you may so hoodwink:
> We have willing dames enough; there cannot be
> That vulture in you, to devour so many
> As will to greatness dedicate themselves,
> Finding it so inclin'd. (IV, iii, 66–76)

Tyranny in nature means disturbance in the metaphorical kingdom of a person's nature but, in the present context, one is likely to think of the effects of the monarch's intemperance on the literal kingdom. Macduff suggests that such behaviour has caused the fall not just of usurpers but of kings, occupants of 'the happy throne'. Despite this danger, he encourages Malcolm 'To take upon you what is yours' – a sinister way of putting it, implying either Malcolm's title to the state in general or his rights over the women he wants to seduce or assault. Fortunately the latter will not be necessary, there are 'willing dames enough': Macduff is ready to mortgage both the bodies and (within the ideology invoked in the play) the souls of women to the monster envisaged as the lawful good king. It will be all right, apparently, because people can be hoodwinked: Macduff allows us to see that the virtues James tries to identify with the Absolutist monarch are an ideological strategy, and that the illusion of them will probably be sufficient to kept the system going.

Nor is this the worst: Malcolm claims more faults, and according to Macduff 'avarice/Sticks deeper' (ll. 84–5): Malcolm may corrupt not merely people but property relations. Yet this too is to be condoned. Of course, Malcolm is not actually like this, but the point is that he well could be, as Macduff says many kings have been, and that would all be acceptable. And even Malcolm's eventual protestation of innocence cannot get round the fact that he has been lying. He says 'my first false speaking / Was this upon myself' (ll. 130–1) and that may indeed be true, but it nevertheless indicates the circumspection that will prove useful to the lawful good king, as much as to the tyrant. In Holinshed the culminating vice claimed by Malcolm is lying, but Shakespeare replaces it with a general and rather desperate evocation of utter tyranny (ll. 91–100); was the original self-accusation perhaps too pointed? The whole conversation takes off from the specific and incomparable tyranny of Macbeth, but in the process succeeds in suggesting that there may be considerable overlap between the qualities of the tyrant and the true king.

Macbeth allows space for two quite different interpretive organizations: against a Jamesian illustration of the virtues of Absolutism we may produce a disturbance of that reading, illuminated by Buchanan. This latter makes visible the way religion is used to underpin state ideology, and undermines notions that established monarchs must not be challenged or removed and that state violence is utterly distinctive and legitimate. It is commonly assumed that the function of criticism is to resolve such questions of interpretation – to go through the text with an eye to sources, other plays, theatrical convention, historical context and so on, deciding on which side the play comes down and explaining away contrary evidence. However, this is neither an adequate programme nor an adequate account of what generally happens.

Let us suppose, to keep the argument moving along, that the Jamesian reading fits better with *Macbeth* and its Jacobean context, as we understand them at present. Two questions then present themselves: what is the status of the disturbance of that reading, which I have produced by bringing Buchanan into view? And what are the consequences of customary critical insistence upon the Jamesian reading?

On the first question, I would make three points. First, the Buchanan disturbance *is in the play*, and inevitably so. Even if we believe that Shakespeare was trying to smooth over difficulties in Absolutist ideology, to do this significantly he must deal with the issues which resist convenient inclusion. Those issues must be brought into visibility in order that they can be handled, and once exposed they are available for the reader or audience to seize and focus upon, as an alternative to the more complacent reading. A position tends to suppose an *op*position. Even James's writings are vulnerable to such analysis, for instance when he brings up the awkward fact that the prophet Samuel urgently warns the people of Israel against choosing a king because he will tyrannize over them. This prominent biblical instance could hardly be ignored, so James quotes it and says that Samuel was preparing the Israelites to be obedient and patient. Yet once James has brought Samuel's pronouncement into visibility, the reader is at liberty to doubt the king's tendentious interpretation of it. It is hardly possible to deny the reader this scope: even the most strenuous closure can be repudiated as inadequate. We are led to think of the text not as propounding a unitary and coherent meaning which is to be discovered, but as handling a range of issues (probably intractable issues, for they make the best stories), and as unable to control the development of radically divergent interpretations.

Second, the Buchanan disturbance has been activated, in the present essay, as a consequence of the writer's scepticism about Jamesian ideological strategies and his concern with current political issues. It is conceivable that many readers of *Macbeth* will come to share this outlook. Whether this happens or not, the theoretical implication may be taken: if such a situation should come about, the terms in which *Macbeth* is customarily discussed would shift, and eventually the Buchanan disturbance would come to seem an obvious, natural way to consider the play. That is how notions of appropriate approaches to a text get established. We may observe the process, briefly, in the career of the Witches. For many members of Jacobean audiences, Witches were a social and spiritual reality: they were as real as Edward the Confessor, perhaps more so. As belief in the physical manifestation of supernatural powers, and especially demonic powers, weakened, the Witches were turned into an operatic display, with new scenes, singing and dancing, fine costumes and flying machines. In an adaptation by Sir William Davenant, this was the only stage form of the play from 1674 to 1744, and even after Davenant's version was abandoned the Witches' divertissements were staged, until 1888. Latterly we have adopted other ways with the Witches – being still unable, of course, to contemplate them, as most of Shakespeare's audience probably did, as phenomena one might encounter on a heath. Kenneth Muir comments: 'with the fading of belief in the objective existence of devils, they and their operations can yet symbolize the workings of evil in the hearts of men' (New Arden *Macbeth*, p. lxx). Recent critical accounts and theatrical productions have developed all kinds of strategies to make the Witches 'work' for our time. These successive accommodations of one aspect of the play to prevailing attitudes are blatant, but they illustrate the extent to which critical orthodoxy is not the mere response to the text which it claims to be: it is *remaking* it within currently acceptable parameters. The Buchanan disturbance may not always remain a marginal gloss to the Jamesian reading.

Third, we may assume that the Buchanan disturbance was part of the response of some among the play's initial audiences. It is in the nature of the matter that it is impossible to assess how many people inclined towards Buchanan's analysis of royal power. That there were such may be supposed from the multifarious challenges to state authority – culminating, of course, in the Civil War. *Macbeth* was almost certainly read against James by some Jacobeans. This destroys the claim to privilege of the Jamesian reading on the ground that it is historically valid: we must envisage diverse original audiences, activating diverse implications in the text. And we may demand comparable interpretive licence for ourselves. Initially the play occupied a complex position in its ideological field, and we should expect no less today.

With these considerations about the status of the Buchanan disturbance in mind, the question about the customary insistence on the Jamesian reading appears as a question about the politics of criticism. Like other kinds of cultural production, literary criticism helps to influence the way people think about the world; that is why the present essay seeks to make space for an oppositional understanding of the text and the state. It is plain that most criticism has not only reproduced but endorsed Jamesian ideology, so discouraging scrutiny, which *Macbeth* can promote, of the legitimacy of state violence. That we are dealing with live issues is shown by the almost uncanny resemblances between the Gunpowder Plot and the 1984 Brighton Bombing, and in the comparable questions about state and other violence which they raise. My concluding thoughts are about the politics of the prevailing readings of *Macbeth*. I distinguish conservative and liberal positions; both tend to dignify their accounts with the honorific term 'tragedy'.

The conservative position insists that the play is about 'evil'. Kenneth Muir offers a string of quotations to this effect: it is 'Shakespeare's "most profound and mature vision of evil"; "the whole play may be writ down as a wrestling of destruction with creation"; it is "a statement of evil"; "it is a picture of a special battle in universal war ..."; and it "contains the decisive orientation of Shakespearean good and evil"'. This is little more than Jamesian ideology writ large: killing Macdonwald is 'good' and killing Duncan is 'evil', and the hierarchical society envisaged in Absolutist ideology is identified with the requirements of nature, supernature and the 'human condition'. Often this view is elaborated as a socio-political programme, allegedly expounded by Shakespeare and implicitly endorsed by the critic. So Muir writes of 'an orderly and closely-knit society, in contrast to the disorder consequent upon Macbeth's initial crime [i.e. killing Duncan, not Macdonwald]. The naturalness of that order, and the unnaturalness of its violation by Macbeth, is emphasized ...' (New Arden *Macbeth*, p. li). Irving Ribner says Fleance is 'symbolic of a future rooted in the acceptance of natural law, which inevitably must return to reassert God's harmonious order when evil has worked itself out' (Ribner 1960, p. 159).

This conservative endorsement of Jamesian ideology is not intended to ratify the Modern State. Rather, like much twentieth-century literary criticism, it is backward-looking, appealing to an earlier and preferable supposed condition of society. Roger Scruton comments: 'If a conservative is also a restorationist, this is because he lives close to society, and feels in himself the sickness which infects the common order. How, then, can he fail to direct his eyes towards that state of health from which things have declined' (Scruton 1980, p. 21). This quotation is close to the terms in which many critics write of *Macbeth*, and their evocation of the Jamesian order which is allegedly restored at the end of the play constitutes a wistful gesture towards what they would regard as a happy ending for our troubled society. However, because this conservative approach is based on an inadequate analysis of political and social process, it gains no purchase on the main determinants of state power.

A liberal position hesitates to endorse any state power so directly, finding some saving virtue in Macbeth: 'To the end he never totally loses our sympathy'; 'we must still not lose our sympathy for the criminal' (Bradley 1965, p. 305). In this view there is a flaw in the state, it fails to accommodate the particular consciousness of the refined individual. Macbeth's imagination is set against the blandness of normative convention and for all his transgressions, perhaps because of them, Macbeth transcends the laws he breaks. In John Bayley's version: 'His superiority consists in a passionate sense for ordinary life, its seasons and priorities, a sense which his fellows in the play ignore in themselves or take for granted. Through the deed which tragedy requires of him he comes to know not only himself, but what life is all about' (Bayley, 1981, p. 199). I call this 'liberal' because it is anxious about a state, Absolutist or Modern, which can hardly take cognizance of the individual sensibility, and it is prepared to validate to some degree the recalcitrant individual. But it will not undertake the political analysis which would press the case. Hence there is always in such criticism a reservation about Macbeth's revolt and a sense of relief that it ends in defeat: nothing could have been done anyway, it was all inevitable, written in the human condition. This retreat from the possibility of political analysis and action leaves the state virtually unquestioned, almost as fully as the conservative interpretation.

Shakespeare, notoriously, has a way of anticipating all possibilities. The idea of literary intellectuals identifying their own deepest intuitions of the universe in the experience of the 'great' tragic hero who defies the limits of the human condition is surely a little absurd; we may sense delusions of grandeur. *Macbeth* includes much more likely models for its conservative and liberal critics in the characters of the two doctors. The English Doctor has just four and a half lines (IV, iii, 141–5) in which he says King Edward is coming and that sick people whose malady conquers the greatest efforts of medical skill await him, expecting a heavenly cure for 'evil'. Malcolm, the king to be, says 'I thank you, Doctor'. This doctor is the equivalent of conservative intellectuals who encourage respect for mystificatory images of ideal hierarchy which have served the state in the past, and who invoke 'evil', 'tragedy' and 'the human condition' to produce, in effect, acquiescence in state power.

The Scottish Doctor, in V, i and V, iii, is actually invited to cure the sickness of the rulers and by implication the state: 'If thou couldst, Doctor, cast / The water of my land, find her disease ...' (V, iii, 50–1). But this doctor, like the liberal intellectual, hesitates to press an analysis. He says: 'This disease is beyond my practice' (V, i, 56), 'I think, but dare not speak' (V, 1,76), 'Therein the patient / Must minister to himself' (V, iii, 45–6), 'Were I from Dunsinane away and clear, / Profit again should hardly draw me here' (V, iii, 61–2). He wrings his hands at the evidence of state violence and protects his conscience with asides. This is like the liberal intellectual who knows there is something wrong at the heart of the system but will not envisage a radical alternative and, to ratify this attitude, discovers in Shakespeare's plays 'tragedy' and 'the human condition' as explanations of the supposedly inevitable defeat of the person who steps out of line.

By conventional standards, the present essay is perverse. But an oppositional criticism is bound to appear thus: its task is to work across the grain of customary assumptions and, if necessary, across the grain of the text, as it is customarily perceived. Of course, literary intellectuals don't have much influence over state violence, their therapeutic power is very limited. Nevertheless, writing, teaching, and other modes of communicating all contribute to the steady, long-term formation of opinion, to the establishment of legitimacy. This contribution King James himself did not neglect. An oppositional analysis of texts like *Macbeth* will read them to expose, rather than promote, state ideologies.

11 *The White Devil*: Transgression Without Virtue*

JONATHAN DOLLIMORE

Where criticism traditionally assumes a 'human condition' and refers Renaissance drama to the supposedly transhistorical and universal concept of 'human nature', **Cultural Materialism** begins from the thesis that there is no essential human core since individuals are products of societies in history. In *Radical Tragedy*, Jonathan Dollimore argued that this awareness was, in fact, shared by Jacobean drama, which dates from a hiatus between a God-centred world-picture and a **humanist** one, when the social process shaping identity was exposed to the enquiry of sceptics such as John Webster. Thus, in Webster's tragedy, *The White Devil*, Vittoria and her brother Flamineo strip church and state of the **legitimacy** of divine sanction. Instead of the 'virtue' of compliance with their oppression, the 'assertive woman' and 'dispossessed intellectual' of Jacobean drama expose by their crimes the workings of a vicious society. They therefore participate in that unhinging of moral absolutes which Hobbes thought 'the core' of the English Civil War. This is a reading of Jacobean drama that draws on the old historicism of Marxists such as Christopher Hill, but with an urgency born of the conviction of the New Left of 1968, that revolution will be led by the socially or sexually **marginalised**.

In *The White Devil* the decentring of the tragic subject is most fully in the service of another preoccupation of Jacobean tragedy: the demystifying of state power and ideology. In no other play is the identity of the individual shown to depend so much on social interaction; even as they speak protagonists are, as it were, off-centre. It is a process of displacement which shifts attention from individuals to their context and above all to a dominating power structure which constructs them as either agents or victims of power, or both.

---

* Reprinted from *Radical Tragedy: Religion, Ideology and Power in the Drama of Shakespeare and His Contemporaries* (2nd ed, London: Harvester, 1989), pp. 230–46.

Religion and state power

For Flamineo religion is the instrument of state power – a facade of sanctity indispensable to its operation. His satire is cynically reductive yet based on accurate insight: 'there's nothing so holy but money will corrupt and putrify it... You are happy in England, my lord; here they sell justice with those weights they press men to death with .... Religion; O how it is commeddled with policy. The first bloodshed in the world happend about religion'(*The White Devil*, III, iii, 24–5, 27–8, 37–9). In the following act Flamineo's assessment is vindicated as we witness 'religion' fronting 'policy'; Monticelso enters *in state* (stage direction) and Francisco whispers to him the news that Brachiano and Vittoria have escaped from the house of convertites; as a result Monticelso makes their excommunication his first act as new Pope:

> We cannot better please the divine power,
> Than to sequester from the holy church
> These cursed persons. Make it therefore known,
> We do denounce excommunication
> Against them both.
>
> (IV, iii, 65–9)

It is an episode which shows how state power is rendered invulnerable by identification with its 'divine' origin – how, in effect, policy gets an ideological sanction. In performance of course we will see that it is an appeal further ratified by the awesome apparatus of investiture – a good instance of the ceremonial keeping of men in awe. Finally there is the masterful foresight of the true politician: 'All that are theirs in Rome / We likewise banish'. Thus at the same time as it consolidates faith, religious ritual is shown to consolidate the power of those who rule, the second being secured in and through the first. Brachiano, in describing Duke Francisco, makes a similar point in relation to the 'robes of state':

> all his reverent wit
> Lies in his wardrobe; he's a discreet fellow
> When he's made up in his robes of state
>
> (II, i, 184–6)

The virtuous and the vicious

In Act I, scene ii, Cornelia, unseen, witnesses the seduction of Vittoria (her daughter) by Duke Brachiano, with Flamineo (her son) acting as pander. At last she intervenes to reprimand all three. As she preaches honour and virtue to Brachiano we realise that she has an entirely false conception of 'The lives of the Princes' (I, ii, 276); she is, in fact, a victim to the myth of courtliness, the myth which disguises the real nature of the court and the elite which dominates it (and her). It is the same myth to which Vittoria refers when she is dying – 'O happy they that never saw the court / Nor ever knew great man but by report' (V, vi, 258–9) – and which surrounds the reputed glory of these great men: 'Glories, like glow-worms, afar off shine bright / But look'd to near have neither heat nor light' (V, i, 40–1).

In both of these so–called *sententiae* there is something quite different from the inappropriate moralising that some critics have detected. In fact, they evince a perceptive awareness that those who are geographically and socially removed from the centre of power are deceived as to its true nature. This is an aspect of the ideological ratification of power which Machiavelli refers to in *The Prince*. If a ruler is consistently virtuous, and behaves accordingly – this will be his ruin, says Machiavelli. On the contrary he must be capable of doing evil while appearing virtuous. The reality is concealed by a carefully constructed myth – Vittoria's 'report' – rendered workable at least in part by the ignorance of those who are ruled. Both *The White Devil* and, here, *The Prince* indicate that this is an ignorance resulting from geographical and social distance:

> To those seeing and hearing him, [the prince] should appear a man of compassion, a man of good faith, a man of integrity, a kind and a religious man. And there is nothing so important as to seem to have this last quality. Men in general judge by their eyes rather than by their hands; because everyone is in a position to watch, few are in a position to come in close touch with you. Everyone sees what you appear to be, few experience what you really are. And those few dare not gainsay the many who are backed by the majesty of state. (Machiavelli, *The Prince*).

In short, *realpolitik* presupposes for its successful operation complicity by the few, ideological misrecognition by the many.

At this same point in *The White Devil* (I, ii) we witness yet again irony in the service of subversion: Cornelia preaches to the Duke precisely the myth which ratifies his exploitation of subjects like her. Having internalised her position as one of the exploited she does not exactly make the rod for her own back, but when the master drops it she is the one who 'instinctively' returns it to him. By embracing the Christian ethic of humility and passive virtue Cornelia endures poverty and reproaches her son's conduct with the question: 'what? because we are poor / Shall we be vicious?' (I, ii, 304–5). Flamineo, indirectly in what he says here, more directly in his actual conduct, answers that question affirmatively: in *this* society the only means of alleviating poverty is a self-regarding viciousness. Here, as in the very first scene of the play, we see the lie being given to the Christian/stoic belief in the efficacy of adversity. In that first scene Antonelli tells Lodovico: 'affliction / Expresseth virtue, fully' (he is referring to the latter's banishment). Lodovico, in his brutal reply – 'Leave your painted comforts – I'll make Italian cut-works in their guts / If ever I return' (I, i, 51–3) – indicates the contrary. We draw the same conclusion when Lodovico and Flamineo agree to a malcontented allegiance: 'Let's be unsociably sociable' (III, iii, 74). It is a mock pact, broken almost as soon as it is made, and parodying, even as it proposes, the resignation characteristic of *contemptus mundi*. They agree to withdraw from the court and tell all those like them – the dispossessed and the failed – 'To scorn that world which life of means deprives'. It is a large group, embracing

> the beggary of courtiers,
> The discontent of churchmen, want of soldiers,
> And all the creatures that hang manacled,
> Worse than strappado'd, on the lowest felly
> Of Fortune's wheel.
>
> (III, iii, 89–93)

Antonelli suddenly announces that Lodovico's fortunes have reversed: he has been pardoned. Instantly Lodovico spurns Flamineo and within seconds they are at each other's throats.

Whereas Cornelia internalises an oppressive conception of virtue, one which keeps her dutifully subservient, Vittoria and Flamineo reject virtue to become, like Lodovico, vicious. It is the tragic contradiction of this society that for those in it virtue involves false consciousness while the struggle for true consciousness entails viciousness. The crimes of Flamineo and Vittoria reveal not their essential criminality but the operations of a criminal society. Most importantly, those who are most responsible for its viciousness – the powerful – conceal this fact *by and through* their power:

> *Vittoria*   If Florence be i'th' court, would he would kill me.
> *Gasparo*   Fool! Princes give rewards with their own hands
>   But death or punishment by the hands of others.
>
> (V, vi, 184–6)

Exploitation – by the prince of his subjects and by them of each other – is a recurring concern of the play (one articulated at, for example, II, i, 317–19; IV, i, 81–6; IV, ii, 134; V, iii, 60–3). Act IV, scene ii, more than anywhere else in the play, uses antagonistic confrontation to reveal the rootedness of power in exploitation. In that scene both Vittoria and Flamineo rebel against their master, Brachiano. More generally Vittoria rebels against her subordination as a woman, Flamineo against the subordination of one forced into service through dispossession.

Sexual and social exploitation

Vittoria lives a society in which women are subordinate to men. But the men are never quite confident of their domination and require that women acquiesce in the role accorded to them: 'A *quiet* woman' says Flamineo, 'Is a still water under a great bridge. / A man may shoot her safely' (IV, ii, 175–7, my italics). The same male insecurity flares into misogyny at the least provocation (Brachiano is here speaking to Vittoria):

> Thou hast led me, like an heathen sacrifice,
> With music, and with fatal yokes of flowers
> To my eternal ruin. Woman to man
> Is either a god or a wolf.
>
> (IV, ii, 86–9)

In her trial scene Vittoria refuses to be 'quiet', provoking Monticelso into a furious diatribe against whores as the bane of man (III, ii, 78–101). Misogyny is further apparent in Flamineo's repeated depreciation of women (eg. at I, ii, 18–20; IV, ii, 147–8; V, iii, 178–84; V, vi, 151–5; V, i, 91–2) and in the fact that evil, lust and jealousy are given female personification by male characters. Isabella laments, 'O that I were a man, or that I had power ...' (II, i, 242). To be male *is* to have power – in particular, power over women. Monticelso has the power, as Vittoria points out, to name her 'whore' (III, ii, 146–8). Not only does the language of the dominant actually confer identity on the subordinate, but the latter can only resist this process in terms of the same language; thus Vittoria determines to 'personate masculine virtue' (III, ii, 135). And yet, because of her different position in relation to power Vittoria's appropriation of that language can only go so far; in a sense the same language is not the same at all: 'O woman's poor revenge / Which dwells but in the tongue!' (III, ii, 281–2). Nevertheless to appropriate masculine virtue was still the most extreme form of female insubordination (in Jacobean England 'assertive women' provoked much controversy; even James I intervened, commanding the clergy to preach against them and threatening more direct action if this failed). The extent of Vittoria's power to defy is captured in her declaration to those trying her: 'I scorn to hold my life / At yours or any *man's* entreaty, sir' (III, ii, 137–8).

Flamineo's dispossession (I, ii, 306–7) has pressed him into service and the search for 'preferment'. In that search he has been disillusioned – first by his university education, second by his attendance at court. Education and service have left him just as poor yet even more dissatisfied: each has given him an insight into what he believes to be the false-consciousness of those like his mother which keeps them poor and 'virtuous' and, at the same time, made him want all the more the preferment he has been denied.

There is a fragile bond of loyalty between brother and sister. Thus Flamineo ruins his standing with Brachiano by reproaching him for calling Vittoria a whore; this leads to a confrontation for which Brachiano never forgives Flamineo (see V, ii, 78). But whatever allegiance Flamineo and Vittoria have through kinship or shared grievance, it is over-ridden – indeed, contradicted – by their respective roles in relation to each other and to Brachiano: she is Brachiano's mistress, he the procurer. Flamineo, challenged by his brother about the role of pander to Vittoria, dissolves kinship into shared ambition: 'I made a kind of path / To her and mine own preferment' (III, i, 35–6). But it is a path hardly enough for two to travel: brother prostitutes sister and she reproaches him accordingly; Flamineo, for his part, repeatedly degrades her sexuality so as to evade his own humiliation as pander. Finally their relationship explodes into outright antagonism with each prepared to kill the other (V, vi). It is a relationship which enacts the process whereby the individual emerges from familial bonds into adulthood only to find in the latter forms of social identity which contradict or destroy the former. The mother is the first casualty. Here, as throughout Jacobean tragedy, the bonds of 'nature' and 'kind' collapse under pressure and, because they break – indeed precisely *as* they break – they are shown to be not natural at all, but social.

The ambivalence which Flamineo and Vittoria feel towards Brachiano is born of their compromised relationship to him. He represents what each wants yet hates. It is an ambivalence which is most apparent in the angry confrontation of Act IV, precipitated by Francisco's letter to Vittoria pretending his love for her. This is intercepted by Brachiano who promptly assumes Vittoria's infidelity. He abuses her in terms which recall Monticelso's denunciation: 'Where's this whore?' (IV, ii, 43). This angers Flamineo who threatens to break Brachiano's neck. In response to the latter's incredulous 'Do you know me?' (ie. 'do you realise who you're talking to?') Flamineo tears away the myth of 'degree' and points to the real basis of hierarchy:

> O my lord! methodically.
> As in this world there are *degrees* of evils:
> So in this world there are *degrees* of devils.
> You're a great Duke; I your poor secretary.

> (IV, ii, 56–9, my italics)

We recall this exchange later when Francisco, disguised as a soldier comments as follows on his anticipated meeting with Brachiano: 'I shall never flatter him: I have studied man too much to do that. What difference is between the Duke and I? No more than between two bricks, all made of the clay: only't may be one is placed on the top of a turret, the other in the bottom of a well, by mere chance' (V, i, 104–8). The force of this repudiation of a Duke's innate superiority is ironically reinforced by the fact that Francisco is one himself. A similar idea is expressed by Bosola, Flamineo's counterpart in *The Duchess of Malfi*: 'Some would think the souls of princes were brought forth by some more weighty cause, than those of meaner persons; *they are deceived*... the same reason that makes a vicar go to law for a tithe-pig and undo his neighbours, makes them spoil a whole province, and batter down goodly cities with the cannon' (II, i, 104–10, my italics).

As Brachiano abuses Vittoria she turns on him with a passionate anger which recalls the confrontation with Monticelso in the trial scene. She attacks Brachiano for his failure to provide:

> What do you call this house?
> Is this your palace? Did not the judge style it
> A house of penitent whores?...
> Who hath the honour to advance Vittoria
> To this incontinent college? Is't not you?
> Is't not your high preferment? Go, go brag
> How many ladies you have undone, like me.

(IV, ii, 109–15)

Vittoria here reveals what she had hoped to get from Brachiano ('high preferment') and what she despises him for (sexual possession – the power to 'undo'; compare lines 129–30 of this same scene when Brachiano declares: 'Are not those matchless eyes *mine*... Is not this lip *mine*?'). Vittoria remains recalcitrant even when the repentant though shameless Brachiano tries to win her around with his reassurance: 'for you Vittoria, / Think of a duchess' title' (ll. 215–16).

The White Devil does not idealise Vittoria. In some respects it even alienates our sympathy for her. But if it does not invite sympathy it invites even less judgement – especially the kind which forecloses the play by relegating problematic figures like Vittoria and Flamineo to the realm of the morally defective. In understanding Vittoria we need to contrast her with Isabella. Isabella has always been a problem for critics who have wanted to identify her as the play's point of moral reference. In their terms she can just about carry moral piety but fails completely to carry moral stature. Throughout her interview with Brachiano (II, i) she evinces a degree of self-abnegation which is the opposite of Vittoria. In the space of thirteen separate utterances – some no more than single lines – she addresses Brachiano nine times as 'my dear lord' or something similar. Finally, despite his callousness, she decides to feign responsibility for the rift even though, apparently, the blame is entirely his. She has a strong desire to be self-sacrificial and to be remembered as such by Brachiano (II, i, 223–4). Hers is sexual subordination taken to an extreme: the 'lesser sex' willingly takes upon itself the guilt of the superior in a ritual of self-sacrifice. The more callous Brachiano is the more she reverences him as god-like. In the first dumb-show – a symbolic enactment of the contradictions and false-consciousness which characterise Isabella's relationship with Brachiano – the self-sacrificial role she has internalised is ritualistically underwritten: 'she kneels down *as to prayers*, then draws the curtains of Brachiano's picture, does three reverences to it, and kisses it thrice'. The ritual element highlights not just her self-sacrifice but the simple fact that she is being brutally murdered by the husband she reverences – in the very act of reverencing him.

The assertive woman

From the outset and especially in the Middle Ages, Christianity had a strong misogynist streak. Woman was the sinful temptress, lustful, vain, and the bane of man. But in the sixteenth century both humanists and reformers were in different ways challenging this estimate of women, especially the basic assumption of their 'natural' inferiority. Recent studies of the Elizabethan feminist controversy amply confirm Louis B. Wright's conclusion in an earlier work that it indicated 'a serious undercurrent of intelligent thinking upon women's status in a new commercial society' (Wright 1964, p. 507). Robert Brustein shows how the satiric denigration of women in Elizabethan drama was an anxious reaction to increasing independence and status on the part of some ('The Monstrous Regiment of Women', pp. 37–8). William Heale, writing in 1609 in defence of women, remarks the ethical double standard which we so often find in the drama: 'The Courtier though he wears his Mistresse favour, yet stickes not to sing his Mistress shame'.

In fact there seems to have been a significant change in attitudes to women in the drama of the second decade of seventeenth century. Linda Woodbridge argues that whereas the first decade witnessed unprecedented misogyny in the drama, a startling change followed whereby assertive women came to be positively celebrated. She argues here for a correlation with the actual behaviour of women in Jacobean England, also a recognition by playwrights and companies of the economic importance of female playgoers (Woodbridge 1983, Chapter 10).

But actual changes for the better in the position of women at this time were distinctly limited. Rightly, the rather complacent but widely held view that some Renaissance women actually achieved equality with men has been challenged in recent years. Joan Kelly-Gadol argues that in the long term the historical changes of that period which were liberating for men resulted in new forms of oppression for women – in particular a diminishing access to property, political power and education, and a greater regulation for their sexuality (Kelly-Gadol 1977).

Certainly in Jacobean drama we find not a triumphant emancipation of women but at best an indication of the extent of their oppression. The form that it takes in Webster's two major plays is important. In particular the figure of Vittoria should be viewed in relation to the image of the disorderly or unruly woman – the 'woman on top' – found extensively in literature, wood-cuts, broadsheets, pictorial illustrations and popular festivity. It was an image which, like other forms of ritual inversion, could legitimate rather than subvert the dominant order (Kelly-Gadol 1977, pp. 25 –8). Yet, as Natalie Zemon Davis has argued, because it was a multivalent image it could also 'widen behavioural options for women within and even outside marriage, and ... sanction riot and political disobedience for both men and women'. Most generally, that image could become part and parcel of conflict resulting from efforts to change the basic distribution of power in society (Davis 1978, pp. 154–5). This seems to describe Vittoria quite aptly. It suggests too that (*pace* Juliet Dusinberre) dramatists like Webster were interested in the exploitation of women (rather than women's rights) as one aspect – and a crucial one – of a social order which thrived on exploitation. So, in a trial in which Vittoria is charged with, among other things, being a whore, we are reminded marriage was itself a form of prostitution.

> 'twas my cousin's fate –
> Ill may I name the hour – to marry you;
> He bought you of your father...
> He spent there in six months
> Twelve thousand ducats, and to my acquaintance
> Receiv'd in dowry with you not one julio.
>
> (III, ii, 234–9)

The Comedy of Errors is another case in point. In that play Shakespeare explores the rationale of female subordination: the sisters Adriana and Luciana disagree about man's domination of woman. 'Why should their liberty than ours be more?' complains Adriana. She complains too that her husband, Antipholus, does not appreciate her servitude: 'when I serve him so, he takes it ill' (II, i, 10, 12). Luciana replies that Adriana's husband is 'bridle of your will', and that among all animals the female species 'Are their males' subjects, and at their controls'. Moreover,

> Man, more divine, the master of all these,
> Lord of the wide world and wild watr'y seas,
> Indu'd with intellectual sense and souls,
> Of more pre–eminence than fish and fowls,
> Are masters to their females, and their lords.
>
> (II, i, 20–4)

Adriana is questioning this explanation when Dromio the servant appears complaining that Antipholus (his master) has been mistreating him too. Adriana, impatient, falls to doing the same and Dromio exits, still complaining: 'You spurn me hence, and he will spurn me hither; / If I last in this service, you must case me in leather'. So: Adriana is abused by her 'master', while she in turn abuses her slave who is in his turn abused by both master and mistress. The episode is a 'comic' yet penetrating critique of authority and service. Two further points are worth noting about it. First, there is the familiar ideological appeal to natural law – the law encoded in nature according to God's providential design: 'heaven's eye' (l.16). Second, we here witness the issue of men's domination of women being put alongside men's domination of men. Thus Adriana, later in the same scene, complains that her husband prefers the company of 'minions' to hers. She adds:

Do their gay vestments his affections bait?
That's not my fault; he's master of my state.
What ruins are in me that can be found
By him not ruin'd?

(II, i, 94–7)

These are powerful lines and their force is increased rather than diminished by the fact that we have just seen how one such minion is as much at the mercy of Adriana and Antipholus as she is of Antipholus.

The dispossessed intellectual

The circumstances which Flamineo struggles against were just as familiar in the first decade of the seventeenth century. He bears some resemblance to the so-called 'alienated intellectuals of early Stuart England' investigated in an article of that name by Mark E. Curtis (Curtis 1965). It was frustration rather than exploitation which characterised these men; leaving university they encountered a society unable to use their talents or fulfil their sense of duty, self-esteem and honour. This 'generated impatience with the old corruption and helped create the body of men who could be among its most formidable opponents' (p. 314). Flamineo is concerned not with duty but survival and gain. His situation is more desperate: he suffers from frustration *and* exploitation and insofar as they can be distinguished the former makes him susceptible to the latter. As Lussurioso remarks in *The Revenger's Tragedy*, 'discontent and want / Is the best clay to mould a villain'(IV, i, 47–8).

Flamineo's education, which on his own confession (I, ii, 320–4) contributed to his discontent, is as important as Hamlet's though for different reasons. Hobbes, discussing the causes of the civil war, laid some of the blame at the door of the universities: 'The core of rebellion, as you have .... read of other rebellions, are the universities'. And in the year before the appearance of *The White Devil* Bacon had written: 'There (are) more scholars bred than the State can prefer and employ, and ... it must needs fall out that many persons will be bred unfit for other vocations, and unprofitable for that in which they were bred up, which fill the realm full of, indigent, idle and wanton people, who are but *materia rerum novarum.'*

In one of his *Essays* Bacon considers 'Seditions and Troubles' in the state. 'The matter of seditions', says Bacon, 'is of two kinds – much poverty and much discontentment.' And among their causes and motives he lists 'general oppression' and 'factions grown desperate'. One of the remedies open to the state is to ensure it does not arise that 'more are bred scholars than preferments can take off'. Bacon also advocates 'great use of ambitious men in being screens to princes in matters of danger and envy ... (and) in pulling down the greatness of any subject that overtops' (F. Bacon, *Essays*, ed. M. Hawkins [Dent 1972] pp. 44–5, 113). This is exactly how Francisco uses Lodovico and Brachiano uses Flamineo. Moreover, it correlates quite precisely with Gasparo's remark to the effect that 'Princes give rewards with their own hands, / But death or punishment by the hands of others'. Bacon then advises on how such men, once used, may be 'bridled': 'There is less danger of them if they be of mean birth than if they be noble; and if they be rather harsh of nature, than gracious and popular; and if they be new raised, than grown cunning and fortified in their greatness'. All such characteristics would tend to isolate such men *from each other* as well as from others unlike them. And this is crucial: potential opponents of the prince must not be allowed to unite since 'whatsoever, in offending people, joineth and knitteth them *in a common cause'* is likely to result in sedition and must therefore be avoided at all cost (*Essays*, p. 45, my italics).

In comparing the theatrical malcontent with his historical counterpart in Jacobean society we are concerned with resemblance rather than exact comparisons – not least because drama gains its realism as much by theatrical exaggeration of essential characteristics as by non-exaggerated representation of surface properties. Thus, just as Flamineo throws the plight of the dispossessed and exploited into exaggerated relief, so too do the two murderers whom Macbeth hires to kill Banquo and Fleance. These murderers are truly *desperate*:

Second Murderer   I am one, my liege,
            Whom the vile blows and buffets of the world
            Have so incens'd that I am reckless what
            I do to spite the world.

First Murderer And I another
So weary with disasters, tugg'd with fortune,
That I would set my life on any chance,
To mend it or be rid on't.

(III, i, 107–113)

As hirelings these men are lethal: misfortune has made them very vicious; they are 'reckless' in the sense of having nothing to lose and therefore being beyond the reach of an appeal to self-preservation. Authority has always had most to fear from those who not only have nothing to gain from it, but also nothing left to lose to it. Of course, each murderer had his life. But life without means comes to mean nothing: 'I would set my life *on any chance,* / To mend it or be rid on't.' The kind of poverty provoking such desperation is graphically portrayed by Robert Burton. Especially relevant is his insistence on the way that extreme poverty is so completely destructive of social standing that no aspect of one's identity, no independently identifiable aspect of oneself, remains untouched; the individual so afflicted is wholly recast in a new role: *'if once poor, we are metamorphosed in an instant,* base slaves, villains, and vile drudges; for to be poor is to be a knave, a fool, a wretch, a wicked, an odious fellow, a common eye-sore, *say poor and say all'* (*Anatomy of Melancholy*, I, 350, my italics). Burton is insistent on this point: 'He must turn rogue and villain ... poverty alone makes men thieves, rebels, murderers, traitors, assassinates' (I,354).

In *All's Well that Ends Well* Parolles asserts: 'Simply the thing I am / Shall make me live .... There's place and means for every man alive' (IV, iii, 310–11, 316). For malcontents like Flamineo and Macbeth's murderers the reverse is true: the position they 'live' makes them what they are, and they kill each other for 'place and means'.

Living contradictions

In death Flamineo and Vittoria remain defiant. Many have interpreted this as tragic affirmation – of self if not of life or the moral order (but sometimes of all three). Yet brother and sister die with the same dislocated identities. Vittoria claims to be 'too true a woman' to show fear (l.220), but as Flamineo observes (ironically recalling Vittoria's own words at III,ii, 135), she is a woman who has appropriated 'masculine virtue' (l. 242). For his part Flamineo sustains defiance only by isolating himself in the moment – removed from the past, the future, almost from consciousness itself; asked what he is thinking he replies:

Nothing; of nothing: leave thy idle questions –
I am i'th'way to study a long silence,
To prate were idle – I remember nothing.
There's nothing of so infinite vexation
As man's own thoughts.

(V,vi, 219–23)

Moments later he declares:

I do not look
Who went before, nor who shall follow me;
No, at myself I will begin and end.

(V,vi, 223–5)

Flamineo dies with a gesture of futile defiance half-acknowledged as such
in his being at once aggressively defiant and masochistically demanding:
'Search my wound deeper: tent it with the steel / That made it' (ll.235–6).
This is not the self-affirmation, the essentialist self-sufficiency of stoicism,
but the stubborn defiance born of a willed insensibility which recalls his
earlier: 'We endure the strokes like anvils or hard steel, / Till pain itself
make us no pain to feel' (III, iii, 1–2). His last words –

farewell glorious villains,–
This busy trade of life appears most vain,
Since rest breeds rest, where all seek pain by pain –

(V, vi, 269–71)

surely allude to Bacon's essay *Of Great Place* (especially if we take 'glorious
villains' to mean villains in search of glory):

It is a strange desire, to seek power and lose liberty; or to seek power
over others and to lose power over a man's self. The rising unto place is
laborious, and *by pains men come to greater pains*; and it is sometimes base,
and by indignities men come to dignities.The standing is slippery; and
the regress is either a downfall, or at least an eclipse, which is
melancholy thing. *Cum non sis qui fueris, non esse cur velis vivere* [When
you are no longer the man you have been there is no reason why you
should wish to live].

(Bacon, *Essays*, p. 31)

It is in the death scene that we see fully the play's sense of how
individuals can actually be constituted by the destructive social forces
working upon them. We have already seen how Cornelia and Isabella
internalised roles of subservience with the consequence that they revere

that which exploits and destroys them. Conversely Vittoria and Flamineo refuse subservience even as they serve and, in so doing, are destroyed as much by their rebellion as that which they rebel against. Perhaps the most powerful contradiction lies in this simple fact: their stubborn, mindless self-affirmation at the point of death is made with the same life-energy which, up to that point, has been life-destructive. So, though directly opposed in many respects, these two pairs (Cornelia, Isabella; Flamineo, Vittoria) resemble each other in being constituted and ultimately destroyed by what Brecht called 'a great living contradiction'. He uses the description in relation to his own play, *Mother Courage and her Children*, with which, for the purposes of this discussion, I must assume acquaintance. The passage is worth quoting at length; it is appropriate not only for *The White Devil* but as a kind of anti-conclusion to this section:

> The trader mother became a great living contradiction, and it was this that defaced and deformed her, to the point of making her unrecognisable .... After the maiming of her daughter, she damned the war with a sincerity just as deep as that with which she praised it in the scene immediately following. Thus she gives expression to opposites in all their abruptness and irreconcilability. The rebellion of her daughter against her ... stunned her completely and taught her nothing. The tragedy of Mother Courage and of her life ... consisted in the fact that here a terrible contradiction existed which destroyed a human being, a contradiction which could be resolved, but only by society itself and in long, terrible struggles .... It is not the business of the playwright to endow Mother Courage with final insight ... his concern is, to make the spectator see. (Quoted from H. Block and H. Salingar (eds), *The Creative Vision*, [New York, 1960], pp. 158–61).

12 Family Rites: City Comedy and the Strategies of Patriarchalism*

LEONARD TENNENHOUSE

Crucial to New Historicism was Foucault's claim that while modern **power** is internalised, early modern power was **spectacular**, an idea it employed to analyse the theatricality of **power** and the power of theatre in the Renaissance. This was the theme of *Power on Display* by the American critic Leonard Tennenhouse, which viewed the Renaissance stage as analogous to the scaffold as a place where the **spectacle** of state was acted out. But Tennenhouse departed from **Cultural Poetics** in his belief that 'such displays were not produced' to the degree that contest was ruled out. Just as a Tyburn crowd might stone the executioner, history would discredit the scenarios of Renaissance plays. In this extract, for example, he describes the tension between the patriarchal endings of Jacobean City Comedies and the teeming metropolis they held at bay. On the stage patriarchy overrules individualist paternalism as father gives way to grandfather or son; but the genre could not thereby represent the 'Jacobean city of night' with its volatile social mix. In stressing the limits of **representation** Tennenhouse shows how art is pressured by social reality: in this case the shift from the dynastic to the nuclear family, a favourite New Historicist topic. His book concludes that so far from dictating history, it would be history that would shut the London theatre down.

Jacobean city comedy acquires its peculiar character by virtue of the fact it excludes the courtly figures found in romantic comedy and absent monarch plays, as well as the rural laboring poor of the pastorals. Jacobean comedy represents the city as a set of social features – neither aristocratic nor impoverished laborer – to be associated with life in the

---

* Reprinted from *Power on Display: The Politics of Shakespeare's Genres* (London: Methuen, 1986), pp. 160–71.

city and its suburbs. So represented, the city of city comedy is staged as a series of distinct character types whose speech indicates social affiliations and sources of income ranging from gentry to servants, from merchants to artisans. And because of the satiric nature of this relationship, when thrown together in this way, the cacophony of voices does not indicate the region of one's origin but the possibility of a character's economic or social vulnerability. Drawn from coneycatching pamphlets, from prose accounts of cant speech, and from the caricatures developed in epigrams and satires so popular among Inns of Court men in the 1590s, these dramatic satires create something of a Dickensian sense that each individual is a particular tic of some massive disruptive force controlling London. City comedy individuates various forms of economic identity and brings each forward to be displayed in sexual or economic relations where inevitably one is either predator or prey. In *A Chaste Maid in Cheapside* – with the notable exception of the goldsmith's daughter of the title and her gallant – we encounter a sterile knight whose wife must be inseminated in order to claim an inheritance, a gentleman impoverished by his fertility, a whoring knight, who would prey on the socially ambitious goldsmith, a wittol who feeds off the whoring knight, a Welsh whore kept by the whoring knight and the pedantic son of the goldsmith she marries, not to mention the avaricious artisan, the drunken puritan women, the greedy promoters who enforce lenten observance, and various minor characters who step forward to present their particular twists and turns of desire. City comedies often have those larcenous figures from the London underworld who may take center stage in such a play as *The Alchemist* or appear briefly as in *The Roaring Girl* to remind us we are witnessing life in the city. Visible for only a moment, these characters seem to be so displayed strictly for the purpose of populating the city. The sheer number of characters – over thirty in *Bartholomew Fair*, for instance – and the narrow range of differences which distinguish one from the other make the exposition of plot nearly impossible. It is difficult indeed, as L.C. Knights observed about Middleton's characters, to remember which of the many characters in city comedy belong to the same play, or for that matter, despite their wit, to distinguish one plot device from another (Knights 1962, p. 258). We must assume the city is represented then not as a backdrop but as the object of display. The city is important, I am suggesting, precisely because it represents the city of early seventeenth-century England in a particular way. City comedy divulges its human content to create the cumulative impression that we have witnessed but a small fraction of a densely populated environment teeming with different types of activity, most of which is corrupt and all of which requires some grand new ordering principal.

Sharing affiliations with no comparable city in Shakespeare's romantic comedies, the city represented in Jacobean comedy undergoes the same transformation when put into writing as representations of the city in nondramatic kinds of writing. The prose pamphlets by the likes of Greene, Nashe, and Dekker, for instance, not only served as source material but also as a model for that behavior of language which is supposed to represent the city. One can see this as well in something as different from the coneycatching pamphlets as that dense and richly textured city Stowe maps in *A Survey of London*. He recounts how aristocratic structures lost their hold on city architecture as the crush of people led to the division and then the subdivision of buildings into meaner accommodations. Here he recounts the fate of 'one large messuage builded of stone and timber' which belonged to the Earl of Oxford during the reign of Henry V:

> in processe of time the landes of the Earle fell to females, amongest the which one being married to *Wingfielde* of Suffolke this house with the appurtenances fell to his lot, and was by his heire Sir *Robert Wingfield* sold to M. *Edward Cooke*, at this time the Queenes Atturney Generall. This house being greatly ruinated of late time, for the most part hath beene letten out to Poulters, for stabling of hourse and stowage of Poultrie, but now lately new builded into a number of small tenements, letten out to strangers, and other meane people.
>
> (J. Stowe *A Survey of London*, ed. C. Kingsford [1908], I, p. 163)

Even more than erecting buildings, the practice of dividing the space within established buildings to create tenements for 'strangers, and other meane people', is the most common way of representing the new city, its buildings and its inhabitants. The same view that depicts the city in Stowe's description gives rise as well to the reductively individuated characters of city comedy. This representation reveals the creation of progressively meaner living accommodations as the distinctive features of older and grander structures are divided and individuated. Such a view of the city appears in Elizabethan and Jacobean royal proclamations, in Privy Council orders, and in the writings of London officials. On 22 June 1602, for example, a royal proclamation was issued 'Prohibiting further Building or Subdividing of Houses in London.' Among the reasons for prohibiting the subdivisions of houses in London was a belief that it increased the size of the population. Overcrowding in turn promoted concern that 'such multitues could hardly be governed by ordinary justice,' much less employed or fed. In such a proclamation the fear is writ large that the plague would spread rapidly where people were so 'heaped up together and in a sort smothered with many families of children and servants in one small house or tenement.' This great mixture of people thus constituted a source of political unease as one historian notes: 'in 1607 the recorder of London described four large buildings which housed eight thousand inhabitants, of whom eight hundred had died in the last plague visitation: "... if it be not reformed, " he stated, "the people cannot have food nor can they be governed" ' (Zagorin 1970, p. 136). In addition to familiar literary materials drawn from Elizabethan drama, as well as the caricatures from satire and epigram, the London of the city comedies was composed out of and thus refers back to these surveys, prose pamphlets, proclamations and chroniclers' reports. This London calls to mind the city under plague in Foucault's account.

I have found his discussion of the city useful in trying to understand what is at stake in the representation of the Jacobean city of night. *Discipline and Punish* argues, among other things, that those in charge of the plague-infested city of the late seventeenth century applied the same disciplinary techniques middle-class culture would eventually use in creating a modern institutional culture. The figure of the city under plague materializes the operations of the plague's destructive power and mobilizes in turn the strategies which finally make the plague a thing of past history. The power of the plague, according to Foucault, lay in its ability to cause confusion. As a contagion, it was transmitted when bodies mingled. It was for this reason associated with other forms of illicit combinations such as rebellions, riots, and vagabondage. 'Against the plague, which is mixture, ' he writes, 'discipline brings into play its power, which is analysis' (Foucault 1977 b, p. 197). The plague ultimately serves the state as it calls forth the disciplinary practices that turn the city into 'a segmented, immobile, frozen space. Each individual is fixed in his place. And, if he moves, he does so at the risk of his life, contagion or punishment' (p. 195). Although the city under plague may appear to an historically later eye like the strategies of a nascent middle-class culture, its differences from that culture are crucial for our understanding of city comedy. In my view, neither the positive nor the negative features of middle-class culture are on display there. To the contrary, a very different political formation can be observed which the emergence of the middle class almost two hundred years later tends to prevent us from seeing.

In his account of the formation of modern society, Harold Perkin reminds us that what we mean by the middle class simply did not exist before the latter part of the eighteenth century. The old society – that of the sixteenth, seventeenth, and early eighteenth century – was largely composed of a group called 'the middle ranks' whose social organization was quite different from that of the middle classes of a modern industrialized society. The older social organization he describes as 'a finely graded hierarchy of great subtlety and discrimination in which men were acutely aware of their exact relation to those immediately above and below them, but only vaguely conscious except at the very top of their connections with those of their own level' (Perkin 1969, p. 24). 'Between the landowners and the labouring poor, ' Perkin writes, 'stretched the long, diverse, but unbroken chains of the "middle ranks".'

These chains determined that socioeconomic differences which bound each individual to those above and below him in a relation of dependency and domination should determine one's identity. We should note, further, that history offers Perkin no positive form for representing this social body. The middle ranks, in his view, 'were distinguished at the top from the gentry and nobility not so much by lower incomes as by the necessity of earning their livings, and at the bottom not so much by higher incomes as by the property, however small, represented by stock in trade, livestock, tools, or the educational investment of skill or expertise' (p. 23). Perkin's description stresses the heterogeneous quality of the middle ranks, and because it is bound within a vertical system of relations, this group can only be defined as neither nobility nor laboring poor. One of the reasons for the absence of a positive ethos for this group clearly has to do with the fact that, in the historically earlier city, power can only be thought of in terms of patronage relations. Any bond other than relations of generosity and service was by definition a distortion of patronage, which made the city appear – even to Perkin – as a Hobbesian universe of greedy people who preyed upon one another. In this respect, he provides a useful corrective to our tendency to read city comedy as if it were about the middle class or the proto-middle class. At the same time, I will insist, Perkin's account is not any less a representation than the relatively homogeneous class which displaced the older notion of the middle rank. What I am suggesting is that this negative representation of the middle rank is itself a product of seventeenth and early eighteenth-century writing.

We might return to the figure of the plague to see how this bit of cultural history was written under the pressure of a particular ideology of representation. Because the plague is viewed as something produced by and reproducing illicit forms, mixtures, boundary violations of all sorts, it must then be met with regulation, documentation, and analysis. To say this, however, is to accede to the belief that the bureaucracy so mobilized threatens the state itself in such a way that only institutional structures provide a remedy. Such thinking would come into its own by the end of the seventeenth century. However, Renaissance England had not yet made such a semiotic move. For one thing, *Measure for Measure* clearly demonstrates that the bureaucracy itself, rather than providing a cure for disease, actually encouraged its spread. This is to say, the city represents disorder in terms that call forth the patriarch whose power alone can regulate the state. A royal proclamation of 22 June 1602 prohibited the building or subdivision of buildings in London. This proclamation affords a glimpse of the ultimate nature of the danger posed by the plague. Having invaded the city and from there dispersed throughout the realm, 'great mortality should ensue to the manifest danger of the whole body thereof, out of which neither her majesty's own person (except by God's special providence) or any other whatsoever could be exempted'. In a word, this passage understands the plague as an assault on the queen's body. To prevent its outbreak, then, the queen must act to protect herself and her subjects. By virtue of the same logic, Jacobean city comedies create a framework sorely in need of patriarchal authority. Indeed, the very constructs which govern the way social historians and literary scholars understand the social alignments composing the middle rank during the seventeenth century no doubt arise in part from Jacobean representations of the city. We might go so far as to think of these comedies as the first instance of the modern use of 'representation, ' in the modern sense of the term. Taken together they determine the way an entire field of economic and social relations will come to be understood and evaluated.

Evidently there was good reason to see London as a place organized according to an inverse principle of patronage and a site where patriarchy would be opposed. Once James came to the throne, the city was placed in a particularly difficult relationship to the Crown. Like other important urban centers, its governance was based on charter, which ideally spelled out something akin to a contractual relationship between the city and the Crown. This notion of power would not have been particularly appealing to such an imperious king as James. The city – as opposed to the outparishes and the liberties which were administered neither by guilds nor by the municipal government – was ruled by an oligarchy whose membership was based on money rather than blood. To qualify as one of the twenty-six aldermen of London required a minimum of ten thousand pounds in property, and once chosen, an alderman sat for life. Although the common council of two hundred and fifty supposedly constituted a more inclusive form of political representation, then, it in fact drew its members from among a small number of wealthy citizens, the selection of which was in the hands of the few. Perez Zagorin describes the process in this manner:

> In theory the choice of councilmen belonged to the freemen – citizens – i.e. to all persons free of any of the city companies and hence possessed of the right to trade – who constituted the wardmote for this purpose. Practice, however, had come to limit the election of councilmen to a minority of well-to-do residents who had usurped the wardmote's power.
>
> (Zagorin 1970, p.127)

At odds with national interests, resistant to Crown demands for loans and entertainments, a haven for dissident religious views, and governed by a principle which substitutes money for the metaphysics of blood, London surely provided one way of representing the opposition to patriarchal authority.

To control this opposition, the Crown sought to establish its model of the state as the only possible form of political order. In 1613, the Privy Council again issued a proclamation to limit building in greater London. Then two years later, in 1615, James officially ordered gentry and aristocracy to return to their country estates where they were expected to maintain centres of hospitality. His speech to the Star Chamber in 1616 returns to the matter of his proclamation of the year before. Leah S. Marcus has demonstrated the importance of this speech to James's policies, as well as to the topography of court entertainments that ensued (Marcus 1978b). After dwelling on problems of the judiciary, he not only encouraged members of the gentry and nobility to display themselves in the countryside, he launched an attack on London as well. The published version of that speech represents the city as a place attracting so many people 'that all the countrey is gotten into *London*; so as with time, England will onely be *London*, and the whole countrey be left waste'. Women, attracted by foreign fashions, forced their husbands and fathers to abandon the country for London only to spend money and tarnish their virtue. To correct these 'forreine toys, ' he says, 'let vs ... keepe the old fashion of *England*: For it was wont to be the honour and reputation of the English Nobilitie and Gentry, to liue in the countrey, and keepe hospitalitie....' Twenty years before, on 2 November 1596, Elizabeth had issued a proclamation similarly ordering hospitality to reign in the countryside, but hers was intended to combat poor harvests as well as to marshal defenses against the threat of an invasion by Spain. Worried about civil disturbances, James saw both the problem and its resolution differently. In response to a a hungry populace and the threat of a Spanish invasion, Elizabeth saw the presence of the aristocracy as a strategic distribution of her force throughout the kingdom. By the time James voiced his concern over the possibility of civil disorder, however, the whole notion of popular power had changed. One might compare the change to that of the figure of festival one can observe in shifting from an Elizabethan history play like *Henry V* to the Jacobean *Henry VIII*. No longer do the materials of festival dramatize forms of resistance. With James, these materials have already been appropriated as an instrument of state authority. Festival is now conceived as a framework for the containment rather than for the release of forces inherently opposed to the patriarchal principle.

My point is to consider aristocratic hospitality as the king's preferred solution to the political problem posed by London and by the isolated political groups who resisted his authority. In his speech of 1616, James expresses the fear, among other things, of a popular rebellion: 'if insurrections should fall out (as was lately seene by the *Leuellers* gathering together) what order can bee taken with it, when the country is vnfurnished of Gentlemen to take order with it?' It is not the people he fears, but a specific political faction, the Levellers, and this fear does not arise because they represent a threat to his power in and of themselves. The fear is they will gain popular support and turn it against the monarch. To oppose the Levellers, James declared the aristocracy must put on a positive show of power through displays of generosity. The attractions of the city appeared to stand in the way of his policy. Thus he describes the problem in terms of sexual corruption and economic loss, the features of city comedies. Of the effects of the city on women he says, 'if they bee wiues, then their husbands; and if they be maydes, then their fathers must bring them vp to *London*: and here, if they be vnmarried they marre their marriages, and if they be married, they loose their reputations, and rob their husbands purses'. Every city comedy accordingly demonstrates how the city inverts patronage relations. Rather than plots that turn on generosity or display economic plenitude, these plays dramatize a profound economic hunger.

In terms of modern culture, we should note, this economic desire appears to be greed where the city comedies call it 'covetousness.' It is important to stress the difference between Jacobean desire and that said to motivate capitalism. Unlike the acquisitive desire which provides a basis in nature of modern political economy, 'covetousness' was neither represented as man's natural legacy nor understood as the agency for his success. The Renaissance understood it to mean a purely destructive hunger that led to rapaciousness. It is highly significant, then, that covetousness takes over social relations in city comedies when patronage relations have been cut loose of their aristocratic base. Inverting the principle of generosity, which insures the harmony of an aristocratic community or court, patronage – no longer tied to blood – defines a situation where one individual preys upon another. Such a situation demands a higher form of authority – a patron of patrons so to speak – who restores the proper relations of patron to client. Yet city comedy feels no compulsion to bring a monarch on stage for purposes of a resolution, nor for that matter does James ever suggest that the king might intervene and impose order on life in the city. No courtly ceremonies materialize within the framework of city comedy. All the same, I will argue, the plays represent the city in a manner that authorizes patriarchy. Consequently, the whole strategy James proposed for dealing with the issue of a corrupt London can be viewed as an adaptation of the dramatic strategies enacted in the theater over the preceding ten to twelve years.

City comedy deliberately turns upon the relationship between patriarchy and paternalism. Indeed, the plays make clear that these exist as separate notions and represent opposing forms of political organization. They mark this difference by demonstrating the general incompetence of natural fathers, uncles, and grandfathers who almost always try to prevent the marriage of a virtuous maid to a reformed gallant. In *A Chaste Maid in Cheapside,* Yellowhammer would marry his daughter to Sir Walter Whorehound and his son to Whorehound's mistress. All this, out of a desire to improve himself by having his children marry up! In *The Roaring Girl,* covetousness also makes Sir Alexander Wengrave prevent his son from marrying. With notable regularity, plays by Marston, Middleton, Jonson and Dekker find paternal characters unable to fill the role of patriarch when they act as the head of household. This principle is underscored by their abuse of the principle of inheritance. Surveying the plots of city comedies from 1603 to 1613, Michael Shapiro writes, 'in the typical satiric city comedy, a prodigal gallant endeavors to regain his land or his money or both from a usurious, miserly father figure.... In all cases, the young man has a moral if not a legal claim to the land or money' (Shapiro 1977, p. 56).

It is in telling the difference between paternalism and patriarchy, furthermore, that inheritance becomes the issue at hand in all of these plays. In *Epicoene,* an attempt to disinherit the nephew presents a challenge to the principle of patrilineal descent. Jonson could not be clearer on this point. To the news Morose would disinherit Sir Dauphine Eugenie, Jonson gives Truewit the following lines: 'I'll tell thee what I would do. I would make a false almanack get it printed; and then have him drawn out on a coronation day to the Tower–wharf, and kill with the noice of the ordinance. Disinherit thee! he cannot, man. Art thou next of blood, and his sister's son?' (B. Jonson, *Epicoene, or The Silent Woman,* ed. L. Beauline [Lincoln, Nebraska, 1966], I, i, 215–20).

The figures of festival seem to side with the interests of 'the next of blood' when Morose is subjected to the noises of coronation-day celebrations and wed to a woman who is a man. By the same token, *A Mad World, My Masters* turns on a benevolent grandfather who is the figure of hospitality itself. He can neither be gulled nor robbed by a grandson who wants to steal his inheritance before it has legally passed down to him. For this attempt to violate the principle of genealogy, the playwright marries off the disrespectful grandson to his grandfather's courtesan – still with the assurance he will inherit in due time.

In keeping with the threat that paternalism poses to patriarchy is the strategy of splitting the female characters. No women in city comedy are allowed to habour the desires which made the Elizabethan romantic heroine politically important. Features that could have combined to make a Hermia, Portia, Rosalind, or Viola, can only provide the stuff of separate and oppositional characters. *Measure for Measure* demonstrates as well as any play this tendency to cut categories where Elizabethan comedy was wont to dissolve boundaries. Comparing this play to its Elizabethan source in Whetstone's *The Historie of Promos and Cassandara* (1578), one finds that Shakespeare has divided the materials comprising Cassandra to form Isabella and Mariana. Similarly, *The Malcontent* sets the chaste wife of Malevole against Pietro's promiscuous wife to create a conflict between chastity and desire. In every case, this conflict nullifies the fantasy of marriage based on desire. Isabella may enter a convent or marry Duke Vicentio, but in contrast with the heroines of romantic comedy, she may never pursue her own desires. The woman of desire is automatically sullied, it appears, while the woman who lack all desire steps forth as the female component of comic resolution. A woman of no desire, like Isabella in *Measure for Measure,* demonstrates the Jacobean relation of submission to patriarchy. Through acts of obeisance, she elicits a display of generosity on Vincentio's part, which is the most positive face of political authority.

So long as kinship remains the language of politics, disruption of its rules is tantamount to political chaos. Thus inversion of patronage relations organizing the city invariably makes itself felt in sexual transgressions, all of which maybe read as assaults against the Jacobean notion of monarchy. In *The Malcontent,* accordingly, the ambitious courtier Mendoza knows that he must seduce Altofront's wife to wrest hold of political power. Just as chastity assumes idealized forms in Altofront's wife, so we find eroticism debased. A few lines from *Measure for Measure* are sufficient to show how desire has been transformed from a force promoting social health to one that proves destructive. As Claudio explains, 'Our natures do pursue, / Like rats that ravin down their proper bane, / A thirsty evil, and when we drink we die' (I, ii, 128–30). The city world generally contains but one virtuous female, as the exception to the rule, who exists in danger controlled by the forces ruling the city. Although this female appears to be a throwback to the earlier comic heroine who aggressively arranged her own marriage, they differ in a basic respect: the women in city comedy who take on this patriarchal prerogative are never aristocratic women. This is crucial – more crucial than their gender – to their use of such authority. Because these women are not aristocratic, they, unlike the women of romantic comedy and Jacobean tragedy, are not in fact usurping the prerogative of the aristocratic male. When Moll Yellowhammer marries Touchwood Junior, then, or when the young Wengrave marries Mary Fitzallard, these women do not present a direct challenge to patriarchal power. To the contrary, they countermand some paternal figure – usually a father – who lacks the ability to properly oversee the exchange of women in his family.

In this light, the comic resolutions that so clearly disturb any attempt to arrive at some moral interpretation of these plays make perfect sense. There is nothing wrong, for example, with Sir Bounteous Passage marrying off his whore to his grandson. Sir Bounteous privileges the principle of genealogy over that of competition as he punishes the grandson for trying to rob his generous grandfather. Satire is aimed at certain corrupt practices, as Margot Heinemann explains, and the city corrupts knights and gallants as readily as merchants. For all the city's power to disrupt and overturn it, however, the aristocratic principle of patriarchy invariably triumphs over paternalism. *A Chaste Maid* is a case in point. It concludes by having the impotent Sir Oliver Kix reward Touchwood Senior for administering the 'magic waters' to Lady Kix which have made his lady pregnant. More than that, the knight offers the impoverished and too-fertile Touchwood Senior the most generous form of patronage:

I am so endeared to thee for my wife's fruitfulness
That I charge you both, your wife and thee,
To live no more asunder for the world's frowns;
I have purse and bed and board for you;
Be not afraid to go to your business roundly;
Get children, and I'll keep them.

> (T. Middleton, *A Chaste Maid in Cheapside*,
> ed. R. B. Parker [London, 1969], V, iv, 79–84).

However uncomfortable the modern reader might feel with this arrangement, as a conclusion to a play riddled with sexual disease and greed, it nevertheless fulfills the Jacobean conditions for comic resolution. Sir Oliver declares the child his, and the child assumes its position within a genealogical system of descent. Through this child, the patrimony remains in the family, and Whorehound is disinherited. The generous Sir Oliver takes a politically appropriate measure, then, when he shares his wealth with the man who cuckolds him. Yet another example can be seen in *A Trick to Catch the Old One*. Wit-Good the gallant may have been a profligate and foolishly pawned his estates to his uncle, but it is the uncle, Lucre who refuses to observe the rules of kinship. For this Lucre is gulled and Wit-Good recovers his patrimony. As the principle of blood once again wins out over the intolerable principle of economic competition, we seem to have a consistent rule guiding the construction of many if not all of these plays: so long as the principles of genealogy are observed, other social and economic violations can go unnoticed in restoring a society to order.

These plays, then, are part of a much larger argument in which the dominant class confronted various practices which authorized a different basis for political authority. I would argue that a middle class as we now understand it does not supply the counterargument of these plays. At the same time, critics who feel those in the middle classes – more properly, the middle rank – were receiving shabby treatment at the hands of Jacobean playwrights are correct. An assortment of groups, sects and factions – neither aristocracy nor laboring poor – were being represented in decidedly negative terms. For another hundred years after the passing of citizen comedy, this group would continue to be so represented. Long after patriarchy gave way to paternalism as the dominant way of thinking political power, the figures of feast table and festival continued to bind the populace to the aristocracy in what E.P. Thompson has termed a 'moral economy' (Thompson 1971).

13 Smithfield and Authorship: Ben Jonson*

PETER STALLYBRASS AND ALLON WHITE

If Foucault provided New Historicism with a sense of the power of **discourses** to write their truths upon the **body**, earlier Marxist critics still influenced those critics who sought to evade the stranglehold of **representations**. In particular, Mikhail Bakhtin's notion of pre-modern culture as a **heteroglossia** or polyphony of voices offered a purchase on Renaissance drama, where clashing dialects and accents are intrinsic to the action. In *The Politics and Poetics of Transgression* Peter Stallybrass and Allon White surveyed the rift between literary and popular culture, which they trace in this extract to the inauguration by writers such as Ben Jonson of the concept of the author as master of a monological text. A play such as *Bartholomew Fair* explicitly turns away from the dirt and laughter of the marketplace, by this interpretation, as literature decontaminates itself of its earthy origins. Henceforth, **carnival** will become a means of social control; but the price paid by high art will be a suicidal etiolation, like the fasting to death of the hunger-artist in a story by Kafka. The allusion seems a corrective to Stephen Greenblatt's Kafkaesque defeatism that subversion is 'not for us' (Chapter 5). Culture deludes itself, we infer, if it thinks its poetics are all-powerful over the crowd that 'hurries on past', eager to satisfy its different desires.

In the last chapter of *Rabelais and his World*, Bakhtin argues that 'the literary and linguistic consciousness of the Renaissance' was formed 'at a complex intersection of languages, dialects, idioms and jargons':

---

* Reprinted from *The Politics and Poetics of Transgression*, (London: Methuen, 1987), pp. 66–79.

The primitive and naive coexistence of languages and dialects had come to an end; the new consciousness was born not in a perfected and fixed linguistic system but at the intersection of many languages and at the point of their most intense interorientation and struggle. Languages are philosophies - not abstract but concrete, social philosophies, penetrated by a system of values inseparable from living practices and class struggle. This is why every object, every concept, every point of view, as well as every intonation found their place at this intersection of linguistic philosophies and was drawn into an intense ideological struggle.

(Bakthin 1968,pp. 470–1).

This dialogic emphasis on what Bakhtin called *heteroglossia* is a more powerful and useful model of cultural formation than his earlier model of popular symbolism simply 'emerging' out of the literary text. The dialogic model inscribes the discourse of the fair within the wider, contestatory arena of the social formation. No one was more conscious of that arena of 'intense ideological struggle' than Jonson. Indeed, Jonson's specific intervention in that struggle contributed significantly to the construction of the domain of 'authorship' in the period. And the notion of 'authorship' to which Jonson dedicated his poetic career was in every way in contradiction to Saturnalia, the grotesque, even to the theatre itself.

There is no easy sense in which Jonson's work can be considered as an extension of the fair or as an immediate 'copy' of popular symbolic practices. On the contrary: all of Jonson's critical comments are resolutely directed against the popular audience and the 'hacks' whom he saw as serving it. If Jonson's early life had been spent 'as an apprentice brick-layer, then as a soldier in Flanders, and finally (and most significantly) as a common player and play patcher' (Helgerson 1983, p. 145), his career as laureate poet was spent in scourging players, play-patchers and 'groundlings'. In the 1607 preface to *Volpone*, he attacks the 'licence' of those mere playwrights who debase 'stage-poetry'; in the 1612 preface to *The Alchemist*, he derided those plays in which 'the concupiscence of dances and of antics so reigneth'. By contrast he proclaimed his own writing to be 'quick comedy refined' or 'a legitimate poem' or 'one such as other plays should be'. Again and again, Jonson defines the true position of the playwright as that of the poet, and the poet as that of the classical isolated judge standing in opposition to the vulgar throng. In this, of course, he was not alone. Few 'serious' poets prided themselves on their plays. Drayton, for instance, 'who had a hand in some two dozen plays, kept all but one from publication and even that one appeared anonymously' (Helgerson 1983, p. 146).

But whilst even such 'elevated' forms of writing as George Chapman's translation of Homer were dismissed by their authors as 'the droppings of an idle humour; far unworthy the serious expense of an exact gentleman's time', Jonson strove to tell the world, as Suckling put it, that 'plainly he deserved the bays./For his were called *Works*, where others were but plays' (quoted in Helgerson 1983, pp. 21, 37). But the problem remained: whom did 'the author' (itself a problematic concept) write for? Who were to be his judges? With extraordinary vituperative energy, Jonson proceeded to answer these questions by a series of negations. *Bartholomew Fair* itself provides an illuminating example of Jonson at work. The title page of the 1631 edition contains the following quote from Horace's epistles: 'If Democritus were still in the land of the living, he would laugh himself silly, for he would pay far more attention to the audience than to the plays, since the audience offers the more interesting spectacle. But as for the authors of the plays - he would conclude that they were telling their tales to a deaf donkey' (*Bartholomew Fair*, ed. G. Hibbard, 1977, p.2). The title page is followed by a prologue 'To the King's Majesty', in which the 'place', the 'men' and the 'language' of the play are mockingly excused as appropriate to a fair.

And then, mediating between the reading-text and the performance-text, we are presented with 'The Induction on the Stage', in which Jonson dramatises the relationship between the author and the fair and between the author and the text. As Jonson demonstrates, the question of whom he writes for (which kind of audience?), what he writes, and how it is to be judged are intimately connected. The Induction opens with the Stage-keeper, whose function is to sweep the stage and to gather up 'the broken apples' (Jonson 1977, *Ind*.: 50) for the bears who alternated with the actors as the attraction of the Hope Theatre. The Stage-keeper appeals to 'the understanding gentlemen o' the ground' (*Ind*.: 47) – i.e. to the groundlings who stood under the stage – against 'these master-poets' who 'will ha' their own absurd courses' and 'will be informed of nothing' (*Ind*.: 25–6). Jonson's play, he claims, 'is like to be a very conceited scurvy one': 'When it comes to the Fair once, you were e'en as good go to Virginia for anything there is of Smithfield. He has not hit the humours, he does not know 'em; he has not conversed with the Bartholomew-birds' (*Ind*.: 9–12). The Stage-keeper's first accusation, then, is that Jonson is simply ignorant of Smithfield. But from attacking Jonson for failing to represent the sights of the fair, he moves to a second accusation: that Jonson has failed in the very methods of his representation. 'In Master Tarlton's time' – in other words, in the age of the improvising clown – things were done better. And the radical break between Tarlton's theatre and Jonson's can be accounted for by the shift from improvisation to 'master-poets' who stand above and detached from their audiences and thus are as incapable of representing the fair on stage as they are of understanding it at Smithfield.

The 'free' conversation of the Stage-keeper with his 'familiars', though, is ended by the entrance of the Book-holder and the Scrivener. As Jonathan Haynes writes in his fine essay on *Bartholomew Fair*: 'The opposition between the popular and coterie theatres is perfectly expressed in this moment: groundlings vs. gentlemen; the Stage-keeper with his memories of an improvisational theatre vs. the Book-holder and Scrivener, men of the master-poet's written text' (Haynes 1984, p. 659). In contrast to the Stage-keeper's familiarity, the Scrivener proceeds to read out a legal contract which will define the obligations of author and audience alike. In fact, this contract is a mock-version of the critical positions which Jonson had ferociously argued in his previous work. As before, these positions are defined negatively. In the contract, the author attacks those who admire old plays like *The Spanish Tragedy* and *Titus Andronicus*, for although that betrays 'a virtuous and staid ignorance' it is still 'a confirmed error' (*Ind.*: 106–11); he attacks contemporary playwrights, like Shakespeare, for their Calibans, their drolleries, their 'concupiscence of dances and of antics' (*Ind.*: 122–7); he attacks informers who would read his plays as political allegories (*Ind.*: 130–40); he attacks those who confuse the author's morality with the scurrility and profanity of his characters (*Ind.*: 143–7).

But above all, the contract attempts to define the nature of Jonson's 'public' (see Salingar 1979: 151–2). On the one hand, the 'Articles of Agreement' insist that the audience is composed of free, rational individuals and that 'every man here exercise his own judgement, and not censure by contagion, or upon trust' (*Ind.*: 94–5). On the other hand, the articles emphasize the division of the audience into separate classes. The patricians, who are themselves divided into 'the curious and envious' and 'the favouring and judicious', are set against the plebeians with their '*grounded* judgements and understandings' (*Ind.*: 72–3). (It is worth noting how the contract punningly conflates rational judgement and the physical positions of the plebeians who 'stood under' on the 'ground', but the conflation is intended only to act as a reminder of the abyss between the author and the vulgar. In the Latin tag on the title page of his *Workes* (1616), Jonson proudly announced that he did not write for the crowd but for the readership of a select few). But if the audience is divided into patrician and plebeian on an imaginary scale of 'wit', it is also divided more crudely between those who can afford to pay for the expensive seats and those who cannot. And Jonson is mockingly prepared to let each spectator buy his or her right to proclaim judgement: 'it shall be lawful for any man to judge his six penn'orth, his twelve penn'orth, so to his eighteen pence, two shillings, half of a crown to the value of his place' (*Ind.*: 84–5). The juxtaposition of judgement and money is curious, though, a reminder that the author, for all his contempt, is a bought man, dependent for his success upon the applause of conflicting social groups. And even as the author attempts to situate his audience, he himself is positioned in multiple and contradictory ways.

Moreover, the very notion of contract which the Induction proposes is subverted in the play which follows. The contract of marriage between Grace Wellborn and the simpleton Bartholomew Cokes is stolen by Edgworth; Justice Overdo's contract to Grace, whom he bought from the Court of Wards, is rewritten by Quarlous in his own favour; Busy makes himself 'feofee in trust to deceased brethren' (V, ii, 65–6) so as to cozen their heirs. In *Bartholomew Fair*, to insist upon contract is to be mad or a fool. It is the lunatic Trouble-All who makes repeated demands to see the fairgoers' licences: 'Have you a warrant?' (IV, i, 98); 'Whither go you? Where's your warrant?' (IV, ii, 2); 'There must be a warrant had, believe it' (IV, iii, 69). And Justice Overdo's attempts to track down the unwarranted, unlicensed doings of the fair lead only to a cudgelling and the stocks. Similarly, Busy's insistence on the godly contract which prohibits 'Fairs and May-games, Wakes and Whitsun-ales' (IV, vi, 81–2) as well as 'stage-players, rhymers, and morris-dancers' (V, v, 9–10) lands him in the stocks.

In the fair, 'judgement' belongs not to the enforcers of contract but to the cutpurse, the bawd, the ballad-singer and the hobby-horse seller. And in the judgements of the fair, it is the language of the the grotesque body which triumphs over the languages of the Scriptures and of the classics. No Latin tags come to Justice Overdo's aid as he is confronted by his drunk wife vomiting, and no Biblical wisdom helps Busy when the puppet Dionysius pulls up his/her skirt to ridicule 'all fundamentalist distinctions between male and female, righteous and unrighteous, saved and damned' (Barish 1972, p.29). It is as if in silencing the censors (Overdo, Busy, Wasp), Jonson is silencing the classical satiric voice of the 'master-poet', a voice for which he, above all contemporary writers, was responsible. Indeed, even the Induction where Book-holder and Scrivener assert the authority of the author's text over the actor's performance, Jonson seems aware that here, for once, he may have produced a play which is in keeping with the grotesque, saturnalian traditions of the Elizabethan theatre. Although the 'rascal' Stage-keeper is dismissed, the Book-holder tells us that the play is written for his understanding and to 'the scale' of the plebeian audience. It is, the Induction rightly claims, a play as 'full of noise as sport' (79), suited to the Hope, sometimes theatre, sometimes bear-pit, a place 'as dirty as Smithfield, and as a stinking every whit' (154).

But this returns us to the contradictions out of which Jonson's 'authorship' was formed. To the extent that *Bartholomew Fair* was a *popular* play, Jonson could scarcely claim it as his own. For within a classical aesthetic, the text was 'contaminated' both by its subject-matter and by its relation to the 'dirt' of the theatre and the theatrical marketplace. This second form of 'contamination' is also imagined by Shakespeare when he is writing in the more 'elevated' form of the sonnet, a form inscribed within a network of aristocratic traditions and patronage:

> O for my sake do you wish fortune chide
> The guilty goddess of my harmful deeds,
> That did not better for my life provide
> Than public means which public manners breeds.
> Thence comes it that my name receives a brand,
> And almost thence my nature is subdued
> To what it works in, like the dyer's hand.

(Sonnet 111)

Jonson wrote obsessively about the contaminating influence of 'public means' and 'public manners', and resented more than Shakespeare the 'brand' which dubbed him a mere playwright. But in *Bartholomew Fair*, Jonson was 'subdued' not only by the Hope audience but also, from the perspective of a classical aesthetic, by his own choice of subject-matter. One consequence of this choice was the kind of arduous labour which Dryden, for instance, undertook to separate Jonson from his material. In Dryden's view, *Bartholomew Fair* is the 'lowest kind of comedy', but then Jonson 'does so raise his matter.... as to render it delightful'. Jonson has made 'an excellent lazar of the fair' and 'the copy is of price, though the original be vile' (*Essays of John Dryden* ed. W. Ker [1926], pp.74–5). But however much the author may be praised for his act of 'elevation', a classical aesthetic remains deeply suspicious of saturnalian comedy: however brilliant, it is 'the lowest kind', however excellent, it is a 'lazar', a beggar with some loathsome disease all too liable to be contagious. Perhaps it was *Bartholomew Fair* which Dryden had in mind when he published *A Parallel of Poetry and Painting* in 1695. There again he approaches comedy as 'a representation of human life in inferior persons, and low subject', comparable to 'the painting of clowns' or 'the representation of a Dutch kermis'. And again, Dryden returns to the image of a diseased beggar: comedy is 'a Lazar in comparison to a Venus'. But here, Dryden goes on to imagine an even lower form of art: farce or 'the grotesque'. The grotesque is 'a very monster in a Bartholomew Fair, for the mob to gaze at for their two-pence'. And laughter itself is now conceptualized as lazar-like: 'Laughter is indeed the propriety of a man, but just enough to distinguish him from his elder brother with four legs. 'Tis a kind of bastard pleasure too, taken in at the eyes of the vulgar gazers, and at the ears of the beastly audience' (*Essays of John Dryden*, pp. 132–3).

What justification can there be, then, for the grotesque or even for comedy? Dryden's answer is that plays serve a *political* function. He concludes his discussion of the grotesque by quoting Davenant's preface to *Gondibert*: ''Tis the wisdom of a government to permit plays [he might have added – farces] as 'tis the prudence of a carter to put bells upon his horses, to make them carry their burthens cheerfully' (Ibid., p. 133). We have moved a long way from Jonson's concept of the true dramatist as the corrector of ignorance and vice; for Davenant *all* plays, and for Dryden comedies in particular, are legitimate only as placebos, suitable to dampen the dangerous political propensities of 'the vulgar gazers' and 'the beastly audience'. From this perspective, plays, fairs and festivals were interchangeable as safety valves: as Sir Henry Wotton commented on the Venetian carnival in 1622, public festivals were necessary because 'the restrained passions [are] indeed the most dangerous'. This was a position which was most vigorously argued after the Civil War. The Duke of Newcastle, for instance wrote to Charles II that 'ther Shoulde be playes to Goe upp and downe the Counterye....The devirtismentes will amuse the peoples thaughtes, and keepe them In harmless action which will free your Majestie from faction and Rebellion.' And Newcastle makes it clear that he thinks of plays as only an extension of morris dances, cakes and ales, May, Christmas and Shrovetide festivities, all of which are conducive to the good order of 'merrye Englande'. Jonson was not unfamiliar with these arguments: James I supported popular festivity, publishing his *Book of Sports* in 1618 and Jonson himself submitted a poem to *Annalia Dubrensia*, a collection which proclaimed the Cotswold Games as 'harmless [i.e. depoliticized] Olimpicke exercises', in opposition to the 'standings, lectures, exercises' of the Puritans. *Bartholomew Fair* itself could be read as a 'harmless action' dedicated to the suppression of 'faction and Rebellion'.

But to do so, of course, would be to conflate festival, fair and theatre as public arenas. And it was precisely against this conflation that Jonson's elevated concept of authorship was directed. One strategy which Jonson adopted was to elide the position of the poet with that of the monarch. As Don Wayne argues, in Jonson

> The place of the author is finally privileged in opposition to that of the theatre audience by an identification of his own judgement with the 'power of judge' of the king. In this way, the place of the king, the highest earthly place, functions as more than just that of another audience of the play; it is the place of final authority.
>
> (Wayne, 1982, p. 118).

Associated with the royal patron, Jonson could adopt a position above groundlings and learned critics alike. Helgerson notes that '*Solus Rex aut poeta non quotannis nascitur*' was 'one of Jonson's favourite Latin tags' (Helgerson 1983, p.50). Jonson believed that ideally there should be a 'consociation of offices' between the monarch and the scholar, in which power was exchanged for learning and learning for power (*Ben Jonson:Works* ed. C. Herford and P. Simpson [Oxford 1925–52], I, p.565).

But the relation of poet to prince was not equitable 'consociation' as Jonson knew to his cost. In 1597, he was arrested for his part in *The Isle of Dogs*; in 1603, 'he was called before the Council for his *Sejanus* and accused both of popery and treason by [Northampton]'; in 1605, he was imprisoned for his part in *Eastward Ho*, and it was reported that he would have his nose and ears cut off. Thus, the epilogue of *Bartholomew Fair* can be read both as an invocation of his royal patron against '[the] envy of a few' and as an ironic acknowledgement that the play, despite having 'the Master of the *Revels*' hand for it' (V, v. 15), could still be adjudged, as Busy says of all plays, 'scurrility' and a production of 'the Master of *Rebels*' (V, v, 16–17). In its address to the king the epilogue turns upon the relation of the licensed to the licentious:

> Your Majesty hath seen the play, and you
>   Can best allow it from your ear and view.
> You know the scope of writers, and what store
>   Of leave is given them, if they take not more,
> And turn it into license. You can tell
>   If we have used that leave you gave us well;
> Or whether we to rage or license break,
>   Or be profane, or make profane men speak.
> This is your power to judge, great sir.

Even if the play did gratify the 'ear and view' of a king, the writer's claim to 'authority' was by no means assured. As Jonson's act of negation antithetically witnesses, the poet's success with the court opened him up to the charges of 'servile flatterie' and of 'smelling parasite' (*Ben Jonson: Works*, VIII, pp. 41,48).

Certainly, Jonson wanted to believe in the alliance between prince and poet whilst rarely showing enthusiasm for his role as a writer in the popular theatre. Against both of these positions however he tried to define a new role in which authority was invested in authorship itself. Hence Jonson's troubled, problematic relationship to both the high and the low symbolic positions of the social hierarchy. We see him trying to stabilize and dignify an emergent place for authorship at a distance both from the aristocracy and the plebeians, and yet this authorial investiture – for that is what it aspired to be – was only locatable, 'groundable', through its symbolic relation to existing hierarchies, existing languages, symbols and practices of high and low. The insertion of professional authorship *between* these was a fraught negotiation of a 'middle' space and a complex contestation of traditional dichotomies. Authorship in this sense required a two-handed fending off of royal and popular patronage alike, since both entangled the poet in symbolic arrangements, rituals and deferences which no longer quite answered his *professional* needs.

The 'contagion of the low' is felt much more pressingly by Jonson, at least when he was writing for the theatre. The 'authorship' of his plays, indeed, was an act performed *on* and *against* the theatrical script, so as to efface its real conditions of production. The *Workes* which Jonson published in 1616 were the result of a labour whereby his plays appeared as literary texts, miraculously freed from the contagion of the marketplace. Stephen Orgel has reminded us of the *collaborative* process through which plays of the period were formed:

> The company commissioned the play, usually stipulated the subject, often provided the plot, often parcelled it out, scene by scene, to several playwrights. The text thus produced was a working model, which the company then revised as seemed appropriate. The author had little or no say in these revisions: the text belonged to the company, and the authority represented by the text – I am talking now about the *performing* text – is that of the company, the owners, not that of the playwright, the author.
>
> (Orgel 1981, p.3)

Orgel then brilliantly demonstrates how Jonson transformed *Sejanus* from theatrical script to literary text:

> The play was first written in collaboration with another playwright; that was the version the actors performed. But in preparing the play for publication, Jonson *took control* of the text: he replaced his collaborator's scenes with ones of his own, and added a good deal of new material, largely historical documentation... Jonson here has succeeded in suppressing the theatrical production, and has replaced it with an independent, printed text, which he consistently refers to, moreover, not as a play but as a poem.
>
> (Orgel 1981, p.4).

The literary text, though, was haunted by these 'suppressions'. The more it strove to be 'independent', the more the author needed to deny the patron, the audience, the collaborators, even the readers upon whom he was dependent. In fact the author remained, like the dyer's hand, subdued to the elements he worked in, but these appear as negated or denied elements, taking on a new and different form under the sign of their negation. This process is analogous to that described by Freud in his essay 'On negation': the content of the repressed image does indeed make its way into consciousness, but on the condition that it is denied, devalued and negated. 'Negation is a way of taking cognizance of what is repressed; indeed, it is already a lifting of repression, though not, of course, an acceptance of what is repressed'. Negation was Jonson's way of taking cognizance, even as he rejected, the hybridization of his medium and his audience. The theatre was, as Dekker observed in *The Gull's Hornbook*, a 'Royal Exchange', and the poet's muses were 'Merchants'. And in the theatre, 'your stinkard has the self-same liberty to be there in his tobacco fumes which your sweet courtier hath and ... your carman and tinker claim as strong a voice in their suffrage, and sit to give judgement on the play's life and death, as well as the proudest *Momus* among the tribe of Critic'. It was from the theatre that Jonson's plays had to be removed so that they could become 'literature' within a classical canon.

For all the deliberate conservatism of this strategy, we should recognize that Jonson was demanding a status which, as Don Wayne has argued, 'was unacknowledged in the traditional social and cultural system from which England was then emerging' (1982,p.129). Jonson was attempting to dissociate the professional writer from the clamour of the marketplace and to install his works in the studies of the gentry and the libraries of the universities. In this, he succeeded. When Sir Thomas Bodley wrote to Thomas James in 1612 about the establishment of his library, he classed plays as 'idle bookes, and riffe raffes': even if 'some little profit might be reaped...out of some of our playbookes, the benefit therof will nothing countervaile, the harm that the scandal will bring into the Librairie, when it shalbe given out, that we stuffe it full of baggage bookes'. In publishing his plays as part of his folio *Workes*, Jonson removes them from the ranks of play-quartos which could be catalogued along with the 'the *Academy of Complements, Venus undress'd, Westminster Drollery* and...a Bundle of *Bawdy* Songs in Manuscript'. His plays were to become fitting companions to the works of Horace and Virgil on the library shelves.

As 'master-poet', then, Jonson constituted his identity in opposition to the theatre and the fair. Through the imaginary separation of the scholar's study and library from the theatrical marketplace, Jonson simultaneously mapped out the divisions between the 'civilized' and the grotesque body, between the stunted quarto and the handsome folio, between the 'author' and the hack, between 'pure' literature and social hybridization. In the image of the fair, the author could rewrite the social and economic relations which determined his own existence; in the fair he could stigmatize the voices which competed against his own and reveal just how 'dirty' were the hands which sullied his 'pure' wares.

But disgust bears the impress of desire, and Jonson found in the huckster, the cony-catcher and the pick-pocket an image of his own precarious and importuning craft. Proclaiming so loudly how all the other plays were mere cozenings, did not Jonson pursue the perennial techniques of the mountebank who decried the deceptions and the false wares of others the more easily to practise his own deceptions and pass off his own productions as the 'real thing'?

In separating self from the popular festive scene, authorship after Jonson gradually developed in accordance with the ideal of the individual which was emerging within bourgeois culture – the individual, that is, as 'the proprietor of his own person and capacities, for which he owes nothing to society' (quoted in Fish 1984, p.26). Authorship became a visionary embodiment of this ideal to the degree that it represented itself as transcendent to the 'common' place of the market. In so far as the author still inhabited the fair, it was increasingly either as an aloof spectator or as spectacle and freak. As the latter, he appears most poignantly in the work of Kafka, himself both hunger-artist and most resourceful of conmen.

In 'A Fasting Showman', Kafka wrote of a hunger-artist who draws large crowds to the cage in which he fasts and where he lives at first in 'visible glory, honoured by the world'. But as the years pass, the crowds dwindle; a fasting showman is not, after all, much of a spectacle. The hunger-artist is reduced to performing at a side-show in the circus and the crowds hurry on past him to see the animals. Finally, he stages a fast unto death, after which he is replaced by a young panther whose 'noble body' is 'furnished almost to bursting point with all that is needed' and whose freedom 'seemed to lurk in its jaws'. But before the hunger-artist dies, the overseer asks him why he has spent his life trapped within the cage of his own wasting body. 'Because I couldn't find any food that I liked', he replied.

Like the hunger-artist, Jonson presented withdrawal as a spectacle. Authorship, as he made it, was a series of leave-takings – from other writers, from theatrical audiences, from actors, even from patrons. In his poetry, as Stanley Fish says, Jonson emphasized 'the notion of the "gathered self" which is always to itself "the same" (Epigram 98), a self which presents such a closed face to the world that it is invulnerable to invasion and remains always "untouch'd" '(Fish 1984, p. 39). Yet within his writings Jonson also projected a self quite antithetical to this, the man 'of prodigious wast', 'laden with bellie', who knew 'the fury of men's gullets' (*Ben Jonson: Works*, I pp.179, 226–30). This was the Jonson who concluded *Every Man Out of his Humour* with the 'violently impatient' Macilente (whose name means 'lean' or 'meagre') turning from his 'envious apoplexy' with the help of the audience's applause to become 'as fat as Sir John Falstaff'. If, as master-poet, Jonson could find no food that he liked, as a dramatist in the popular theatre he knew the appetites, if not of the panther, at least of the pig.

Yet *Bartholomew Fair*, his 'pig-wallow', was, for whatever reason, excluded from the 1616 *Workes*. Although we know that Jonson worked on producing a copy of the play for the 1631 Folio, the play was printed, but never distributed, in Jonson's lifetime. Not attaining the status of 'literature', it remained until 1640 simply a play that had been performed in the popular theatre. And that seems appropriate, for with its enormities, abominations and its intimacy with 'low' forms, it would certainly have compromised the haughty individuation of the classical to which Jonson so avidly aspired. Dryden was right to see *Bartholomew Fair* as 'the lowest kind of comedy'. Inheriting (in part from Jonson) a classical aesthetic by then deeply committed to separation from the repertoires of the fair and marketplace, Dryden could conceptualize the 'low' only negatively. After the Restoration, the 'logic' of excess, of the lower bodily stratum, of the fair, even of popular theatre itself, was re-inscribed as the 'bastard pleasure' of 'vulgar gazers' and 'beastly audiences'.

Postscript
Richard Dutton

New Historicism is not without its critics; an approach to literary and cultural studies so stimulating and so iconoclastic could hardly fail to stir up controversy. It has met with resistance from traditional schools of criticism, particularly those whose own credentials it seeks to challenge; these span the entire conventional political spectrum – from entrenched conservatives dedicated to preserving the integrity of the literary 'canon', through liberal humanists who see literature as the testing ground of essential values, to orthodox Marxists who relate literature primarily to the economic base of its production. There has also been a marked equivocation in the response of some – notably the feminists – with whom New Historicism would seem to share a degree of common cause. And there has been a sometimes rancorous debate within the ranks of its own proponents as to ultimate aims and strategies. I wish here briefly to address some of the issues raised by these controversies.

The defence of humanist values, the essentialist status of the text and the privileged status of canonical authorship were all explicit issues in Charles R. Forker's review of *Political Shakespeare* (1985), the collection of broadly New Historicist essays edited by Jonathan Dollimore and Alan Sinfield:

> A monochrome high seriousness virtually annihilates all Shakespearean wit, charm, and sense of humour unless these can be harnessed vulgarly to some ulterior social moralism. Obsessive class-and gender-consciousness make for a kind of inverse snobbery. One would never guess from reading these commentaries that sacrificial love, self-surrender, renunciation, forgiveness, chastity, unselfishness, chivalric courage, or Christian humility and submission could have any honorable place in Shakespeare's complex of values. Power and oppression become exclusively and reductively the theme. Implicit also in this school of academic discourse is the arrogant assumption that the interpretive act, if it can be sufficiently startling and revisionist, somehow displaces and ought to displace the work interpreted, even if (or perhaps because) it comes from the pen of Western civilization's supreme literary genius.

Similar themes occur in Harry Keyishian's review of Dollimore's own *Radical Tragedy: Religion, Ideology and Power in the Drama of Shakespeare and His Contemporaries* (1984), which praises his thesis as ' exhilarating and seductive, since it requires us to take these playwrights at their word', but simultaneously undercuts the praise by an appeal to common sense and collective wisdom (key values in the liberal humanist tradition which New Historicists have consistently called into question): 'If they had, in fact, been doing what Dollimore thinks, they certainly were greater, more courageous, and keener than we have thought them.' He finishes on a note of condescension, implicitly diminishing the wider movements to which Dollimore belongs by trying to implicate them in an attack on his personal deficiencies as a critic: 'Unfortunately, even readers who share Dollimore's orientations are generally likely to be unconvinced by his readings of individual plays.'[2]

For all Forker's and Keyishian's conviction that they were addressing a 'school of academic discourse' or a group of people with shared 'orientations', there remains a problem about the identity of the movement as a whole. Is it indeed a movement, with a shared agenda? This is an issue that sceptics have not been slow to exploit. As Louis Montrose suggests, New Historicism narrowly defined is predominantly an American enterprise in origin, post-structuralist in emphasis, looking particularly to Foucault as a mentor; the British wing of the movement (with some transatlantic support) generally prefers the term Cultural Materialism, looking to such as Gramsci, Althusser and Raymond Williams for its foundations.[3] Both camps stress the subversive implications (for modern society) of the ways in which literary texts demonstrate the discursive construction of power relations, but the former have been much more sceptical than the latter about the potential in this for generating political activism for any real change. These are, however, differences about which the parties have been able to communicate amicably and constructively; see, for example, Alan Sinfield's late, considered review of Stephen Greenblatt's seminal *Renaissance Self-Fashioning* (1980).[4] Jean E. Howard, in this collection, confesses that her 'main reservation about much of this work is its failure to reflect on itself. Taking the form of the reading, a good deal of this criticism suppresses any discussion of its own methodology and assumptions.' This seems rather truer of the American New Historicists, notably Greenblatt and Montrose, who are centrally in her sights here, than of the Cultural Materialists, though Greenblatt has taken such strictures to heart and addressed them in his *Shakespearean Negotiations* (Oxford, 1988), while Jonathan Dollimore has taken stock of objections to Cultural Materialism in the second edition of his *Radical Tragedy* (London, 1989).

Rather more contentious has been an on-going debate about the methodologies and ultimate orientations of the movement as a whole, about whether it is essentially an off-shoot of Marxism and whether it has the courage of its (sometimes tacit) convictions. As this volume tries to demonstrate, the two wings concur and overlap in their convictions about the materiality of discourse, about its positive role in the shaping of cultural forms and structures, about its function as an agency of power. This is perhaps sufficient common ground to justify the use of a single label, though Steven Mullaney's objections to 'New Historicism' as that label, that it implies a more unified theoretical movement than actually exists, that it encourages 'false dichotomies (old vs.new, history vs. literature)' (p. xi) are not without weight. Carol Thomas Neely proposes a possibly ironic conflation of labels, 'cult-historicists', to deal with this difficulty, but she also points to a more fundamental problem in observing that other 'new' critical approaches (specifically Lacanian and deconstructive ones) are 'theoretically quite different but practically not entirely separate' from those of her 'cult-historicists.'[5] The borders of New Historical theory and practice, it has to be admitted, are not easy to define or to marshal.

The supposed reduction by New Historicists of all history (and of all literary discourse within history) to matters of power is the central theme of a much more wide-ranging, sceptical review of the whole movement by Edward Pechter. He defines it as 'a kind of "Marxist criticism"' inasmuch as it 'views history and contemporary political life as determined, wholly or in essence, by struggle, contestation, power relations, *libido dominandi*', a proposition which he finds problematic.[6] Unravelling what he sees as a sequence of flaws, incoherencies and self-contradictions within a wide range of texts, he acknowledges 'the enormous interest and energy this kind of criticism has generated', but concludes: 'Putting the text back into history (or better, histories: our histories, its histories) is clearly a valuable project. Maybe it is the only project. In any case, it is far too important to be left to the new historicists' (p. 302). An over-narrow concentration on New Historicism may obscure the fact that historians of a more traditional stamp have also 're-politicised' the English Renaissance over the past decade, but on entirely different premises. The so-called 'revisionist' historians concentrate on such matters as aristocratic factions and the processes of patronage in propounding a view of Tudor and early Stuart politics (especially the politics of the court) very different from earlier accounts, both Whig and Marxist, which in their different ways had emphasised the corruption, imminent break-down and revolutionary potential of the system. Among the key authors and texts here are Conrad Russell, *The Crisis of Parliaments: English History, 1509–1660* (Oxford, 1971); Kevin Sharpe (ed.), *Faction and Parliament: Essays on Early Stuart History* (Oxford, 1978), his own *Sir Robert Cotton, 1586–1631* (Oxford, 1979), and (with Steven N. Zwicker, eds), *Politics of Discourse: Literature and History in Seventeenth–Century England* (Berkeley, Ca. 1987); E.W. Ives, *Faction in Tudor England* (London, 1979); Linda Levy Peck, *Northampton: Patronage and Policy at the Court of James I* (London, 1982); R. Malcolm Smuts, *Court Culture and the Origins of a Royalist Tradition in Early Stuart England* (Philadelphia, 1987); and David Starkey *et. al.*, *The English*

221

Court (London, 1987). In such works, the 'revisionists' have tended to stress the continuities and pragmatic accommodations within the system as it operated, providing a view of the practical mechanics of politics and power which in many ways is radically at odds with the New Historicist emphasis on ideologically charged structures of authority and subjection.

Leeds Barroll has pointed out the tendency of New Historicists to accept 'old' historical explanations of such matters of the Richard II play performance before the Essex rebellion and James I's supposed love of theatre, rather than enquire what 'revisionist' perspectives would reveal about such matters. Their concern with crises in power relations inclines them to favour older, more confrontational, explanations of what went on - even though their epistemological premises purport to be very different from those of the Whig and Marxist historians on whom they tacitly draw:

> It would be unfortunate were we to restrict the new historicism to those approaches to Shakespeare built upon the unquestioning acceptance of an extremely narrow set of documents, creating a configuration of events ensconced in traditional narratives and premised upon elementary concepts of political process. A new history does not ask us to follow one overarching theory of culture: it asks us to deal with the profound problems posed by the notion of the historical event.[7]

Annabel Patterson similarly castigates Stephen Greenblatt, among others, for a predisposition to configure Renaissance theatre within narrow, faceless and uniform structures of power:

> We need to return to a less impersonal, less totalitarian account of how Shakespeare's theater probably functioned, in a network of power in the abstract and in nobody's hands, but rather of local ordinances, unwritten and unstable policies, fads, fashions, pretexts, improvisations, human impulses, and the occasional application of discipline and punishment both to texts and to persons, by other persons whose names and motives are not indecipherable.[8]

More generally, Pechter's article, mentioned above, also draws attention to apparent inconsistencies in New Historicists' treatment of historical data and the question of whether some kinds of evidence have priority over others, given their conviction that all information is subsumed within a uniform system of discourse. Analogous problems were highlighted in papers given by Stanley Fish and Howard Felperin at the Convention of the Modern Language Association of America in New Orleans in December 1988. The New Historicists and traditional academic historians distrust each others' premises so much (not least on the status of literary texts, the former regarding them as powerful voices, the latter as more marginal evidence) that they have rarely confronted each other directly. But their interests overlap in key areas where literature and politics indisputably overlap, such as courtly and civic theatricals, patronage and censorship. The differences between them (highlighted, for example, by the distinguished historian, Lawrence Stone, in a paper on 'The Future of History ' given at the University of Lancaster in May 1990, which was openly sceptical of the credentials of literary critics to pursue historical topics) certainly require further investigation.

One notable constituency which seemed initially to have much in common with the New Historicists, but latterly have distanced themselves somewhat, are the feminists. Both groups are concerned, to a degree, with questions of the cultural construction of identity and subjectivity, not least in the area of gender, and their aims overlap on many specific issues; there seemed initially every possibility of making common cause. Essays like Catherine Belsey's 'Disrupting Sexual Difference: Meaning and Gender in the Comedies' and Phyllis Rackin's 'Androgyny, Mimesis, and the Marriage of the Boy Heroine on the English Stage' are both feminist and Cultural Materialist.[9] But the continued fixation of the (mainly male) New Historicists with the established canon and their persistent concentration, where they have introduced new 'texts' at all, on male-authored and male-centred ones (which 'do not much concern themselves with women, sexuality, gender relations, marriage and the family, and when they do, their concern is to master women') has led to a distinct disenchantment, voiced most cogently here by Carol Thomas Neely:

> All of the topoi of the new approaches: the historicity and intertexuality of texts; the constriction of history to power, politics, and ideology ... have the effect of putting woman in her customary place, of re-producing-patriarchy – the same old master plot. In it, women continue to be marginalized, erased, displaced, allegorised, and their language and silence continue to serve the newly dominant ideology. The new approaches are not new enough.[10]

This in many ways mirrors a fairly acrimonious debate within New Historicism itself over an issue central to the joint 'cult-historicist' agenda, which is the question of the privileging of texts. A repeated article of faith in this critical practice is that the high-literary texts (the works of Shakespeare, Spenser, Jonson, Donne and Milton, for example), previously given 'canonical' status by earlier theorists, had no right to such exclusive attention, which effectively repressed other forms of discourse and the voices of more marginalized groups (especially radicals and women): the New Historicists would change all that. But they have not done so, although this has been on their agenda for a decade now: study continues to be focused overwhelmingly (in the name of freeing them from earlier 'appropriations') on authors who were already canonical. As James Holstun complains, in a wide-ranging and rigorous critique: 'If we bracket new historicist studies focusing on More, Sidney, Spenser, Milton, the Elizabethan and Jacobean lyric poets and playwrights, only a handful of books and articles remains'. He argues that more attention should be paid to the radical pamphlet literature that managed to get into print during and after the Civil War for a truer picture of the repressed voices of the Renaissance: 'the new historicism should stop policing so vigilantly the borders between itself and Marxist criticism and should start examining more carefully the voices of popular resistance that become more and more audible at mid-century'.[11] Analogous concerns are voiced by Carolyn Porter, who argues that the movement 'has generated forms of critical practice that continue to exhibit the force of a formalist legacy whose subtle denials of history – as the scene of heterogeneity, difference, contradiction, at least – persist', preferring herself 'to hypothesize a continuous, but continuously heterogeneous discursive field in which dominant and subjugated views occupy the same place, as it were'.[12]

Ironically, but inevitably, Shakespeare continues to enjoy the lion's share of attention in all this, as successive writers try to appropriate him to their own cause though not without some embarrassment. Note, for example, the defensiveness of a self-proclaimed Cultural Materialist like Steven Mullaney, who in confessing that 'my focus is on Shakespeare' hurries on to explain that this is only because he is 'one of the few playwrights whose career encompassed both the height and the decline of popular theatre in Elizabethan and Jacobean England', not simply because of his culturally created reputation.[13] Given the strength of reaction to their works (itself no small testament to the power of discourse, which is such a central theme for them) the New Historicists have had to define and defend themselves as best they can, constantly going back to first principles. This is well demonstrated in an issue of *New Literary History*, where Richard Levin has focused his long-running crusade to denounce supposed cant and muddle in all new readings of Renaissance drama on the New Historicists and Cultural Materialists. He clinically dissects a number of representative assertions by them about concepts of the self, 'literature' as a separate high category of writing, the biological determination of gender, and the non-illusionistic nature of Elizabethan theatre: ' There is, however, one idea that I suspect really was unthinkable to (the Elizabethans)–that anyone in the future would seriously maintain that they were unable to think of the relationship of gender to biology, or of a unified and continuous self, or any of the other alleged nonideas-of-the-time presented in these discoveries'. Levin's conservative common sense is a useful corrective, but hardly the last word. The issue might not be what was thinkable so much as what ideas carried most weight at the time. And if the New Historicists have sometimes over-stated their cases, they were ones which for many years did not receive a hearing at all. Catherine Belsey and Jonathan Goldberg confidently make these and other points in their invited responses to Levin's argument.[14]

Jonathan Dollimore was invited to join in this battle, but chose to fight another one instead, responding to complaints such as those by Carol Thomas Neely that the 'cult-historicists' have marginalized women. He defends materialist readings of gender difference and of the cultural construction of human nature, focusing his case on an imaginary cross-dressed production of *Antony and Cleopatra* that would give all conservatives apoplexy, but gives the lie to Forker and others who believe that such criticism is always too po-faced.[15]

Others declare themselves better disposed than Levin or Neely to New Historicist ambitions, but have reservations about aspects of their agenda or wish to propose ways of refining it. Howard Felperin declares himself a deconstructionist and 'of the Left' (and so implicitly in the same camp), but is worried that American New Historicism in particular is a form of fiddling while the humanities burn: ' The problem of relativism ... looms large at a moment when the value of the humanities within an increasingly utilitarian and implicitly reactionary culture is in serious question.' His main concern is their wish to abolish not only the present 'canon' of literary texts but the concept of canonicity itself (though some, like Holstun, have roundly condemned them precisely because, whatever they profess, they have pointedly failed to do this): 'without a canon and its record of re-inscription, there would be no ground on which literary studies could oppose the state and its strategies of containment by teaching the curriculum against the grain. Nor would there be any basis without it on which to construct the newer historicism some of us might envision.'[16] His case might be stronger if he gave us some idea of what this 'Newer Historicism' he more than once envisions might consist of. Theodore B. Leinwand tries this on a small scale in wishing to take New Historicism through the impasse it may be said to have reached in the debate about 'containment' and 'subversion' models of social energy, suggesting that a 'negotiation-based model of social relations' that 'can account for change or for resistance to change has the significant advantage of recognizing that the lower orders are not limited to a choice between quietism and insurrection'.[17] More substantially, Alan Liu, in a major ground-clearing exercise for his own reading of Wordsworth, has argued sympathetically but perceptively that the whole new historicist enterprise is in fact a version of neo-formalism, applying the methodologies of New Criticism not simply to the texts of canonical literature but to the 'text' which is history itself and to the cultural structures within which it is inscribed.[18] This is not an argument for its rejection, but for its purposeful refinement and development as a mode of cultural analysis.

It is perhaps the fact that New Historicism, broadly defined, remains so central a factor in *everyone else's* agenda as a catalyst or point of departure which guarantees its continuing importance in Renaissance literary studies (and, increasingly, in the literary studies of other periods) for the forseeable future.

NOTES

1. *Medieval and Renaissance Drama in England*, III (AMS Press, New York, 1986), 315.

2. *Medieval and Renaissance Drama in England*, II (AMS Press, New York, 1985), 314–20, 320.

3. LOUIS A. MONTROSE, 'Renaissance Literary Studies and the Subject of History', *English Literary Renaissance*, 16 (1986), 5–12. On the question of 'transatlantic support', see Steven Mullaney in *The Place of the Stage: License, Play and Power in Renaissance England*, (Chicago and London, 1988), pp. x–xii.

4. *Medieval and Renaissance Drama in England* II (AMS Press, New York, 1985), 324–8.

5. See 'Constructing the Subject: Feminist Practice and the New Renaissance Discourses', *English Literary Renaissance*, 18 (1988), 5–18, 6, n.

6. 'The New Historicism and its Discontents: Politicizing Renaissance Drama', *PMLA*, 102 (1987), 292–303, 292.

7. 'A New History for Shakespeare and His Time', *Shakespeare Quarterly*, 39 (1988), 441–64, 464.

8. ANNABEL PATTERSON, '"The Very Age and Body of the Time its Form and Pressure": Rehistoricizing Shakespeare's Theater', *New Literary History*, 20 (1988), 83–104.

9. CATHERINE BELSEY, 'Disrupting Sexual Difference: Meaning and Gender in the Comedies', in *Alternative Shakespeares*, ed. John Drakakis (London, 1985), pp. 166–90; Phyllis Rackin, 'Androgyny, Mimesis, and the Marriage of the Boy Heroine on the English Stage', PMLA, 102 (1987), 29–41.

10. 'Constructing the Subject: Feminist Practice and the New Renaissance Discourses'. The quotations come, respectively, from pp. 8 and 7.

11. 'Ranting at the New Historicism', *English Literary Renaissance*, 19 (1989), 189–225, 192, 193.

12. CAROLYN PORTER, 'History and Literature: "After the New Historicism"', *New Literary History*, 21 (1990), 253–72, 253, 265.

13. In *The Place of the Stage*, Preface, p. x.

14. RICHARD LEVIN, 'Unthinkable Thoughts in the New Historicizing of English Renaissance Drama'; Catherine Belsey, 'Richard Levin and In-Different Reading'; Jonathan Goldberg, 'Making Sense', *New Literary History*, 21 (1990), respectively 433–47 (quotation p. 444), 449–56, 457–62. Levin's 'Reply' (463–70) only continues, and does not conclude, the argument.

15. 'Shakespeare, Cultural Materialism, Feminism and Marxist Humanism', *New Literary History*, 21 (1990), 471–93.

16. HOWARD FELPERIN, *The Uses of the Canon: Elizabethan Literature and Contemporary Theory* (Oxford, 1990), quotations pp. viii, 190.

17. 'Negotiation and New Historicism', *PMLA*, 105 (1990), 477–90.

18. ALAN LIU, 'The Power of Formalism: the New Historicism', *ELH* 56 (1989), 721–71.

Key Concepts

Agency The social determination of history; hence, the capacity of men and women to **resist** or rewrite the meanings culture assigns them. In **Cultural Materialism**, a crucial concept as a counter to the New Historicist tendency to view cultural forms as all-powerful.

Body In New Historicism, a site of struggle between competing **discourses** and not a transhistorical human property. New Historicism follows Foucault's thesis that science merely assumes the place once occupied by torture in inscribing on the body its version of truth. By this interpretation the body is a palimpsest continually rewritten to produce new meanings, and its pleasures and desires the products of power rather than its innate drives. Shakespearean drama can therefore be viewed as a laboratory where modern meanings of what it is to be human are tested on Renaissance bodies.

Canon The 'great tradition' of English literary works assembled since the Renaissance as a vernacular complement to the Bible and Latin classics. Bound up with the British nation-**state**, the primacy of the canon has been challenged by proponents of multi-ethnic culture in both Britain and America, and its hierarchy, with Shakespeare at the apex, has been questioned by some New Historicists, while explained by others as a fact of history which it is naively late to challenge.

Carnival Historically, the Shrovetide festival prior to Lent, culminating in Shrove Tuesday with a final 'farewell to the flesh': *carne vale*. Renaissance drama was acted at court during this period and incorporates its movement to penance from indulgence. The Russian critic Mikhail Bakhtin idealised 'the battle between Carnival and Lent' as the moral economy of the pre-capitalist marketplace, and interpreted art as the liberating spirit of the carnivalesque. Carnival thereby became synonymous with popular culture; but this nostalgia has been checked by Foucault's critique of the **repressive hypothesis**, on which Bakhtin's utopian theory of carnival would seem to depend. The result has been a New Historicist reading of Renaissance drama that stresses the way that power licenses, rather than liberates, carnival for its own ends. Meanwhile **Cultural Materialism** has gone back to Bakhtin's less utopian concept of **heteroglossia** for a dialectical account of desire and repression in the Renaissance text.

Cultural Materialism The mainly British wing of New Historicism, which affirms that because culture is a material determinant of history, it is a site of ongoing struggle, and how it is reproduced today is as crucial as its original production. Cultural Materialism accepts the textuality of history, but insists equally on the historicity of texts. This dialectical theory of culture makes it more Marxist in its commitment than **Cultural Poetics**.

Cultural Poetics The mainly American wing of New Historicism, of which it is a formalist refinement. Unlike **Cultural Materialism**, Cultural Poetics emphasises the textuality of history over the historicity of texts, and tends to view cultures anthropologically, as self-regulating sign systems, distinct in their **difference** from the present. A concern with the **power** of representations and cultural forms makes it more structuralist than Marxist.

Decentring The theoretical displacement by postmodern theory of humanist assumptions of the sovereignty of the individual **subject** as author of his/her own meaning. Likewise, the displacement of the Eurocentric and patriarchal privileging of white, male language over other human languages.

Difference In linguistics meaning is binary, so identity is defined by its opposite (or Other): West by East, male by female, power by resistance, etc.. In **Cultural Poetics** differential meaning tends to be seen as a deadlock, whereas in **Cultural Materialism** difference (of race, religion, gender, etc.) is celebrated. Both views are qualified by the 'deconstructive' premise that polar opposites collapse into each other, but the New Historicist usage should not be confused with the concept of difference as it is understood in Deconstructionism.

Discourse The socially regulated form of language: hence, a way of speaking or writing that is specific to particular practices or institutions. Foucault used the term to denote the power-laden materiality of privileged areas of language, of which Literature or History would be instances. Discourses are rule-governed sets of statements which make truth-claims in opposition to other discourses, and as such they are, for New Historicists, the objects as well as the means of power struggles.

Essentialist humanism The assumption, dating from the eighteenth century, that there is a bedrock 'human condition' that is universally shared, anterior to history, and which constitutes 'human nature'. This assumption naturalises racial and gender differences, but it has been **decentred** by existentialist philosophy, with its insistence that there is no *essence* prior to existence, and by structuralism, with its axiom that there is no nature outside culture.

Heteroglossia The concept, developed by Mikhail Bakhtin, of early modern culture as a cacophony of competing languages, like the festive mêlée of the marketplace. Out of this intersection of voices, a monological literary language would emerge triumphant, but not without carrying the marks of linguistic struggle. By extension, therefore, the notion of heteroglossia has been applied, particularly by **Cultural Materialist** critics, to Renaissance dramatic texts as sites of dialogic meaning, where élite and popular discourses, or official and marginal accents, vie with each other and interpenetrate.

Histories The notion, developed by the *Annales* school of French historians, that there is no 'grand narrative' of history, since different cultures, classes or genders 'fiction' their own separate histories. Extra bite was given to this idea by Foucault, who popularised it with his 'genealogy' of discrete domains of **discourse**. Where 'history' was privileged over 'story', the Foucauldian concept of histories refuses the distinction, maintaining that the past is never available to the present as pure, unmediated fact, but always as a text.

Humanism The **ideology** of the West since the seventeenth century, which presupposes a human being to be a sovereign and spontaneous individual **subject**, who is the origin and author of her/his own meaning. Termed 'liberal humanism' when associated with capitalism, this ideology was problematic for the absolutist **state**, and it has been rendered theoretically untenable by Saussurean linguistics, with its structuralist premise that 'we do not speak language, it is language which speaks us'.

Ideology For contemporary theory, the automatic assumptions of a culture. Whereas Marx stigmatised ideology as 'false consciousness', **Cultural Materialism** follows Althusser in theorising it is as the conceptual framework through which a social order reproduces itself. Raymond Williams' theory of overlapping dominant, residual and emergent ideologies has been important for the **Cultural Materialist** account of the contest between social blocs represented in Renaissance drama. Foucault, however, disputed the existence of ideology, and it is not a concept employed by **Cultural Poetics** in its account of the power of **representations**.

Legitimacy The sanction claimed by authority for its actions, whether divine, in an absolutist state, or natural, in a parliamentary one. In early modern **states**, such as Tudor or Stuart England, there was often a *legitimacy crisis*, when real power was usurped from the sanctioned authorities, and according to New Historicism this eclipse was the central subject of Renaissance tragedy and the cause of its formal instability.

Marginality The condition of subordination or exclusion by which power defines itself in relation to that which opposes it. New Historicism follows the French New Philosophy in idealising history's victims – American Indians, blacks, Jews, women, homosexuals – but has a tendency to sentimentalise them as powerless to resist their oppression. **Cultural Materialism** has reacted with a strong emphasis on the potential for **resistance**, reading back into Renaissance drama the voices of the demonised poor, for example, or silenced women.

Power/will to power The fundamental category of human experience for Foucault and his New Historicist followers, the so-called *libido dominandi*, or drive for domination. This Nietzschean concept replaces Marx's class struggle in **Cultural Poetics**, where power is an effect of **discourse**, rather than of control of the means of production. For Foucauldians power is inescapable. **Cultural Materialism** continues, however, to define it in Marxist terms as the object of struggle.

Repressive hypothesis The **humanist** assumption, discredited by Foucault, that desires or pleasures are spontaneous. Where the human sciences have seen sexual desire, for instance, as latent or repressed, Foucault argued that they construct it as the means through which they operate. Liberation turns out, by this reading, to mean a new form of oppression: a view that has been influential over the New Historicist interpretation of **carnival**, festivity and art.

Representation The term, particular to **Cultural Poetics**, for the signs and signifying practices through which reality is mediated. *Representations* is the title of the American New Historicist journal, and the so-called *Representations* school has become known for a preoccupation with the textuality of history and the unavailability of the past except in the form of representations. Postmodern theorists such as Jean Baudrillard also describe 'the disappearance of reality' in an age of electronic images; but **Cultural Materialists** strongly disagree with the premise of **Cultural**

Poetics that representations circulate among themselves like transactions on the currency market.

Resistance The struggle of those on whom power operates against their own oppression or **marginalisation**. A term particularly important to **Cultural Materialism**, which insists that cultures are not self-regulating, as **Cultural Poetics** tends to assume, but that meanings may be challenged and altered through social **agency** and struggle. For the critic, this means that texts are never closed, no matter how much they may, like Shakespearean comedy, appear to foreclose on social or sexual transgression.

Spectacle The form in which, according to Foucault, **power legitimates** itself in pre-modern cultures. According to this view, the Renaissance state displayed its omnipotence in spectacular rituals, such as the public execution, which had nothing to do with law or reason, but everything to do with the visibility of kingship. In the Shakespearean playhouse, therefore, New Historicism finds a complex awareness that 'princes', as Queen Elizabeth declared, 'are set on stages in sight and view of the whole world'. Theatre is power, in this scenario, power theatre; whereas modern power is interiorised as conscience by those who are the objects of surveillance rather than spectators.

State New Historicism follows Foucault in his anti-statism. This bias reverses a conventional admiration for authority figures in Renaissance drama, such as Shakespeare's rulers. These are seen instead as leaders of a nascent nation-state founded on conquest, coercion and incarceration. But **Cultural Materialists** stress that state building is represented in Renaissance plays as incomplete. England was never an absolute monarchy, with **power** concentrated in the king, and the attempt to make it one provoked the Civil War: an outcome prefigured, in the view of some New Historicists, on the Shakespearean stage.

Subject/subjectivity The sense of self developed by humanist ideology which presupposes the human individual to possess an autonomous, unified and interior identity, whose object is an unmediated, empirical and exterior world. Subjectivity thus assumes that language is expressive rather than constitutive of reality, an assumption superseded by Saussurean linguistics, with its proposition that meaning is not a given but an effect of **difference**.

Subversion/containment debate A central disagreement between American **Cultural Poetics** and the mainly British **Cultural Materialism** over the question of whether culture is all-powerful over social **agency**

or whether these are interactive. Proponents of the former read Renaissance playtexts for authoritarian closure, while the advocates of the latter see them as sites of open contention. The containment thesis depends on Foucault's fetishising of **power**; the subversion argument draws on the Marxist concept of **resistance**.

Notes on Authors

FRANCIS BARKER is Senior Lecturer in Literature at the University of Essex and the author of the *The Tremulous Private Body: Essays on Subjection* (1984). He has published widely on the politics of Renaissance literature.

CATHERINE BELSEY is Professor of English at University College, Cardiff and the author of *Critical Practice* (1980) and *The Subject of Tragedy: Indentity and Difference in Renaissance Drama* (1985). She has written many essays on critical theory and medieval and Renaissance literature.

JONATHAN DOLLIMORE is Reader in English in the School of English and American Studies at the University of Sussex. He is author of *Radical Tragedy: Religion, Ideology and Power in the Drama of Shakespeare and his Contemporaries* (1984,1989); and co-editor with Alan Sinfield of *Political Shakespeare: New Essays in Cultural Materialism* (1985). He has edited the plays of John Webster (1983), and written numerous essays on transgression and deviance.

RICHARD DUTTON is Professor of English at Lancaster University. He is the author of *Ben Jonson: to the First Folio (1983), William Shakespeare: A Literary Life (1989),* and *Mastering the Revels: the Regulation and Censorship of English Renaissance Drama* (1991). He has edited *The Selected Writings of Sir Philip Sidney* (1987), and has published widely on issues relating to modern readings of Renaissance texts.

STEPHEN GREENBLATT is The Class of 1932 Professor of English Literature at the University of California, Berkeley. He is the author of *Sir Walter Raleigh: The Renaissance Man and His Roles* (1973); *Renaissance Self-Fashioning: From More to Shakespeare (1980); Shakespearean Negotiations: The Circulation of Social Energy in Renaissance England (1988);* and *Learning to Curse: Essays in Early Modern Culture* (1991). He is the editor of *Representations*, the flagship of New Historicism, and has edited *Representing the English Renaissance*, a selection of essays from the journal (1988).

JEAN E. HOWARD is Professor of English at Syracuse University, where she teaches Renaissance literature and critical theory. She is author of *Shakespeare's Art of Orchestration* (1984) and co-editor with Marion O'Connor of *Shakespeare Reproduced: The Text in History and Ideology* (1987).

LOUIS ADRIAN MONTROSE is Professor of English Literature at the University of California, San Diego. He has published numerous articles on the politics of Renaissance literature and is presently completing a book entitled *The Subject of Elizabeth: Relations of Power and Cultural Practices in Elizabethan England*.

ALAN SINFIELD is Professor in the School of English and European Studies at the University of Sussex. He is the author of *Literature in Protestant England 1550–1660* (1982) and co-editor with Jonathan Dollimore of *Political Shakespeare: New Essays in Cultural Materialism* (1985). He has published widely on Renaissance literature and ideology.

PETER STALLYBRASS is Professor of English at the University of Pennsylvania. He is the co-author with Allon White of *The Politics and Poetics of Transgression* (1986), and he has published widely on Shakespeare, Sidney and Renaissance popular culture. He is presently working on enclosures and transgression in the Renaissance.

LEONARD TENNENHOUSE is Professor of English at Wesleyan University, Connecticut. He is the author of *Power on Display: The Politics of Shakespeare's Genres* (1986), and co-editor with Nancy Armstrong of *The Ideology of Conduct* (1987) and *The Violence of Representation: Literature and the History of Violence* (1989).

ALLON WHITE was Lecturer in English at the University of Sussex until his death of leukemia in 1988. He was co-author with Peter Stallybrass of *The Politics and Poetics of Transgression* (1986) and left an autobiographical memoir, *Too Close to the Bone*, published in 1991.

RICHARD WILSON is Lecturer in English at Lancaster University. He has published essays on Shakespeare and early modern popular politics and is the author of the volume on *Julius Caesar* in the Penguin Masterstudies Series (1992). A collection of his essays entitled *Will/Power: Essays on Shakespearean Authority* will be published in 1992.

Further Reading

(1) Theory

Any consideration of New Historicism takes place within a wider debate about the impact of literary theory on the study of Renaissance texts and on the status of history. A collection of essays edited by Patricia Quint Parker and David Quint, *Literary Theory/Renaissance Texts* (Baltimore: The Johns Hopkins University Press, 1986), offers a stimulating introduction to the field and a survey of the different theoretical issues raised for the interpretation of Renaissance texts by the post-structuralist critique of humanist ideas of the subject and the author. The argument of many of these essays is that there is an elective affinity between contemporary theory and Renaissance literature, because they both assume that reality and identity are constructed through language. Another collection, edited by Margaret Ferguson, Maureen Quilligan and Nancy Vickers, *Rewriting the Renaissance: The Discourses of Sexual Difference in Early Modern Europe* (Chicago: The University of Chicago Press, 1986), also addresses the power of rhetoric in Renaissance culture, specifically the language of and about women, gender and sexual difference. And a further collection, *The Historical Renaissance: New Essays on Tudor and Stuart Literature and Culture,* edited by Heather Dubrow and Richard Strier (Chicago: The University of Chicago Press, 1988), provides a conspectus of the ways that history is interpreted both as a rhetorical construction by New Historicist criticism and as an unproblematic background by traditional Renaissance scholarship.

   Three collections of essays assemble differing views about and applications of New Historicism. *Renaissance Historicism: Selections from English Literary Renaissance,* edited by Arthur F. Kinney and Dan S. Collins (Amherst: The University of Massachusetts Press, 1987), presents a sequence of searching analyses of the movement, its implications and its blindnesses, followed by a range of specialised essays on key issues in the New Historicist agenda, such as patronage, censorship and family politics. *Representing the English Renaissance,* a selection of articles from

Representations, the leading New Historicist journal, edited by Stephen Greenblatt (Berkeley: University of California Press, 1988), comprises a more daring and committed prospectus of the work of the school. Here the emphasis is on the 'shaping power' of the Renaissance text, and the 'cultural poetics' that define its meaning. This is an invigorating volume which aims to perambulate, without fixing, what its editor calls 'the boundary stones' of Renaissance studies. But 'beating the bounds' of the disciplines of literature and history is more contentious in *New Historicism*, a collection edited by H. Aram Veeser (London: Routledge, 1989), that is intended as a symposium on the anthropological methods and Foucauldian philosophy which underpin the movement. Some of the contributions are sceptical of its assumptions about the primacy of culture; others question its privileging of the anecdote; many worry about the blunting of its radical edge within the academic institution. That this worry may be justified is suggested by the note of breezy commercialism in the last words, accorded to the Reader-Response theorist, Stanley Fish: 'Try it, you'll like it.'

(2) Theatre

As an account of the history of signifying practices, New Historicism has gravitated to those moments, such as that around 1800, when there occurred a shift in the way the world and the self were represented. The Renaissance was such a period of semiotic revolution, when a symbolic sign system was giving way to a realist one in the institutions of literature and the theatre. For this reason, some of the most effective historicist criticism of Renaissance drama focuses on the actual situation of the Elizabethan playhouse. Outstanding in this analysis is *The Place of the Stage* by Stephen Mullaney (Chicago: The University of Chicago Press, 1988), a compilation of anthropological sightlines on the Shakespearean stage, composed in the idiom of the *Annales* school of earthy history, which reveal just how 'peculiar' (in the legal and literal senses) its position was. Mullaney follows a Foucauldian reading of works of art as licensed play. More idealist, but richly documented, is the view of the Shakespearean playhouse in Michael Bristol's *Carnival and Theater: Plebeian Culture and the Structure of Authority in Renaissance England* (London: Methuen, 1985; paperback ed. London: Routledge, 1989). This is an interpretation which applies the theory of the Russian Formalist Mikhail Bakhtin to early modern London, arguing that the world of carnival comprised a counter-culture that energised dramatic writing. Like Bakhtin, Bristol sentimentalises popular festival, but his book is a vigorous contribution to the ongoing debate about subversion and containment in the licensed liberties of the Elizabethan Bankside. This is a debate hinging on the question of the degree to which culture shapes society, and it is unlikely to be answered without recourse to the material gathered by Andrew Gurr in his pre-theoretical but invaluable *Playgoing in Shakespeare's London* (Cambridge: Cambridge University Press, 1987; paperback edn, 1988).

(3) Language

Renaissance England is often seen as in transition between oral and literary cultures. But the New Historicist emphasis on the power of language and the post-structuralist critique of phonocentrism (the privileging of speech) have radicalised the interpretation of Shakespearean playtexts. They also make it hard to draw a line around New Historicist, as opposed to other historicising criticism. A number of the essays collected by John Drakakis in *Alternative Shakespeares* (London: Methuen, 1985) take a lead from the deconstructionist Christopher Norris, for example, in reading Elizabethan drama as a final fling of pre-Enlightenment representation ('where words "go on holiday" ') that would later be drilled by editors into files of rationalistic common sense. Postmodern culture has more in common with its delinquent pre-modern grandparent, the argument goes, than it has with the intervening epoch of stable and universal 'truth'. This is likewise the starting-point of a rousing 'red letter' by the Marxist Terry Eagleton. *William Shakespeare* (Oxford: Basil Blackwell, 1986) hurtles through the canon in the grip of a thesis that the conservative ideology of Shakespearean drama is undercut by the transgressive language with which it is expressed, which itself figures the relentless energy of capitalism. Eagleton is a sworn adversary of New Historicism, but like Brecht, he is 'that rare thing, a Marxist who meditates on signs', and this makes his eclectic work a vital part of the historicising tendency. At the other extreme, Jonathan Goldberg offers, in *Voice Terminal Echo* (London: Methuen, 1986), a postmodern prospectus of Shakespearean plays as an infinite circuit of voice and writing. 'Life, in these texts, is lived *à la lettre*', in Goldberg's view, and character is 'signed, sealed and delivered'. Thus, for a computerised New Historicism, there is truly nothing outside the text, and history is a dead letter.

(4) History

New Historicism's notion of 'histories' chimes with a trend towards localism in Anglo-American historiography, while its concern with textuality coincides with an alertness among historians to the *pretexts* that give meaning to events and how they are reported. Natalie Davis's study of pardon pleas in early modern French courts, *Fiction in the Archives* (Berkeley: University of California Press, 1988), shows, for instance, how much theatre was a life-and-death matter for Renaissance culture. In such a work, the wall between history and criticism is all but down. Likewise, *Revel, Riot and Rebellion: Popular Politics and Culture in England,* by David Underdown (Oxford: Oxford University Press, 1987), traverses the same country as the critics: the Shakespearean Midlands, with their rites of ownership and passage. Cattle, trees and commoners turn out to be branded or bound with texts for such history, which gives parish-pump actuality to the question of subversion and containment. But if research, such as that edited by Anthony Fletcher and John Stevenson on *Order and Disorder in Early Modern England* (Cambridge: Cambridge University Press, 1985), confirms the resolve of Tudor and Stuart judges to tame the scold or Ranter, critics of Renaissance drama have sought to prove that people make history by breaking bridles and interdictions. Thus, Annabel Patterson risks anachronism in *Shakespeare and the People's Voice* (Oxford: Basil Blackwell, 1990) to argue that the *vox populi* articulates a call to democracy in the plays of the Warwickshire landowner. This is a reading at odds with that of Jonathan Goldberg in *James I and the Politics of Literature* (Baltimore: Johns Hopkins University Press, 1983), which views Jacobean drama through a prism of state power. But as Leah Marcus admits, in *Puzzling Shakespeare: Local Reading and its Discontents* (Chicago: Chicago University Press, 1988), the jury is still out on the question of Renaissance power and resistance.

(5) Marginality

The awareness of the extent to which Renaissance culture was a patriarchy aligns New Historicism with feminism; an alliance that was never, however, an easy one, as Lisa Jardine recalled in *Still Harping on Daughters: Women and Drama in the Age of Shakespeare* (London: Harvester, 2nd ed, 1989). Her book was a milestone in the historicising of gender as its study of the Globe's boy-actors cut across feminism's faith that 'Shakespeare's vision of women transcended his time and sex '. The custom of cross-dressing condenses the question of subversion and containment in early modern society, and the debate over its meaning is reviewed by Jonathan Dollimore in the second edition of *Radical Tragedy* (London: Harvester, 1989). If *The Matter of Difference: Materialist/feminist Criticism of Shakespeare,* edited by Valerie Wayne (London: Harvester, 1991), charts how far feminism has in fact historicised concepts of gender, two earlier books by Simon Shepherd had demonstrated how the marginality of women was materially tied to male fears of emasculation in Renaissance England. *Amazons and Warrior Women: Varieties of Feminism in Seventeenth-Century Drama* (Brighton: Harvester, 1981) gave indispensable insight into characters such as Shakespeare's Joan of Arc; while *Marlowe and the Politics of Elizabethan Theatre* (Brighton: Harvester, 1986) stated a thesis begging to be made: that Marlowe's plays register both the marginalisation of homosexuality and the instability of gender. If men are made, Renaissance drama remains one of the templates that programmes them. It does this via the transcendental clichés debunked in *The Shakespeare Myth* (edited by Graham Holderness, Manchester: Manchester University Press, 1988). For alone of the arts, the theatre remains a temple of modernism. Thus, *The Tempest*, opined the theatre director Peter Brook in 1990, is not about power, but the 'human spirit' divined 'behind the words'. That he was applauded by his profession proved the urgency of a New Historicist reading of Renaissance drama.

Bibliography

AERS, D., B. HODGE and G. KRESS (1981): *Literature, Language and Society in England, 1580–1680*, Dublin.

ALTHUSSER, L. (1971): 'Ideology and Ideological State Apparatuses' in *Lenin and Philosophy and Other Essays*, London and New York.

ANDERSON, P. (1974): *Lineages of the Absolutist State*, London.

AUERBACH, E. (1968): *Mimesis*, trans. W. Trask, Princeton.

BAKHTIN, M. (1968): *Rabelais and his World*, trans. H. Iswolsky, Cambridge, Mass.

– (1976): (under the name of V. Volosinov) *Freudianism: a Marxist Critique*, trans. I. Titunik, ed. N. Bruss, New York.

– (1981): *The Dialogic Imagination: Four Essays*, ed. M. Holquist, trans. C. Emerson and M. Holquist, Austin.

BARBER, C. (1964): '"The form of Faustus' fortunes good or bad"', *Tulane Drama Review*, 8.

– (1980): 'The Family in Shakespeare's Development: Tragedy and Sacredness', in M. Schwartz and C. Kahn (eds), *Representing Shakespeare*, Baltimore.

BARISH, J. (1972): 'Feasting and Judging in Jonsonian Comedy', in *Renaissance Drama*, 5, 3–35.

– (1981): *The Anti-Theatrical Prejudice*, Berkeley.

BARKER, F. (1981): *1642: Literature and Power in the Seventeenth Century*, Colchester.

– (1984): *The Tremulous Private Body: Essays on Subjection*, London. (See this volume.)

BARTHES, R. (1972): 'The Great Family of Man', in *Mythologies*, trans. A. Lavers, London and New York.

– (1975): *S/Z*, trans. R. Miller, London.

BARTON, A. (1967): *Shakespeare and the Idea of the Play*, Harmondsworth.

BAYLEY, J. (1981): *Shakespeare and Tragedy*, London.

BEIER, L. (1985): *Masterless Men: the Vagrancy Problem in England 1560–1640*, London.

BELSEY, C. (1980): *Critical Practice*, London.

– (1982): 'Re-Reading the Great Tradition', in *Re-Reading English*, ed. P. Widdowson, London.

– (1985): *The Subject of Tragedy: Identity and Difference in Renaissance Drama*, London. (See this volume.)

BENNETT, T (1979): *Formalism and Marxism*, London

– (1981) : 'Marxism and Popular Fiction', *Literature and History*, VII, 138–65.

BLUESTONE, M. (1969): '*Libido Speculandi*: Doctrine and Dramaturgy in Contemporary Interpretations of Marlowe's *Doctor Faustus*', in N. Rabkin (ed.), *Reinterpretations of Elizabethan Drama*, New York.

BRADLEY, A. C. (1965): *Shakespearean Tragedy*, 2nd edn, London.

BURKE, P. (1978): *Popular Culture in Early Modern Europe*, London.

CALABRESI, G. and P. BOBBIT (1978): *Tragic Choices*, New York.

CASSIRER, E. (1968): *The Individual and the Cosmos in Renaissance Philosophy*, New York.

CLARK, P. (1985)(ed.): *The European Crisis of the 1590s: Essays in Comparative History*, London.

CURTIS, M. (1965): 'The Alienated Intellectuals of Early Stuart England', in T. Aston (ed), *Crisis in Europe 1560–1660*, London.

DAVIES, T. (1982): 'Common Sense and Critical Practice: Teaching Literature', in P. Widdowson, *Re-reading English*, London.

DAVIS, N. (1975): 'The Reasons of Misrule', in *Society and Culture in Early Modern France*, Stanford.

– (1978): 'Women on Top: Symbolic Sexual Inversion and Political Disorder in Early Modern Europe', in B. Babcock, *The Reversible World: Symbolic Inversion in Art and Society*, Ithaca and London.

DELEUZE, G. (1968): *Différence et répétition*, Paris.

DERRIDA, J. (1973): *Speech and Phenomena*, trans. D. Allison, Evanston.

– (1976): *Of Grammatology*, trans, G. Spivack, Baltimore and London.

DOLLIMORE, J. (1984, 1989): *Radical Tragedy: Religion, Ideology and Power in the Drama of Shakespeare and his Comtemporaries*, Brighton. (See this Volume.)

DOLLIMORE, J. and A. SINFIELD (1985a) (eds): *Political Shakespeare: New Essays in Cultural Materialism*, Manchester. (See this volume.)

– (1985b): 'History and Ideology: The Instance of *Henry V*', in J. Drakakis (ed.), *Alternative Shakespeares*, London.

DRAKAKIS, J. (1985) (ed.): *Alternative Shakespeares*, London.

DUSINBERRE, J. (1975): *Shakespeare and the Nature of Women*, London.

ECO, U. (1984): 'The Frames of Comic Freedom', in T. Seboek (ed.), *Carnival!*, New York.

EVANS-PRITCHARD, E. (1940): *The Nuer*, Oxford.

FISH, S. (1984): 'Authors-readers: Jonson's community of the same', *Representations*, 7, 26–58.

FOUCAULT, M. (1970): *The Order of Things: an Archaeology of the Human Sciences*, London and New York.

– (1977a): 'Nietzsche, Genealogy, History', in *Language, Counter-Memory, Practice*, ed. D. Bouchard, Oxford.

– (1977b): *Discipline and Punish: the Birth of the Prison*, Harmondsworth.

– (1978)(ed.): *I, Pierre Rivière....* Harmondsworth.

– (1979): *Power, Truth, Strategy,* ed. M. Morris and P. Patton, Sydney.

– (1981): 'The Order of Discourse', trans, I, McLeod, in R. Young (ed), *Untying the Text: a Post-Structuralist Reader,* London.

GEERTZ, C. (1977): 'Centers, Kings and Charisma: Reflections on the Symbolics of Power', in J. Ben-David and T. Nichols Clark (eds), *Culture and its Creators: Essays in Honour of Edward Shils,* Chicago.

GINZBURG, C. (1980): *The Cheese and the Worms: the Cosmos of a 16th-Century Miller,* London.

GOLDBERG, J. (1983): *James I and the Politics of Literature: Jonson, Shakespeare, Donne, and their Contemporaries,* Baltimore.

GREENBLATT, S. (1980): *Renaissance Self-Fashioning,* Chicago. (See this volume.)

– (ed.)(1982): 'The Forms of Power and the Power of Forms', Genre, 15.

– (1985): 'Invisible Bullets: Renaissance Authority and its Subversion', in J. Dollimore and A. Sinfield, *Political Shakespeare,* Manchester. (Included in this volume.)

HAYNES, J. (1984): 'Festivity and the Dramatic Economy of Jonson's *Bartholomew Fair',* English Literary History, 51, 4, 645–68.

HEINEMANN, M. (1981): *Puritanism and Theatre: Thomas Middleton and Opposition Drama Under the Stuarts,* Cambridge.

HELGERSON, R. (1983): *Self-crowned Laureates: Spenser, Jonson, Milton and the Literary System,* Berkeley.

HILL, C. (1975): *The World Turned Upside Down: Radical Ideas during the English Revolution,* Harmondsworth.

– (1986): *Society and Puritanism in Pre-Revolutionary England,* Harmondsworth.

HOLLAND, N. (1965): Introduction to the Signet Classic edn. of *2 Henry IV,* New York.

JARDINE, L. (1983): *Still Harping on Daughters: Women and Drama in the Age of Shakespeare,* Brighton.

KAHN, C. (1981): *Man's Estate: Masculine Identity in Shakespeare,* Berkeley.

KELLY-GADOL, J. (1977): 'Did Women Have a Renaissance?' in R. Bridenthal and C. Kroonz (eds), *Becoming Visible: Women in European History,* Boston.

KINNEY, A. and D. COLLINS (eds) (1987): *Renaissance Historicism: Selections from English Literary Renaissance,* Amherst.

KNIGHTS, L. (1962): *Drama and Society in the Age of Jonson,* London.

LACAN, J. (1977): *Ecrits,* trans. A. Sheridan, London.

LaCAPRA, D. (1983): 'Rethinking Intellectual History and Reading Texts' in *Rethinking Intellectual History: Texts, Contexts, Language,* Ithaca.

LADURIE, E. (1981): *Carnival at Romans: a People's Uprising in Romans 1579–1580,* Harmondsworth.

LENTRICCHIA, F. (1983): *Criticism and Social Change,* Chicago.

LEVER, J. (1971): *The Tragedy of State,* London.

LEVIN, R. (1979): *New Readings vs. Old Plays: Recent Trends in the Reinterpretation of English Renaissance Drama*, Chicago.

LONGHURST, D. (1982): '"Not for all time, but for an Age": an approach to Shakespeare Studies', in *Re-Reading English*, ed. P. Widdowson, London.

LUKÁCS, G. (1971): *History and Class Consciousness*, trans. R. Livingstone, Cambridge, Mass.

MACHEREY, P. (1978), *A Theory of Literary Production*, trans. G. Wall, London.

MACK, M. (1965): Introduction to the Signet Classic ed. of *1 Henry IV*, New York.

MARCUS, L. (1978a): *Childhood and Cultural Despair: a Theme and Variations in Seventeenth-Century Literature*, Pittsburgh.

– (1978b): '"Present Occasions" and the Shaping of Ben Jonson's Masques', *English Literary History* 45, 201–25.

MAROTTI, A. (1982): '"Love is not love": Elizabethan Sonnet Sequences and the Social Order', *English Literary History* 49, 396–428.

MARX, K. (1963): *Early Writings*, ed. T. Bottomore, New York.

– (1972): *The Marx-Engels Reader*, ed. R. Tucker, New York.

MCLUSKIE, K. (1983): 'Feminist Deconstruction: the Example of Shakespeare's *The Taming of the Shrew*', *Red Letters*, 12.

MONTROSE, L. (1981): '"The Place of a Brother": *As You Like It*: Social Process and Comic Form', *Shakespeare Quarterly* 32, 28–54.

MULLANEY, S. (1983): 'Strange Things, Gross Terms, Curious Customs: the Rehearsal of Cultures in the Late Renaissance', *Representations*, 3, 40–67.

OLSON, P. (1957): '*A Midsummer Night's Dream* and the Meaning of Court Marriage', *English Literary History*, 21, 95–119.

ORGEL, S. (1975): *The Illusion of Power: Political Theater in the English Renaissance*, Berkeley.

– (1981): 'What is a text?' *Research Opportunities in Renaissance Drama*, 2, 4, 3–6.

PARKER, P. and QUINT, D. (eds)(1986): *Literary Theory/Renaissance Texts*, Baltimore and London.

PERKIN, H. (1969): *The Making of Modern English Society 1780–1880*, London.

POULANTZAS, N. (1973): *Political Power and Social Classes*, trans. T. O'Hagan, London.

RIBNER, I. (1960): *Patterns in Shakespearean Tragedy*, London.

RUBIN, G. (1975): 'The Traffic in Women: Notes on the "Political Economy" of Sex', in R. Reiter (ed.), *Toward an Anthropology of Women*, New York.

RYAN, K. (1984): 'Towards a Socialist Criticism: Reclaiming the Canon', *LTP: Journal of Literature Teaching Politics*, 3, 4–17.

SALINGAR, L. (1979): 'Crowd and Public in *Bartholomew Fair*', *Renaissance Drama*, 10, 141–59.

SCRUTON, R. (1980): *The Meaning of Conservatism*, Harmondsworth.

SHAPIRO, M. (1977): *Children of the Revels: the Boy Companies of Shakespeare's Time and their Plays*, New York.

SHEPHERD, S. (1981): *Amazons and Warrior Women: Varieties of Feminism in Seventeenth-Century Drama*, Brighton.

SINFIELD, A. (1982): *Literature in Protestant England*, London.

STALLYBRASS, P. and A. WHITE (1986): *The Politics and Poetics of Transgression*, London. (See this volume.)

STONE, L. (1977): *The Family, Sex and Marriage in England, 1500–1800*, London.

TENNENHOUSE, L. (1980): 'The Counterfeit Order of *The Merchant of Venice*', in *Representing Shakespeare: New Psychoanalytic Essays*, ed. M. Schwartz and C. Kahn, Baltimore.

– (1982): 'Representing Power: *Measure for Measure in its Time*', in S. Greenblatt (ed.) *The Forms of Power*, 139–56.

THOMPSON, E. (1971): 'The Moral Economy of the English Crowd in the Eighteenth Century', *Past and Present*, 50, 76–136.

TILLYARD, E. (1943): *The Elizabethan World Picture: a Study of the Idea of Order in the Age of Shakespeare, Donne and Milton*, London.

TODOROV, T. (1984): *The Conquest of America: the Question of the Other*, trans. R. Howard, New York.

TOMPKINS, J. (1980): 'The Reader in History: the Changing Shape of Literary Response', in J. Tompkins (ed.), *Reader Response Criticism: from Formalism to Post-Structuralism*, Baltimore and London.

TURNER, V. (1974): *Drama, Fields, and Metaphors: Symbolic Action in Human Society*, Ithaca.

VEESER, H. A. (ed.) (1989): *The New Historicism*, London and New York.

WAYNE, D. (1982): 'Drama and Society in the Age of Jonson: an Alternative View', *Renaissance Drama*, 13, 103–29.

– (1984): *Penshurst: the Semiotics of Place and the Poetics of History*, Madison.

WHITE, H. (1973): *Metahistory: the Historical Imagination in Nineteenth-Century Europe*, Baltimore and London.

– (1978): *Tropics of Discourse: Essays in Cultural Criticism*, Baltimore.

WILLIAMS, R. (1973): *The Country and the City*, London.

– (1977): *Marxism and Literature*, Oxford.

– (1980): *Problems in Materialism and Culture*, London.

WOODBRIDGE, L. (1983): *Women and the English Renaissance: Literature and the Nature of Womankind 1540–1620*, Brighton.

WRIGHT, L. (1964): *Middle-Class Culture in Elizabethan England*, London.

ZAGORIN, P. (1970): *The Court and the Country*, London and New York.

Index

Absolutist state, 15, 46, 108, 128–9,
    158–62, 167–80, 182, 200
Althusser, L., 2–3, 12, 15, 30, 37, 46, 167,
    220, 230
America, Elizabethan colonisation of,
    6–7, 83–93, 121–3, 155
Anderson, P., 168–9
anthropology, as influence on New
    Historicism, 63, 108, 114
Arden, A., Elizabethan murderess, 13,
    131–44
Arden of Faversham, 132–44
Auerbach, E., 81

Bacon, F., 31
    on female rulers, 124
    on power, 193
    on seditious intellectuals, 191
Bakhtin, M., 7–8, 16, 32, 150, 207–8, 227,
    229, 236
Barber, C.L., 64
Barish, J., 24–5
Barker, F., 14, 146, 153–5, 157–66
Barroll, L., 222
Barthes, R., 2–3, 8, 10, 24, 36
Barton, A., 151
Baudrillard, J., 5, 230
Bayley, J., 179
Beier, L., 149
Belsey, C., 12–14, 33–44, 131–44, 223, 224
Benjamin, W., 7
Bennett, T., 31, 40
Bluestone, M., 66
Bodley, T., rejects plays from his library,
    216
Brecht, B., 15, 194, 237
Brighton Bombing, 14, 167

Bristol, M., 150, 236
Brook, P., 239
Brooks, H., 114, 121
Brustein, R., 188
Bucer, M., on divorce, 140
Buchanan, G., 173–4, 176–8
Bunny, E., on divorce, 140
Burckhardt, J., 11, 21
Burke, P., 147–8, 156
Burton, R., on alienated intellectuals, 192

Calvert, S., accuses theatre of sedition,
    51
canonicity, 33, 41–3, 47, 167, 223–5, 227
carnival, 8, 15, 32, 46, 83, 145–56, 201,
    207–8, 213, 227, 236–7
Cassirer, E., 59
Cecil, R., and cult of Elizabeth I, 123, 129
censorship, 155
Chapman, G., 208–9
Charles I, 154, 168
Charles II, 213
Christianity and Marlowe, 73, 76–7
City Comedy, 195–206
Clark, P., 148
Collins, D.S., 235
Communism, French, 2, 4
confession, 9
Cortez, H., conquers Amerindians, 6
Coverdale, M., and marriage, 141
Curtis, M.E., 190

Darnton, R., 10
Davenant, W.,
    Gondibert, 212–13
    Macbeth, 177
Davis, N.Z., 10, 122, 150, 189, 238

245

Debray, R., 5
deconstructionism, 5–6, 36–7, 225, 237
de Gaulle, C., 2–3
Dekker, T.,
    The Gull's Hornbook, 216
    Page of Plymouth, 137
    The Roaring Girl, 196, 203
Deleuze, G., 3, 79
Deloney, T., *Mistress Page of Plymouth*,
    137
Derrida, J., 5–6, 32, 36–7
Descartes, R., 165
divorce, 138–42
Dollimore, J., 15, 19, 21–2, 31, 45–56, 151,
    169, 181–94, 219–20, 225, 238
Donne, J., as examination subject, 34
Dove, J., on divorce, 140
Drakakis, J., 237
Dryden, J., 212, 218
Dubrow, H., 235

Eagleton, T., 237
Eco, U., 4, 150
Edwardes, A., writes love letter to
    Elizabeth I, 129
Eliot, T. S., 33
Elizabeth I,
    and absolutism, 168
    as an Amazon, 121–5
    and *A Midsummer Night's Dream*,
        109–13, 127–30
    and plague, 199–200
    and *Richard II*, 51
    and theatricality, 108, 231
Elyot, T., on tragedy, 52
Essex, Earl of, 51, 53, 169
Essex, husbands frightened in, 136, 138
Essex University conferences on the
    Sociology of Literature, 33, 43
Evans-Pritchard, E., 63
examination questions, 34–5

Falklands War, 12–13, 37
family as institution, 38–9, 43, 116–21,
    131–44, 185–8, 195–206
Felperin, H., 222, 225
Feminism, 13, 53, 188, 223
Filmer, R., *Patriarcha*, 142
Fish, S., 222, 236
Fletcher, A., 238
Forker, C.R., 219–20, 225

Forman, S., 109–13, 129
Foucault, M., 1–16, 24, 26, 29, 37–40, 46,
    83, 109, 148–9, 195, 198, 230, 232
Frankfurt School of Sociology, 4–5
Fukuyama, F., 9, 11, 16

Geertz, C., 108
Ginzburg, C., 54
Glücksmann, A., 4–5
Globe Playhouse, 145–56
Goldberg, J., 19, 224, 237, 238
Gordon, D.J., 10–11
Gramsci, A., 2–3, 15, 46, 220
Green, R., 197
Greenblatt, S., 1, 5–6, 9–11, 14, 19, 22, 24,
    47–8, 51, 54, 57–108, 151, 220–2, 236
Greville, F., 53, 128
Guattari, F., 3
Gunpowder Plot, 14, 153, 170, 173
Gurr, A., 237

Hakluyt, R., and colonialism, 89
Harington, J., on Elizabeth I as
    temptress, 127
Hariot, T., and colonialism 83–93, 100
Harman, T., on argot, 100–3
Heale, W., 188
Heinemann, M., 204–5
Helgerson, R., 213–14
Henry VIII, most powerful Tudor, 168
Henslowe, P., closes theatre on sabbath,
    147
Herrick, R., on carnival, 150
Heteroglossia, 32, 37, 207–8, 228, 229
Heywood, T.,
    Apology for Actors, 50–1
    Troia Britannica, 132
Hill, C., 33, 147, 150, 154, 181
history, 8–16, 19, 23–30, 33, 38–9, 44,
    167–80, 221–3, 229, 237–8
Hobbes, T., on subversive literature, 181
Hobsbawm, E., 34
Hogarth, W., *Southwark Fair*, 148
Holinshed, R., 176
    on the Arden murder case, 132–5
Holstun, J., 223–5
Hooker, R.,
    his doctrine of order, 49
    on God, 80
Hope Theatre, 209
Howard, J., 19–32, 220

human nature and essentialist myth of
  Man, 13, 24–5, 43, 47, 131, 162–6, 181,
  229

ideology, 30–2, 49–50, 229
Ives, E.W., 221

James I, 23
  and absolutism, 200–2
  and *Bartholomew Fair*, 209
  Basilikon Doron, 170
  Book of Sports, 150, 213
  defends theatres, 147
  and divorce, 139
  and *Macbeth*, 167–80
  and theatricality, 51
  and women, 185
Jameson, F., 9
Jardine, L., 19, 238
Jews, as marginalised group, 66–73
Jonson, B., 207–18
  The Alchemist, 28, 196
  Bartholomew Fair, 16, 28, 196, 207,
    209–14, 217–18
  Eastward Ho, 214
  Epicoene, 203
  Every Man Out of his Humour, 217
  The Isle of Dogs, 214
  Page of Plymouth, 137
  Sejanus, 53, 214–15
  Volpone, 208
Kafka, F., 7, 16, 217
Kelly-Gadol, J., 188
Keyishian, H., 220
Kinney, A.F., 235
Knights, L.C., 196
Kyd, T., *The Spanish Tragedy*, 210

Lacan, J., 3–4, 157, 221
LaCapra, D., 26, 32
language as system, 35–7
Leavis, F.R., 33
Leicester, Earl of, Elizabeth I puts him in
  his place, 124
Leinwand, T.B., 225
Lentricchia, F., 55
Le Roy Ladurie, E., 152
Levin, R., 224
Levi-Strauss, C., 3
Liu, A., 11–12, 225
Lukács, G., 10

Macherey, P., 31, 46
Machiavelli, N., 85–7, 183
Machyn, H., and Arden murder case, 132
Mack, M., 94
Marcus, L., 19, 201, 238
Marcuse, H., 4–5
Marlowe, C., 7, 57, 81–2, 83, 239
  Dido Queen of Carthage, 75
  Doctor Faustus, 60–6, 75
  Edward II, 60, 64, 66, 75–6, 79–80
  The Jew of Malta, 66–73, 75, 78
  Tamburlaine the Great, I and II, 58–66,
    73–6, 80
Marotti, A., 19
Marston, J., *The Malcontent*, 203–4
Marx, K., 16, 47, 57, 67–70, 72
Marxism, 2–3, 6, 8–9, 30–1, 33, 38,
  219–21, 232
Mary Queen of Scots, 168, 173
McLuhan, M., 5
McLuskie, K., 53
Middleton, T.,
  A Chaste Maid in Cheapside, 196,
    204–5
  A Mad World, My Masters, 203
  with Dekker, *The Roaring Girl*, 196,
    203
  A Trick to Catch the Old One, 205
Milton, J., 35
  on divorce, 139–41
Montaigne, M., 81, 84
Montrose, L., 8, 19, 22, 24, 109–30, 220
More, T., on politics as theatre, 108
Muir, K., 177–8
Mullaney, S., 19, 221, 224, 236
Munday, A., and Saunders murder case,
  136

Nashe, T., 197
  defends theatre, 147
Neely, C.T., 221, 223, 225
New Criticism, 12, 20
New Philosophy, 4
Nietzsche, F., 4, 11, 57, 230
Norfolk, Duke of, plots against
  Elizabeth I, 168
Norris, C., 237

Olson, P., 114
Orgel, S., 10, 19, 215
Orwell, G., 4

Parker, P.Q., 235
Patterson, A., 222, 238
Pechter, E., 221
Peck, L.L., 221
Peele, G., *Arraygnment of Paris*, 125
Pepys, S., as typical bourgeois subject, 14, 157, 162, 165
Perkin, H., 198–9
plague, 198–200
Plato and Marlowe, 77
Platter, T., and *Julius Caesar*, 145–6, 149
Porter, C., 224
Postman, M., 5
psychoanalysis, New Historicism's resistance to, 9, 109
Puttenham, G., on drama, 52

Quilligan, M., 235
Quint, D., 235

Rackin, P., 223
Rainolds, J., on murderous wives, 140
Raleigh, W.,
    and America, 121–3, 129
    and Marlowe, 82, 86
    on writing, 52
Reagan, R., 5
Rembrandt, *Anatomy Lesson of DrTulp*, 153–4
Revisionist Historiography, 14–15, 221
Ribner, I., 178
riots and rebellions, 147–8, 156, 168, 173, 191
Rubin, C., 114
Russell, C., 221
Russian Formalism, 31, 236

Sabbatarian controversy, 146–7
Said, E., 5–6
Sanders, A., Elizabethan murderess, 136
Sarracoll, J., 57–8
Saussure, F. de., 35–6, 229
Scruton, R., 179
Seltzer, M., 10
Shakespeare, W.,
    All's Well That Ends Well, 192
    Antony and Cleopatra, 59, 225
    The Comedy of Errors, 189–90
    Coriolanus, 75
    Hamlet, 14, 43, 146, 157–66

1 Henry IV, 7, 59, 94–100
2 Henry IV, 98–106, 201
Henry V, 106–8, 169
1 Henry VI, 239
Henry VIII, 51, 201
Julius Caesar, 13, 145–56
King Lear, 8, 108, 120, 160–2
Macbeth, 13, 15, 41–2, 94, 167–180
Measure for Measure, 27, 94, 199, 203–4
The Merchant of Venice, 120
A Midsummer Night's Dream, 8, 109–30
Othello, 7, 93
Richard II, 51, 54, 169
Richard III, 93
The Tempest, 11, 93, 239
Titus Andronicus, 210
The Winter's Tale, 120
Shapiro, M., 203
Sharp, K., 221
Sheehan, M.M., 138
Shepherd, S., 238–9
Sidney, P., 53, 128–9
Sierra Leone, Elizabethan exploration of, 57–8, 115
Sinfield, A., 14–15, 167–80, 219–20
Smith, H., on divorce, 140
Smuts, R.M., 221
space and time, Renaissance sense of 59–64
Spenser, E., 58, 79
    The Faerie Queene, 65, 115, 122, 137, 173
Stallybrass, P., 16, 207–18
Starkey, D., 221
Stevenson, J., 238
Stone, L., 24, 29, 38, 48–9, 223
Stow, J.,
    and Arden murder case, 132
    A Survey of London, 197
Strier, R., 235
Stubbes, P., against theatre, 147
subversion/containment debate, 45–7, 53–6, 225
Suckling, J., 209

Tarlton, R., 146, 209
Taylor, J., *The Unnatural Father*, 132, 138
Tennenhouse, L., 16, 19, 195–206
Thatcher, M., 12, 15
Thomas, K., 24
Thompson, E.P., 33, 206

Tillyard, E.M.W., 20, 23, 33, 41, 48–9, 52
Todorov, T., 6, 25, 155
Tompkins, J.P., 51
Tourneur, C., *The Revenger's Tragedy*, 190
Trilling, L., 5

Underdown, D., 238

Veeser, A.H., 236
Vickers, N., 235

Warning for Fair Women, A, 136
Wayne, D., 19, 30, 213, 216
Wayne, V., 238
Webster, J.,
    The Duchess of Malfi, 187
    The White Devil, 15, 181–194
Whetstone, G., *History of Promos and
    Cassandra*, 203

White, A., 16, 207–18
White, H., 11, 25, 27
Williams, R., 15, 45–9, 55, 229
Wilson, R., 13, 145–56
Wiseman, J., executed recusant, 170
witchcraft, 40, 115, 174–5, 177
women,
    as Amazons, 121–4, 188–90, 239
    marginalised by New Historicism,
        131, 225
    as subordinated group, 8, 13, 53,
        114–21, 131–44, 185–7, 238
Woodbridge, L., 188
Wotton, H., 213
Wright, L.B., 188

Zagorin, P., 200